WRITINGS ON THE
**Asian
City**

ORO Editions
Publishers of Architecture, Art, and Design
Gordon Goff: Publisher

www.oroeditions.com
info@oroeditions.com

Published by ORO Editions

Text by Peter Cookson Smith
Drawings by Peter Cookson Smith
Project Manager: Jake Anderson

Book Design by CircularStudio.com
Direction, Pablo Mandel
Typesetting, Micaela Carraro

10 9 8 7 6 5 4 3 2 1 First Edition

ISBN: 978-1-957183-52-7

Color Separations and Printing: ORO Group Inc.
Printed in Hong Kong

ORO Editions makes a continuous effort to minimize the overall carbon
footprint of its publications. As part of this goal, ORO, in association
with Global ReLeaf, arranges to plant trees to replace those used in the
manufacturing of the paper produced for its books. Global ReLeaf is an
international campaign run by American Forests, one of the world's oldest
nonprofit conservation organizations. Global ReLeaf is American Forests'
education and action program that helps individuals, organizations,
agencies, and corporations improve the local and global environment
by planting and caring for trees.

Peter Cookson Smith

WRITINGS ON THE
Asian City

ORO Editions — Novato, California

Contents

Introduction

At a writer's forum in Hong Kong SAR several years ago one of the panelists, Stephen Fry, was asked about the creative writing process and its almost mystical means of linking an idea or "story line" to a final written product. He characteristically replied in part by quoting T. S. Eliot, that "between desire and performance lies a shadow," so that a substantive part of the creative process must be to bring clarity to the initial indistinct realm of promising ideas. It occurred to me at the time that this might also be an apt way of examining the equally elusive relationship between writing and urban design, or perhaps between theory and practice. After all, it used to be said of the early 20th-century Bloomsbury literary set in London, that they lived in squares, moved in circles, and loved in triangles.

Urban thinkers, planners, and designers must share a strong desire and motivation to improve the city. We employ our well tested design principles to set out fanciful objectives, but for various metaphysical reasons the performance rarely, or at least only partly, matches the desired end state. To dispense with a shadow we have to direct a light toward it, particularly as recent evidence has shown how vulnerable global cities are to both climate change and pandemics.

Punctuating the head of Zhongshan Road in Tianjin, the onion-domed Xikai Church forms a formidable landmark.

Cities grow and evolve in ways that often defy pre-determined outcomes for better or worse, and can be remarkably robust in withstanding centuries of urban change that conveniently by-pass the honored classical ideals of city building. The Asian city is in transition, from a situation where the slow stream of influences over the centuries has generated a precarious balance between flourishing but very different urban cultures and subcultures, to what we are now experiencing as a surge of commonalities generated through the dominant forces of globalization. From an immediate post-colonial situation where embedded traditions were insinuated in modernizing programs to meet rising aspirations, rapid economic development has produced a force field that continues to induce an unprecedented sequence of changes to long-standing development patterns. Despite Western-inspired design influences, cities throughout Asia now display a necessary pragmatic and expressive vocabulary of values related to different economic, cultural, and behavioral settings, together with the miscellany of everyday use that reflects the simultaneous but paradoxical existence of complexity and sameness.

Asia itself has little overall historical unity—it embraces large land masses and archipelagos divided by the Indian Ocean, the Andaman Sea, the South China Sea, and the Pacific Ocean, and is bisected by massive riverine systems such as the Yangtze, Pearl, Mekong, Irrawaddy, Ganges, Brahmaputra, Indus, and Chao Phraya, around which capitals and port cities came into being. It is separated from Europe by the Ural Mountains and the Caspian Sea, but can be further defined by breaking it down into sub-regions that vary significantly, and which for many centuries were relatively isolated from each other. The book broadly concentrates on East and Central Asia including the People's Republic of China[1] (which includes the Special Administrative Regions of Hong Kong SAR and Macao SAR), South Korea, Japan, and Chinese Taipei; South Asia, that comprises India, Pakistan, Nepal, Sri Lanka, Bangladesh, the Maldives, and Bhutan; and Southeast Asia that covers the Indo-Chinese states of Myanmar, Thailand, Vietnam, Cambodia, and Laos, together with the archipelago that embraces Malaysia, Singapore, Indonesia, Brunei, the Philippines, Timor, and Papua New Guinea.

These sub-regions embody topographical and climatic extremes, unique indigenous traditions, overlapping ethnic and linguistic patterns, together with complex religious rituals and ideologies that are both embodied and expressed in the contemporary city. Asian cities include some of the largest physical conurbations in the world but also the most populated, including Tokyo (37 million), Beijing (21 million), Shanghai (26 million), New Delhi (29 million), Mumbai and Dhaka (20 million each), and Kolkata (15 million). A number of Asian countries now house more than 60 percent of their people in cities, and some will house up to 70 percent over the coming decades, with China already achieving an urbanization rate of 64 percent. Urban design in these mega-cities becomes the public face of human settlement and spatial organization, historically expressed through elusive narratives of past and present in articulating long-term aspirations for the future. Writings on the city must therefore address the whole—how places came about, how they are perceived, how they work, and what sustains them. The values that result from this are key to understanding the urbanity of the Asian city and the ability to bring about its betterment.

---

1   In further chapters these references are shortened to 'the PRC', 'the Hong Kong SAR' and 'the Macau SAR'

The Asian city has, in the past, been the historic repository of monumental religious edifices, palace citadels and fortifications that signified concentrations of power and elitism. Today it must interface with the wider values of urbanism with its integral but often elusive blend of cultural factors, economic functions, social structures, political processes, and other related urban issues that include sustainability and resilience. The three-dimensional outcome is therefore an identifiable and occasionally symbolic result of past attributes and the ability to cope with economic and social change that merge in the distinctive character of urban places.

An important aspect of this is not merely to retain traditional references, but to embrace adaptability and ensure a constantly changing mix of uses and ownerships—a "structured turbulence" that remains a strong characteristic of the traditional multi-layered Asian neighborhood. What might at first appear organic or informal in its present state, might just as easily be the result of early settlement imprints, regulatory regimes, land ownership structures, or trading trajectories. Cultural expression in terms of urban form is not merely the natural outcome of these but the result of their past interfaces that I have explored in a previous book, *The Urban Design of Intervention.*

Amidst the vast interventions that form the contemporary urban landscape, with its towering business districts and high-rise residential estates, contained and often defined by primary circulation corridors, we can find a parallel universe of indigenous urban spaces. This might include the remaining Ming dynasty hutongs of Beijing, the *hanok* quarters of Seoul, the *lilong* and *sichuyen* neighborhoods of Shanghai, the narrow *roji* of Tokyo and Kyoto, the *travessas* of Macao SAR, the durbar squares of Kathmandu, the *mohallas* of Delhi, the chowks of many Indian cities, the *thamel* of Nepal, the *Sois* of Bangkok, and the pasar *malam* in Singapore, Malaysia, and Indonesia that help to establish nighttime identity. In contrast, Hong Kong, China's high-density vertical urbanism operates through an intense three-dimensional matrix of mixed uses, each interfacing in both a private and public juxtaposition, dictated by compressed convenience and the ebbs and flows of the free market.

Saskia Sassen suggests in *The Global City* that an increasingly globalized economy is creating new strategic functions: first as "concentrated command points" of headquarter functions, second as specialized service and finance centers, and third as areas of new industrial production. To these we might add the large population sectors of urban residents and newcomers who occupy a somewhat disconnected margin and are the mainstay of informal economies. All of these continue to have a significant impact on changing urban form and elaborate ways in which the social and economic order of Asian cities are being restructured and reshaped through new forms of capital investment, overlapping divisions of labor and redirected spatial patterns. In most Asian cities almost constant population growth over several decades has been accompanied by increased pressure on infrastructure and housing, along with a polarization of socio-economic sectors in the achievement of overall material welfare and social justice, that in many cases has tended to threaten or erode both civic and social capital.

Increasingly innovative organizational systems based on information and communication technologies relating to production, finance, management, and advanced corporate and professional service industry, are transforming the ways in which activities are carried out in Asia, accompanied by a continual shift of manufacturing industries to countries or cities with lower production costs. Primate cities, in the throes of increasing competition for investment, therefore become fueled by both local and foreign capital that is transforming city space and establishing new cultural meaning for built environments. In this sense, the process of globalization is in some cases leading to increasingly homogenized city quarters, while in others it stimulates more transformative and heterogeneous qualities, further accentuated by informal settlements created through large-scale migration of labor.

While inner urban zones have experienced a high level of transformation through redevelopment, in many cases peri-urban areas previously associated with agricultural activities have been subject to informal configurations made up of temporary or makeshift structures. The availability of urban services such as clinics and hospitals does not therefore correlate with the needs of all urban residents. At the same time, in poorer cities child labor, and its impact on educational development, creates an enduring poverty trap.

In November 2022, the world passed the 8 billion population mark, that represented a growth of 1 billion people in just 11 years. A further rise of some 2.4 billion is projected before the end of the 21st century, that will place a daunting pressure on resources. Middle-income countries, mostly in Asia, account for the majority of this growth. By way of comparison, the Sub-Saharan Africa population is projected to increase 95 percent by mid-century—a degree of growth that is technically unsustainable in terms of food production. Environmental well-being is often a neglected aspect of urban growth. The World Bank estimates that deterioration of environmental quality in Asian cities can cost up to 10 percent of urban GOP. While major cities have an adequate water supply, particularly for their core developed areas, delivery infrastructure of piped water in the lower ranked cities can be as low as 30 percent. The situation is particularly acute in squatter communities, where potable water supply is often threatened by contamination, and drinking water has to be purchased at high cost. This can also be affected by seasonal flooding where large bodies of water are subject to periodic inundation. Disposal of solid waste and hazardous material from industry, together with uncollected garbage, is a further problem, even in major cities. Landfill sites are usually in short supply and expensive forms of incineration then become the only option, while waste recycling requires significant public initiatives in terms of effective collection and processing.

The built environment is a more or less accurate register of our prevailing social values, and there is a need to direct the emphasis on urban design to ways in which we can satisfy community concerns for environmental quality and to replicate, as far as possible, the inherent complexity and vibrancy of the city itself. This process must therefore be concerned with the entire range of forces that subscribe to the physical make-up of cities, including their subsequent care and management. The term "Urban Design" was first used by the American Institute of Architects in 1957, and lies at the interface of a number of professional disciplines and urban thinkers who lay claim to it. Its essential role is to manage the public interactions of human life into physical forms regulated by complementarity and, as far as possible, a reconciliation of conflicting elements. Its ideology is one of social responsibility that resonates with other aspects of the physical and natural sciences and is perhaps why we most often refer favorably to the formal layout of classical cities, but also to the organic patterns and artistic principles of medieval ones. A typical "figure ground plan" of a long-established urban core with its amalgam of incidental spaces, passageways, and precincts has rarely emerged as part of a definitive plan, but as a by-product of indeterminate development processes, diverse investment decisions, and evolving spatial inter-relationships and user flows, continually modified over time. In this way we look to the past to reimagine the memory of the city, but must inevitably also look to the future through its capacity for change and adaptability.

Urban design tends to suggest an emphasis on values inherent in physical constructs and their underlying morphology as they collectively contribute to spatial organization. It can just as easily relate to a place marked by architectural heritage as to an established gathering space possessing the informal cultural connotations of use. The city itself is more than just material form and must relate equally to the wider values of urbanism with its integral blend of historical and aesthetic factors, economic functions, social structures, and other related urban processes. The three-dimensional outcome is therefore an identifiable and occasionally symbolic result of these inter-relationships and attributes that merge in the distinctive character of urban places. In Asia, as elsewhere, this represents the public face of human settlement expressed through narratives of expression, memory, and aspiration, and essentially relates to the public domain, so that its emphasis is on streets and spaces, with a connective framework that is shared by the community. The public are therefore at the core of successful urban design for the obvious reasons of comfort and convenience, but also on more elusive grounds that satisfy a diversity of stakeholder interests.

Urban design can represent both a description and an activity, but it is in the achievement of holistic approaches to the latter that we can encounter difficulties in terms of administrative hurdles, policy silos, and overarching regulatory processes that too often pre-determine design outcomes. In fact, the ways in which cities and their institutions in Asia deal with urban regeneration is a clear indicator of their civic health.

The design, implementation, and regeneration of city fabric in the creation of sustainable places generally involves input from a range of stakeholders and interested parties that include city authorities, owners, regulators, and users across multiple scales. In essence the "urban" and the "design" processes are not necessarily concomitant, but they are metaphorically joined at the hip to ensure a process that is contextually responsive through a range of contested values. The ecology of urbanism is therefore a continuing challenge during an era of concern for sustainable planning in response to climate change, together with the forces of rapid urbanization across international cities where dangers of eco-collapse must be countered through resilience.

There is a distinction to be made between public space and urban space, both of which have a social as well as a spatial dimension. The former is the accessible public realm of the community, established by territorial limits and distinctions. The latter includes public space but also complementary privately owned space; for example, commercial complexes that are open to the public but subject to management restrictions. An additional and highly disparate spatial type in Asia is the sacred place. As urban space is a continuum that connects both private and public, no part of the urban realm can exist in a state of self-contained exclusion, and this allows for the open space system to be subject to creative order and regulation. The high-density layering of uses that we see in the dense Asian cities can comprise below-grade transport concourses, ground-level dispersal, and above-ground shopping systems as part of a connective framework. Above this we might also find a semi-private realm of commercial, residential, and podium-level recreational uses, largely separate from the public realm and privately managed. In combination these produce "tree" and "semi-lattice" structures, induced by regulatory systems that establish ordering principles of access and connection, accepted as essential for cities with high population densities and commensurately high land values. This embraces and articulates the essential dynamism of urban life but inevitably creates some ambiguity in the integration of genuinely livable streets and public places. In this way perceived space therefore becomes linked with cognitive experience and subjective associations.

In general we might say that historical urban space, defined by distinguishable building fabric, nourishes our urban association with both past and present, shaped by memory, meaning, and identity, but also highlighted by the incongruous energy fields associated with both building and population density. A dialogue with the older urban environment signals our emotional relationship with the city, where the ornamental surfaces of pre-industrial architecture often sit in a less than comfortable proximity to the more austere and anonymous representations of an ubiquitous international style.

While the New Urbanism approach is correctly based on a transect in terms of land use and development scale from rural to urban, the Asian city of multiple neighborhoods of different socio-economic mix requires a creative interconnection so that community identity is bolstered by allowing for diversity of choice across a wide spectrum. However, this must also be responsive to ongoing processes, that can accommodate growth and change in order to meet a technologically and sustainably charged future.

Cities spread knowledge and ideas precisely because of the scope for interface and interaction over time. All of these hold challenges for urban design. In exploring some of these aspects, the general modes of inquiry comprise a necessary combination of measures: descriptive based on the historical evolution of cultural, economic, and political dynamics that have jointly created the conditions for urban design action; empirical through observation of key characteristics that relate to different spatial entities; and theoretical based on various degrees of research.

The book seeks to address both the characteristics and complexity of Asian cities, together with the issues facing them in terms of growth and development in the 21st century, that collectively represent overlapping aspects of urban design. They have been assembled in an updated and re-edited form, and condensed into twelve chapters from a series of presentations and discussion papers made over a number of years at various forums on city planning and urban design.

CHAPTER 1

Ascendancy of the Asian City

Formative City-building Regimes

Early Asian cities were based on the ideological relationship of a ruling elite and its associated military and religious bureaucracy. Prior to the European arrival in Asia, there were three predominant urban settlement types that had flourished for many hundreds of years. The first was the "sacred" settlement, which generally served as both a capital containing a seat of kingship, and as an organizational center related to surrounding patterns of agricultural development, overland trade routes, and economic administration. Cities such as Angkor, Ayutthaya, Luang Prabang, Borobudor, and Majapahit, along with Xian in the PRC, functioned as symbolic hubs of divine authority and bureaucratic government, where morphologies reflected both celestial intersections and religious imagery broadly related to Hinduism and Buddhism. The second settlement type was the port city that acted as an entrepôt in relation to strategic sea routes and long-established maritime relationships with other Asian cities. The third type was the fortified city laid out within a walled perimeter.

The colonial capital of India was transferred from Kolkata to Delhi in 1931. It was designed by Edwin Lutyens and Herbert Baker to encapsulate an "eternal" concept of British sovereignty. Its spatial order was focussed on Government House (now Parliament House).

Much of Asia was predominantly rural until almost the beginning of the 16th century, although there were of course some impressive early city settlements dating from medieval times—Ankor Wat in Cambodia, Edo in Japan, and the Han and Tang cities of the PRC. Bangkok, for example, literally means "place of olive plums" and was a small farming community on the banks of the Chao Phraya River, until it was established as a city in 1782 by King Rama I. Much of the urban form that we see in Asian cities today stemmed either directly or indirectly from the city building regimes of colonial occupation; Hong Kong SAR, Macao SAR, Singapore, Malaysia, Indonesia, Cambodia, Vietnam, India, and the Philippines all spent many years under either Dutch, French, Spanish, Portuguese, or British colonial regimes, which in most cases had a significant urbanizing impact. Other cities were open to foreign trading entities by what was dubiously known as "gunboat diplomacy."

Almost all major Asian cities had pre-colonial origins, but in most cases it was essentially the advent of European settlement that brought about the planned urbanization that we can experience today. Colonial intervention in Asia has been a colossal factor in the generation of city form, along with political and cultural transformation. Above all it was responsible for major migration of labor, new ethnic configurations, and in most cases a new governmental and capitalist order. The remains of foreign fortifications are still discernible on a number of city plans with public open space taking the place of moats and military areas. A typical "figure ground plan" of the dense Asian city illustrates a duality of both fine- and course-grained patterns that have come about through a long sequence of city building and redevelopment processes. Indigenous cultural institutions were in general absorbed rather than subordinated, but from the mid-16th century the result over several centuries was a transformation of city form.

The early maritime economy linked together a vast geographical and geopolitical sphere, opening up layers of complex cultural and commercial realms that extended from the East and South China Seas to the Arabian Gulf. These same maritime forces and emerging sea routes were also the means by which European exploration, closely associated with its new naval powers, entered a diverse but sophisticated Asian maritime world, not unlike a new set of actors intervening on an already crowded stage. During the early period of western intervention urban centers were developed in the coastal communities of Asia, founded by trading companies. In this sense the intermingling of technologies, design, and economic practices fashioned patterns of urbanization based on cross-cultural pollination, where the driving forces of maritime trade and business development were reflected in the spatial characteristics of port and primate cities.

The status of cities such as Malacca, Macassar, Timor, and Brunei came not from territorial gain, but from economic power arising from commercial alliances through a far-flung network of trading centers that Western interests were later able to plug into, and in many cases exploit. What is sometimes known as the "Asian Corridor" broadly corresponded to the continental and maritime Silk Route, together with the "Mongolian Corridor," along trajectories that were most propitious to the transport of merchandise. The discovery of the route from Europe to India by Vasco da Gama in 1497 gave rise to new port cities in the West such as Venice and Genoa, and the birth of world maritime empires that were to have a significant role in the emergence of new Asian townships.

A bronze statue of Queen Victoria marks the entrance to the northern drive of Government House in Kolkata. Her carved stone is decorated with representations of Art, Literature, and Justice; the Lion of Britain; and the Tiger of India.

Colonial policy of one kind or another prompted a swift transition toward more dynamic economic trajectories that still resonate in contemporary urban situations, fashioned from the driving forces of maritime trade, exploration, and the underlying proselytizing forces of religion. European adventurism was closely associated with new naval powers, reflected by the images of Spanish galleons and British schooners depicted on tombstones and early paintings. During this mercantile period new urban centers were developed, first by the Spanish in Intramuros (now Manila); the Portuguese in Goa, Malacca, and Macao SAR; the Dutch in Batavia (now Jakarta); the French in Indo-China; and the British in the Indian sub-continent, the Straits Settlements, and Concession Areas around the Chinese coast that from the mid-19th century that have come to represent some of the largest cities in Asia. Colonization was not just a Western prerogative. Chinese rule predominated in Vietnam for several centuries, and Japan annexed Korea in 1910, causing Seoul to lose much of its historic fabric but later to adopt a new restoration and modernizing agenda.

The first European colonizing regimes in Asia were the Spanish and Portuguese, motivated not merely by financial gain but by a religious ideology, underscored by forms of social control and the cultural assimilation of the indigenous populations into new urban communities as an integral aspect of a proselytizing mission. This was propelled by the forces of religious conviction and praxis to the extent that in Goa even Hindu temples took on very similar design characteristics to the Catholic churches built by the Portuguese. The city-building process in the Philippines was codified through the Spanish *Ordienzas*, the first examples of planning and design guidelines, which attempted to equate urban design parameters with land use controls as part of the planning process. An important example of this in terms of spatial planning was the *Plaza Mayor*, a distinctive urban design feature introduced by the Spanish city builders that can still be seen for example in front of Manila Cathedral and Quiapo Church.

The later British, Dutch, and French regimes were drawn to Asia primarily for trading benefit, including early commercial transactions with Japan where the Portuguese and Spanish were trading in the 17th century, and the Dutch a century later. The initial process of opening up trading trajectories was not merely carried out through aggressive tactics, but was often assisted by gifts. The Chinese demanded tribute from foreign delegations to the Emperor, but probably the most remarkable feature was the centerpiece of the Grand Palace in Phnom Penh—a gift from Empress Eugene of France in 1869, in the form of a prefabricated cast iron palace, dedicated to King Norodom I, who had opened the door for a French protectorate to be established with special trading rights.

Batavia was formed by the Dutch East India Company in 1619, based on the city of Amsterdam, and parts of modern-day Jakarta retain traces of its initial canal alignments

The Gateway of India Arch incorporates an amalgam of neo-Gothic and Indian styles intended to convey the ties between Britain and India, built to commemorate the visit of King George V to Mumbai in 1911.

because of the high water table. The older part of the city, Sunda Kalapa, still has restored Dutch buildings, which when they were constructed had to accord with Dutch building regulations.

More than 70 percent of Western colonial territory, and even more if we include the Chinese Concession Areas, was acquired between 1850 and 1914, and effectively governed under the process of extraterritoriality. Much of this was initially through bodies such as the Dutch and British East India Companies, that unleashed forces of modernization and urbanization, and determined new modes of social formation. The French Plan for Pondicherry around Fort Louis in 1755 illustrates the grid-iron layout that became associated with later military cantonments. The British similarly built new Civil Stations, based on gridded settlements that then became almost standard colonial models.

Cadastral mapping and the concept of place in city building had much to do with the ways in which this was conceived in the West so that city planning in Asia took on the elusive ideological significance of a "Civilizing Mission," overlaying surfaces with predominantly European,

The Quan Chuong Gate—
(the last surviving gate tower)
to the old city of Hanoi.

and in some cases utopian city forms, while at the same time physically annexing local place values and re-inscribing place names. Colonization brought with it a shift in traditional economies from a form of production based on local markets and relative self-sufficiency, to an export market of resources and an import market for foreign goods. This in turn brought with it colossal shifts in infrastructure emphasis, assimilated within new patterns of land use that often had grand colonial connotations. Perhaps the most ambitious undertaking was the plan that linked the Old Mughal City of Delhi to New Delhi, designed by Edwin Lutyens and Herbert Baker, but influenced by the garden city theories of Ebenezar Howard that were prevalent in Britain at the time.

New patterns of architecture and urban design emerged in Neo-Classical styles, as Western planners reconstructed and reconnected older cities to serve the forceful interests of colonizing powers. In some situations, particularly on the Indian sub-continent and in Malaysia, architects and engineers attempted to marry Western layouts with indigenous ones, creating new architectural form such as *Indo-Saracenic*, a combination that left an identifiable urban presence, but one that was only marginally associated with the culture of the indigenous city. In India, for example, the styles came to be known as Bombay Gothic, Calcutta Corinthean, and Bengal Baroque. Ernest Hébrard, the head of the technical council in Hanoi in the 1920s, formulated an urban design code for Vietnam's main cities based on climatic responsiveness through amalgamating indigenous architectural characteristics with modern design innovations. This combined characteristics of Hanoi's terraced shophouses into an adaptable *indochinois* neo-classical style with characteristic shaded terraces, overhanging eaves and high shuttered doorways and was applied to buildings within a new government quarter in Hanoi.

Urbanization grew rapidly during the mercantile era in response to an ideology of material accumulation and industrialization that saw the emergence of a new middle class, as city

Government House in Kolkata
built by Lord Curzon in 1921
in a mix of European, Baroque,
and Indo-Saracenic with
Mughal corner turrets. It was
largely funded by Indian princes
twenty years after the death
of Queen Victoria in 1921. It is
described in some quarters as
the "Taj of the Raj" and now
documents the history of the
British in India, complete
with statues of political and
military figures.

The Victoria Rail Terminus, now known as the Chhatrapati Shiraj Terminus is the most monumental of the neo-Gothic Victorian buildings in Mumbai, featuring an exuberant combination of domes, spires, turrets, flying buttresses, and allegorical friezes.

economies developed to include government employment, specialist institutions, banks, and shipping companies. This helped to lay the foundations for some of the largest cities in Asia, and was responsible for major migration of labor, including far-reaching patterns of international trade. Above all it restructured and, in most cases, redirected the process of city building, with indigenous cultural institutions generally absorbed within imperialist development programs. Some cities had little choice in the matter, having to house vast numbers of refugees from civil war or invasion.

From the turn of the 20th century, primate cities began to massively outstrip second tier cities in terms of both economic and demographic growth, largely through their development as centers of government and administration. However, large-scale rural to urban migration was largely a phenomenon of post-independence situations that tended to reflect political instability, and later a transfer of power to an urban elite that in most situations has sustained a capitalist outlook toward the economic challenges of industrialization and globalization. At the end of World War II only 17 percent of Asians lived in cities. By the mid-1970s Japan, with its reconstructed industries, was the largest post-war economy in Asia. In 2022 urban populations have grown to more than 50 percent and in certain situations, particularly in the PRC, have evolved through expanded metro areas and mega-urban regions as a result of concentrated economic development. Globalization might have meant the decline of much of the manufacturing industry in the West, but in turn it has proceeded to supercharge what have become the behemoth industrial economies of Asia, where the flow of ideas continues to be kindled by a growing international knowledge and service economy. This has led to something of an urban reinvention in many Asian cities, introducing an urbanism of increased density, innovation, and interaction.

The economic strength of Asian cities make them magnets that attract urban migration from less-advantaged areas and then from higher educated and entrepreneurial backgrounds, that demonstrate the strength of the urban system, even through the COVID pandemic, as a source of betterment in the 21st century. Cycles of supply and demand have a secondary impact in driving up levels of density through redevelopment in order to maximize floor area ratios. Preservation policies that act to accelerate gentrification of older heritage quarters therefore come at a certain cost. Restrictions on construction need to be carefully weighed against the value of the existing urban environment in terms of its aesthetic significance but also in terms of its massive economic value built around visitation and tourism.

In the process, densely populated rural enclaves on the peri-urban fringe have been drawn into the city ambit through continuing urban expansion and industrial development. The spatial consequence of this is a mix of dense but dispersed settlements, increasingly consolidated and integrated through primary road and service infrastructure. In some cases this has led to environmental and ecological degradation, and the relocation of productive agricultural land to areas farther afield. On the positive side, spatial dispersion has brought about wider capital accumulation, increased job opportunities, and housing choice.

The majority of cities in Asia's developing economies have, on average, three times the population density of global cities elsewhere. Urban housing is arguably top of the development agenda, which means overcoming something of a paradox whereby rapid economic growth brings about changing social structures and a polarization in terms of wealth and well-being, and with increasing numbers at the extremes creating a segmented population structure. At the lower end this can be accompanied by forced evictions and involuntary resettlement. This reflects a structural demographic shift in the wealthiest Asian cities, where household sizes are falling. While the PRC has over 500 million registered households, 15 percent consist of only one person. In Japan the rate is 33 percent, in South Korea 24 percent, 21 percent in the Hong Kong SAR, and 13 percent in Singapore. Together with aging populations, urbanization is one reason for this, with small urban apartment sizes and the high cost of raising children also given as reasons for single lifestyles.

Henri Lefebvre in *The Urban Revolution* has stated that the "urban" is both form and receptacle, but is always a forum for aspiration. The urbanization process continues to be brought into focus as many parts of South Asia continue to extricate themselves from under-development and deprivation. There is an obvious danger that some Asian cities will become less of an economic springboard for their populations, but rather places of refuge as worldwide production processes become increasingly polarized. In many cases a blurring of the traditional distinctions between city and periphery is accompanied by a mutation of the older cores as

The Nanjing Road pedestrian artery establishes an effective link between the Bund and People's Square in Shanghai.

spiraling land costs lead to high-rise redevelopment and building intensification, but also in some situations to competition between center and sub-center employment hubs. At the same time city expansion is leading to patterns of urbanization increasingly dominated by emerging development axes associated with international growth corridors.

These multiple landscapes reflect a range of subcultures endowed with different needs and building requirements at a time when civil society is asserting changing social agendas and political reform movements in the wake of the centralized and authoritarian regimes of the immediate post-colonial period. However, in most Asian countries the state assumes a major role in transforming urban space and delineating its symbolic qualities. In the process, public investment has entailed the adoption of ever more complicated measures to control city design and to accommodate increased development densities through zoning, building regulations, planning ordinances, and resumption mechanisms.

Post-Colonial Trajectories

The foreign political presence probably achieved its zenith in the late 19th century, and while its secular attributes were appropriated in different degrees within various countries, this gave way to new waves of nationalism over the course of the 20th century. In the period immediately following World War II, western powers withdrew from most Asian countries either voluntarily or under siege.

In the post-colonial period, after erecting statues to freedom fighters and appointing new political leaders, economic policies have varied between Asian countries, but with several commonalities—the requirement to attract investment, to diversify economically, and in most cases a need to concentrate on urbanization programs of mass housing and business development.

This was scarcely the end of western intervention, however. The Cold War brought military confrontation that enveloped entire sub-regions in conflict. In recent years Asia's alignment with new globalizing forces, registering a powerful regional bloc, has assertively focused on economic growth and development. In many cases this continues to involve a physical as well as an economic intervention—with ample evidence of a comfortable co-existence between old and new. However, imported modernizations can act to overwhelm time-honored routines and social customs, often reflecting the inability of prevailing planning systems to control the politically inspired impetus of rapid growth and change that stems from the global marketplace.

Fort Santiago built in 1714 occupied a site at the mouth of the Pasig River in Intramuros, Manila, and was named in honor of Spain's patron saint, the Apostle James. The bastion of Santa Barbara was named after the patron saint of artillerymen and constructed in 1592 to protect the entrance to the river.

The civil service administration of the Hong Kong SAR from 1997 effectively took control of an established governmental hierarchy, and both consolidated and extended its means of urban control and management. It has, however, shown little aptitude to align this with adequate responses to urban design challenges, so that an institutional mindset tends to put process before product in terms of achieving city betterment objectives. Land itself remains as a commodity, manipulated through a combination of zoning and building/planning regulations, and the high return to government from land sales to developers that have contributed to some of the world's highest property prices. Civic engagement and community empowerment are made secondary to a simplistic set of urban values oriented around top-down urban management, bereft of necessary levels of coordinated decision-making.

A fundamental difference between Western and Asian city regions from the 1990s is that the latter situation includes densely populated rural enclaves on the peri-urban fringe that have been drawn into the city ambit through industrialization. These often-present perennial problems of land use control, ineffective use of land through "brownfield" uses, lack of adequate development control mechanisms, and in many cases an undermining of traditions. On the positive side, spatial dispersion has brought about wider capital accumulation, increased job opportunities, and housing choice provided by both government and private investment. However, this is somewhat open to external events, and the extent to which the process has been intelligently handled through effective city management.

A further aspect is that in many post-colonial situations, the older planning and land mechanisms have, with little modification, been left broadly in place for dealing with the changing needs of the contemporary city. These have been applied to the accommodation of new and far-reaching development agendas that serve to meet different requirements and pressures, while maintaining political legitimacy. At the same time, innovation in design has been primarily geared to incorporating new prototypes to achieve housing targets in a uniform and often standardized way, marginalizing the complicated qualities of symbolism and ritual associated with traditional urbanism. There is therefore, in many cities, a challenging connection to be made between modern-day planning, urban design, and the history of place.

The growth of a significant middle class through urban-industrial growth and the rise of multifarious business interests has transformed many Asian cities from centers of production to theaters of accumulation, consumption, visitation, and tourism. This has created a commodification of culture through a new architecture of retail, entertainment, and recreation reflecting changing social agendas, while at the same time the indigenous elite have also belatedly acquired, at least in part, the cultural capital of imperialism, including its pomp and circumstance.

In most Asian countries the state assumes a major role in transforming urban space and delineating its symbolic qualities. In the process, city making and renewal procedures have become increasingly absolutist and expedient. In making room for new development, what should be a community-sensitive approach to regeneration has been implemented through comprehensive redevelopment, where past urban forms and built entities give way to those that reflect constantly escalating land prices.

The Spatial Impact of Intervention

Urban interventions, in one form or another, represent a direct change or interruption to social, economic, environmental, and cultural conditions. At some stage over the past 500 years virtually all Asian societies became subject to significant Western interventionist forces through forms of military invasion, trading programs, colonizing ambitions, authoritarian control, or the proselytizing zeal of imported religious beliefs. This has, until relatively recent times, led to a Eurocentric conceptualization of urban values. The perceptual barriers between East and West were generally tinged by conflict between the expansionist regimes from the West that often disguised imperialist intentions, and the weight of tradition in Asia that emphasized philosophical belief systems and sacred strictures that are still deeply embedded in society, culture, and ruling patterns.

Changing social and economic circumstances produced periodic waves of immigration and emigration within Asia itself, importing or exporting building styles, and amalgamating these with prevailing development conditions to produce new or hybrid forms of urban design. These have in turn become manifested in sequences of growth and change, influencing the predominant scale, form, and architectural design of the urban settlements that we can perceive today, despite the regimented impact of contemporary globalizing forces. In certain situations rationalization of land use for "new" city development through city building initiatives carried out by relatively benevolent occupying powers left older city cores intact so that urban development progressed as a duality of both informal and planned growth. In most situations urban design was, of necessity, highly ideological, whether through enforced trading structures or military inducement. This has left a rich and complementary residue of contrasting urban forms and equally different versions of political economy.

The Asian city itself is a complex interaction of impositions and everyday choices that shape its physicality, increasingly governed by the economics of the marketplace. The modernizing city is a product of two important factors—a precipitate demand for improved and expanded accommodation, and an accompanying opportunity for urban design innovation. This can achieve purposeful regeneration initiatives, new waterfronts and upgraded heritage enclaves,

Gynongdong Sijiang Market in Seoul, a precinct notable for herbal medicine and traditional cooked food.

but also the vertiginous battlements of new high-rise housing enclaves stretching behind them to the horizon. In planning for the public good there must clearly be some degree of control and balance over development interests—in particular the social and economic rights associated with free market mechanisms to which most Asian societies now broadly subscribe. This in turn relates to the degree to which the community perceives that its well-being is a priority of government, and equally that private interests are made secondary to the public good.

Across Asia different customs and traditions that are emphasized and re-fashioned to meet contemporary needs and values are themselves embedded in new lifestyles. Possibly the most enduring characteristics shaped by this process are the design prototypes and adaptations that both symbolically and functionally relate architectural "substructures" to climatic and environmental factors. As urban environments are being constantly reinterpreted, they tend also to evolve into separate and increasingly polarised enclaves echoing growing wealth gaps. However in general the plural character of Asian society helps to build bridges between communities, contributing to the cosmopolitan heterotopia of cities. Gardens by the Bay in Singapore for example constitutes not merely a park but a bold statement on the city's long-term green and sustainable intentions.

The character of socio-cultural change in Asia also varies considerably according to changing political models. There is, in many cities, an inadequate connection between modern-day planning, and the co-ordinates of history and cultural heritage. Freedom from colonial authority has by no means coincided with democratic rule. Vietnam, Cambodia, and Laos emerged from long periods of colonial domination to extremes of socialism and occasional violent conflict before opening their economies to modernization. Some cities have had to reconcile competitive forces for access to urban land while at the same time putting in place more liberal planning and land management mechanisms. This is increasingly underscored by international investment, and the refurbishment of older and iconic landmark structures, such as Ernest Hébrard's imaginative old market building in Phnom Penh, and Hanoi's grand opera house. Some colonial era civic buildings can therefore be welcomed and appreciated by post-independence regimes, while in other situations political decisions have had a different impact. A large number of beautiful old buildings in Yangon, such as the Secretariat and High Court, are now looking for new uses after the government moved the capital to Nay Ryi Tau in 2005.

It is estimated that cities in Asia will, in combination, extend their population size by up to one billion new inhabitants by the mid-21st century, and in the PRC it is projected that in excess of 70 percent of its population might be living in cities within the same timeframe. Cities must therefore renew and regenerate but also expand. As there is a continuing tendency in virtually every Asian country toward reduced household size, housing programs must cater for increased numbers and sizes of dwellings to reflect growing urban wealth. At the same time more institutional and community buildings must reflect improved standards of urban care, and greater numbers of commercial structures are needed to cater for the continued growth in service industry and global economic ties. Environmental action must accord with internationally agreed resolutions including the integration of different modes of transit and the achievement of livable and pollution-free cities.

The Driving Forces

Asia produces around one-third of global Gross Domestic Product, and is projected to account for more than 50 percent by the mid-21st century. GDP is closely linked with the spatial dynamics associated with the process of urbanization and the interconnections between cities that stimulates growth and innovation through flows of people, goods, and services. In addition, geographic factors are also important to the spatial distribution of economic activities, in particular proximity to international markets. Due to differences between individual countries in terms of population size, economic variables, and urban characteristics, national urbanization levels are not necessarily comparable, although urban agglomeration rates can be

Covered markets serve as informal pedestrian connectors that follow the mid-section of the Cheonggyecheon River in Seoul.

Chinatown to the south of the Singapore River was laid out for the Chinese community under the Raffles Plan of 1824.

broadly determined using satellite imagery comparisons. While established Asian cities such as Shanghai, Hong Kong, Singapore, Tokyo, and Mumbai play a major role in global markets, new cities such as Shenzhen and Bangalore have, over the past 30 years, became the new technological epicenters.

An Asian Development Bank Working Paper from 2020 on urbanization rates demonstrates an increase in the total urbanized area of the 43 Asian economies studied, from 230,000 sq kilometers in 1992 to 610,000 sq kilometers in 2016—an average annual growth rate of 4 percent, amounting to 2.4 percent of total land area. At the same time the growth of urban habitation considerably outpaced growth of the overall population of 4.1 billion. The People's Republic of China and India in combination accounted for 75 percent of the regional population that moved to cities from rural areas, and overall urbanization rates continue to be driven by these two countries. Unsurprisingly this also correlates with income levels, representing a broad increase in GDP per capita. In the PRC, changes of land use from rural to urban continues to be an important fiscal revenue source to local government as urban densities increase. However, in Indian cities, the low floor area ratio in older city cores has in general resulted in urban sprawl and inefficient use of land.

Of the five largest countries in terms of population, the PRC has 680 cities, India 320, Indonesia 93, Japan 68, and Pakistan 63. However, of the largest cities with a population in excess of five million people, the PRC had 13, almost tripling the original total over a 20-year period. Over the same timeframe cities with a population below 500,000 decreased considerably.

Of 33 primate cities, 27 are national capitals. Individual cities have not only expanded in terms of physical area and population but also in terms of urban clusters, connected by efficient transport infrastructure to form interlocking metropolitan configurations. This presents certain challenges in terms of administrative coordination of urban design, traffic, and environmental management. The most extreme example in Asia is Shanghai, which incorporates 53 cities within the Yangtze River Delta Area. Altogether, 29 city cluster have been identified across the region, each having in excess of 10 million people, while the largest of these city clusters with total populations exceeding 20 million are set out in the following table:

The Largest City Clusters in Asia with Populations above 10 Million

Rank	Economy	City Cluster	Total Population (million)	Total Area (km²)	Number of Incorporated Cities	Number of Level-1 Administrative Divisions
1	PRC	Shanghai-Nanjing	91.5	45,445	53	4
2	Japan	Tokyo-Osaka	73.3	27,798	2	20
3	PRC	Guangzhou-Huizhou	52.3	19,465	12	4
4	India	Delhi-Chandigarh	43.4	15,379	10	6
5	Indonesia	Jakarta-Bandung	38.6	6,981	11	3
6	PRC	Beijing-Tianjin	37.8	17,023	12	4
7	Korea, Rep of	Seoul-Taejon	32.2	18,330	9	11
8	India	Mumbai-Pune	30.8	5m514	4	2
9	Philippines	Metro Manila-Angeles	26.5	3,313	4	4
10	India	Kolkata-Habra	24.7	4,769	3	1
11	Taipei, China	Capital City of Taipei, China-Puli	21.7	12,135	2	20
12	Thailand	Bangkok-Nakhon Pathom	20.7	16,864	10	5
13	Bangladesh	Dhaka-Sabhar	18.1	2,128	3	2
14	Pakistan	Lahore-Faisalabad	16.5	4,814	9	1
15	Viet Nam	Ho Chi Minh-My Tho	16.0	8,768	5	4
16	Indonesia	Semarang-Cirebon	15.0	4,121	14	4

17	PRC	Quanzhou-Xiamen	14.3	5,752	9	1
18	India	Bangalore-Tumkur	13.7	4,779	4	2
19	PRC	Jinan-Zibo	12.5	7,516	11	1
20	Malaysia	Kuala Lumpur – Johor Bahru	12.4	8,922	7	5
21	India	Ahmadabad – Vadodara	12.3	3,954	4	1
22	India	Chennai-Vellore	12.2	3,538	3	1
23	Indonesia	Surabaya-Malang	11.9	3,867	8	2
24	Korea, Rep of	Pusan-Taegu	11.6	8,925	6	7
25	India	Agra-Aligarh	11.4	6,211	6	1
26	PRC	Shantou-Chaoyang	11.2	3,310	6	2
27	Viet Nam	Ha Noi-Hai Phong	10.3	3,839	3	4
28	PRC	Zhengzhou-Xinxiang	10.3	4,758	10	1
29	PRC	Chengu-Xindu	10.0	2,967	6	1

Source: ADB Working Paper 618: Spatial Dynamics and Driving Forces of Asian Cities, August 2020

Transformative Processes and Changing Values

The Asian city represents substantial cultural change in its 21st century manifestation, with new and different values superimposed on long established patterns of urbanization. Mega-urban regional growth patterns provide for different degrees of co-existence and overlap, and frequently reflect dual economic structures where both cutting-edge technologies and pre-industrial interconnected networks of small businesses operate virtually side by side. This leaves open the notion of how urban design should respond to situations where cultural bonds with the past are being steadily eroded through the homogenizing tendencies of globalization, or sustained only artificially as tourist attractions.

The majority of East Asian societies share Buddhist and Confucianist traditions that emphasize community ideals, manifested in cultural and social values. While this might arguably have been diluted by the advancement of materialistic influences associated with the new global economy, cultural differences shape the dimensions of urban transformation and even political sensitivities, and the city has become the vehicle through which the forces of change are acted out. At the same time, as cities take on similar spatial signatures, there is a commensurate resurrection of cultural heritage to form beacons of identity and foci of visitation that establish a particular urban chemistry.

Rapid change in these values together with globalizing forces have tended to bring about a pragmatic sensitivity toward other contemporary priorities such as a sustainable environment. A realization of this helps to guide new urban planning processes, and reinforces the value of urban places and the need to protect them. The city is the space where local indigenous forces meet new political and economic hierarchies that control national resources. This has created, in various degrees, political, social, and economic transformations, reflected by distinctive spatial patterns but also diverse development pressures and conflict over urban space.

The specter of redevelopment can present an acute threat in virtually all Asian cities, where the demolition of older buildings and neighborhoods with both necessary amenities and cultural value to longstanding communities, is often deemed necessary to provide urban land at much increased building densities for both commercial and residential purposes. This frequently reflects inadequate or inappropriate planning and land-use control mechanisms, coupled in many cases with the influence wielded by development and land-owning interests. The demolition of buildings and relocation of citizens is generally accompanied by a spatial intensification that brings with it a commensurate degree of social and community change that in effect polarizes societies in both social and economic terms. The often-homogenized result conveys less about city-building and more about global image-building, grounded in strategies that prioritize the privileged but disregard the marginalized in society who are relegated to a secondary existence represented by overcrowded slums.

Cities that have evolved without the organizational discipline of an underlying growth strategy have come to represent a series of adaptations and superimpositions interfacing with natural characteristics that contribute to a localized blending of both the formal and informal. This in turn influences the way in which cities are used and experienced. Historical persistency continues to inject a considerable spatial presence in the form of sacred places, even as

questions arise as to the extent to which deeply embedded social customs and belief systems can continue to be insinuated as core values.

Henri Lefebvre questioned the organization of space from a philosophical perspective as being too important to be left to architects and planners, and posited a situationist focus relating to the process of urbanization. This involves exploring the relationship between the "representation of space" and "spaces of representation"—that is between the *conceived* and the *lived* experience. Every space therefore has a social dimension.

As transformative processes become more tangible and predictable there is a need to sustain the narratives of successful urbanism, and this implies a sense of dissonance common in the traditional asian city where business and residence are frequently combined – the chance of interaction and encounter, the unexpected, the complex and the indeterminate. These have created patterns of use and ownership that cannot be neatly defined by either master planning or urban design, but which exert a considerable influence on local economies, community perception and the relationship of urban quarters to the city as a whole. But in situations where renewal and redevelopment procedures are increasingly institutionalized, the tendency is for urban design to become more absolutist, personified by two sets of economic operations which overlap and occasionally conflict: the growing commercial requirements of the service economy through its emphasis on virtually self-contained commercial environments; and the bazaar economy that has traditionally evolved around strong retail interfaces associated with active city streets that form part of distinctive urban quarters. A reconciliation of these factors creates opportunities to retain or introduce ad-hoc aspects of place with distinctive forms of expression that help to break down uniformity.

Asian cities do not necessarily have the formalist configuration of spaces and the highly defined urban public realm generally bequeathed to Western cities. Instead the "street," the progenitor of Asian city form, tends to display complex interactions including an emphasis on social rituals, ceremonial uses, and informal commercial operations that relate more to patterns of activity than conceived physical form. In acknowledging the vast historical and cultural differences between cities, and with limited commonalities in the urban landscape, it is

The former Legislative Council Building in the Hong Kong SAR. Now the Court of Final Appeal.

prudent to steer away from normative models. The utopian city, with its historicist references, is an unobtainable ideal quite simply because it is impossible to envision an ideal state in the face of society's continual struggles to innovate, renew, and modernize. There is also, however, a paradox, in that deterministic urban expansion and wholesale renewal is often an expedient process, not necessarily responsive to cultural or even social ideals. Urban design should therefore be about facilitating, balancing, and invigorating the process and must maintain a balance between past imperatives and future expectations so that the process of regeneration and growth relates simultaneously to physical fabric, social aspirations, economic conditions, and environmental sustainability.

Indigenous urban traditions are but one of many constitutive layers that relate to post-modern Asian city building, necessary to ensure a stable social order, with a duality between informal production processes and modern use of capital and management. This has produced a spiraling rate of consumption in relation to increasing wealth and expenditure patterns, and a realm of urban design built around lifestyle—shopping, food, and entertainment together with a massive growth of private housing estates. It has also produced a situation where cities, even within the same countries, compete for investment and the attractions that encourage it—new airports, station "gateways," science parks, container ports, and convention centers that are large enough in extent to provide nodes of special but interlinked activities. New divisions of labor have accelerated massively since the 1980s, and this has produced major sectoral shifts in national economies along with corresponding socio-economic and class divisions. As Asian cities compete for investment, this ignites an emphasis on transactional flows of capital, people, commodities, and the facilities that service these.

Cities in Transition

Asian cities that traditionally acted as gateways for material export and product delivery are now vehicles for global influences and ideologies. Different forms of capital growth are creating requirements for new types of urban space such as sports stadia and cruise terminals, each with distinctive urban design representations and place identities. The Hong Kong Convention and Exhibition Centre is the busiest of its kind in the world, and the new airport that was built 25 years ago on an offshore island, linked by rail with the urban area, has recently been extended to cater to 100 million visitors a year, and is only one of five airports within the Pearl River Delta. As Edward Soja has reminded us in *Post Metropolis,* density is no longer the necessary marker of centrality. City regions are being assembled with multiple realms of concentration along new growth corridors, and this is breaking down the older distinction between "rural" and "urban."

Globalization brings with it a need to compete at an international level so that cities become shaped less by the natural forces of adaptive urbanism and more by the competitive expansionism of transnational capital and franchised consumerism. Such a situation narrows both social and economic production of space and deflects the intrinsic processes of societal advancement. In turn it impacts urban design priorities and livability associated with diverse realities on the ground that produce the distinctiveness and identity traditionally associated with the Asian city. In hyper-dense cities this is replaced by a pre-zoned expediency that signifies the spatial consequence of rapid transformational processes. This should rather equate economic growth with diverse channels of improvement, at least partly through established local practices, coupled with place-based initiatives that favor incremental growth that consolidates urban character directed toward a process of urban betterment.

In some ways the global economy has picked up where colonialism left off, in forging the dominance of a globalized but predominantly Western worldview but with single-minded political approaches that can all too easily exacerbate social and economic divisions in societies rather than resolving or reconciling them. In part this reflects Western systems of planning control, expediently transferred to many Asian countries, and selectively adapted through top-down government structures to suit changing perceptions of growth and development. As land values increase, often reflecting the leverage of international funding organizations, the more urban design control mechanisms are necessary to introduce coordinated calibrations in city building that equate with higher gains in development ratio and subsequently higher population densities.

There is no single urban model or consistent planning procedure that can apply equally under Asia's hegemonic umbrella, and the convenient broad separation of Asia into several major regions disguises very different political and economic hegemonies. In the global marketplace the majority of countries must maximize their various resources in competition with each other, where the scale of urbanization differs only through governmental ambitions and economic capabilities. We must therefore recognize the transnational flow of knowledge and economic motivations across the region as they are integral to urban design processes, where development and under development might be stated as being two sides of the same coin.

Around 60 percent of national GDP in Asia is now produced within mega-urban regions that are tending to double their populations every 15 years. The Bangkok Metro Area covers around 1,500 square miles but the extended mega-urban region covers some 2,970 square miles and includes six cities within a 62 mile radius of Bangkok. The Jabotabek region around Jakarta encompasses some 2,394 square miles with a population of around 26 million. In Manila the National Capital Region brings together 16 other cities and municipalities within 238 square miles, with an industrial dispersal policy that has encouraged temporary settlements to metamorphosize within the wider city region. The PRC's Greater Bay Area of Guangdong Province in the PRC, consolidated within the Pearl River Delta, encompasses 10 cities and Special Administrative Regions within its 21,658 square mile area.

Contestation represents a realm of uncertainty brought about by conflicting priorities related to aspects such as conservation, maximization of land value, heritage, and housing need. This requires careful moderation of the rate of economic change, which is easier said than done. It has been suggested by Peter Rowe that the "past-present-future" balance can

Orchard Road—the major shopping and entertainment spine in Singapore takes its name from an old fruit growing valley. Urban design strategies have been instrumental in cementing the spine as a series of interlinked spaces for exhibitions, performances, and events.

be manipulated through an emphasis on the past in terms of preservation, the past-present in terms of conservation, and the present-future that represents a fundamental contrast with the past, even as it conserves and connects with it. Perhaps an interesting example of this is Singapore, which includes the preservation of older terraced street forms on Emerald Hill, the upgrading of shop-houses in Chinatown and Little India, and the integration of new high-rise forms that provide for necessary population density.

In areas that do not have to meet increasingly high operational specifications, certain things persist—the sacred places, gathering spaces, and palace compounds, together with indigenous mixed-use quarters. These represent "locales of complexity" that characterize many older neighborhoods where different interest groups compete for priority and space through layering and overlap. They remain according to their capacity to adjust to conditions within the new contested urbanism, where different interest groups compete for priority and space, and where the high and low-order components often experience a less-than-stable relationship, usually existing together in informal allegiances. In these situations commercial transactions

Zhongshan Road in the French Concession Area of Tianjin with the Quan Ye Department Store, built in 1908. Its massive interior space housed around 200 vendors, entertainment uses and restaurants. The corner tower was intended to achieve a characteristic landmark status for the area.

are fragmented, but with symbiotic connections; for example between street-market opera-tors and shops alongside. This juxtaposition of uses tends to be increasingly limited to older mixed-use quarters, as more specialized zones of homogeneous land use such as central busi-ness districts, industrial estates, and technology parks that must meet increasingly high oper-ational specifications. The labor-intensive "cottage" industry in the wealthier cities tends to be now restricted to certain older or ethnic quarters where sympathetic zoning and adaptable lease conditions permit this type of use, while in the poorer cities this remains something of a necessity. In these situations the relationship between architecture and city space often be-comes overwhelmed by forces that have little to do with design and more with expressive qual-ities introduced by constant public encounter.

City space in much of Asia has for the most part traditionally functioned as networks of both official and unofficial economic transactions, and a significant part of economic exchange remains through mobile traders, hawkers, and cooked food operators that form part of a large labor market. As the Asian city undergoes both physical growth and change in response to economic parameters, the informal sector doesn't disappear but tends to operate in parallel. The *pasar malam* and *pojang macha* engender both local employment and social interaction in Southern and East-Asian cities such as Singapore, Thailand, and Malaysian cities, often in specially demarcated outdoors areas that are set aside for vendors under hygienic condi-tions. But as wealth and social gaps increase, there is a tendency to circumscribe the informal

A selection of Art Nouveau Gateways, Gulangyu, Xiamen. Transition spaces do not necessarily imply a strict demarcation between public and private but a robust intervening area that can take on multi-layered functions. Its relationship to the public realm provides the opportunities for distinctive treatment, with a sense of contrast, variety, and transparency that contribute to distinctive urban quarters.

colonization of space. It is also necessary to look hard but sympathetically at these environments because many of the problems to be encountered infer both social and economic polarization, and the potential for future contestation.

In most Asian countries placid cultural traditions, ethnic loyalties, and a history of colonial and "strong arm" rulers have tended to induce a top-down approach to planning. This does not necessarily imply that this is oblivious to public need, but that urban processes often prioritize aggressive urbanization strategies that favor vested interests and short-term returns, and frequently include policies that are more politically expedient than necessarily responsive to actual needs or opportunities. The concepts of land ownership and urbanization are inextricably linked, and access to urban land is through one of only four means: family relations, public housing, the real estate market, or squatting. A direct result of colonial intervention in many countries was the registration of land, which often instigated conflicts through regularizing the distinction between individual property rights and native land rights. This to a large extent still remains, particularly in situations where urban populations are made up of different ethnic groups. Native land holders are often vulnerable to development speculation, and slum conditions become almost permanent fixtures, having evolved their own systems of use and business structures.

The problem of squatter settlements became acute in most Asian cities during the post-war industrialization process, and although partially resolved in economically advanced cities, are still a characteristic of large cities such as Manila, Jakarta, Bombay, Calcutta, Dhaka, and Bangkok, compounded by rising rates of urbanization. This involves either the occupation of public land, or rental of lots on private land, making tenants vulnerable to eviction and where lack of services and infrastructure generate considerable public health and environmental problems. A further factor is the "floating populations" facilitated by increased opportunities for low-income workers. In many cities this is compounded by a lack of funding for adequate urban infrastructure—something that the Asian International Investment Bank is continually called upon to address.

Cities can best respond to risk if urban management is built into planning activities, in particular the need to deal proactively with hazard-prone areas. It is then possible to identify sustainable resilience strategies in terms of preparedness, response, and recovery. Between 1980 and 1994, 163,000 acres around Jakarta were converted from agriculture to building use, which led to forms of development that often violated environmental regulations over use of the floodplain and now leads to periodic water inundation within the city itself. Smog frequently envelopes cities emanating from vehicular traffic. And there is a further aspect of risk— that of adequate disposal of urban waste, and the most sustainable and cost-effective means of designating locations for essential landfills, incineration, or reclamation at a time when communities unsurprisingly adopt a NIMBY attitude.

Reinforcing the Urban Design Process

The Asian city represents a composite interrelationship of both the formal and informal, reflecting an assembly of built references, both old and new. This co-exists with a multitude of individual service providers, authorized or otherwise, whose activities spill out into the public realm of streets and urban places. The precise nature of urban design is therefore transfigured through constant changes of use and involves a maelstrom of trajectories that sustain a sense of consistent activity within the often-impermanent terrains of the city. The casually appropriated public realm situated in a relatively ordered urban setting establishes a cultural duality that tends to encapsulate the experience of the Asian city, reflecting longstanding but also ad hoc functions that shape its use in very diverse urban contexts and situations.

The process of urban design therefore should not be entirely devoted to prescriptive physical solutions but rather integrative community building in consideration of contextual values, levels of use, and activity patterns acceptable to the resident population. Over regulation and compromises to urban efficiency must, in most situations, combine aesthetic consideration with behavioral settings that establish a robust fit between local identity and complexity without recourse to formulaic determinations. Urban informality might appear complex but

Dunlop Street forms part
of the low-rise shophouse
matrix within Singapore's
'Little India."

participants, in the main, have clear agendas, while older street buildings with their periodic insertions, interventions, and additions create a familiar but idiosyncratic streetscape that can be read through patterns of shape, texture, and color. These are not necessarily part of a composed totality, but act to heighten perception and understanding of the city in a pictorial sense, together with an affinity with the wider qualities of use. Operational parameters must therefore achieve an urban design based on both process and product.

In following a new urbanism on the back of the old it is necessary to consider a range of issues that should include some or all of the following:

— An assimilation of what is characteristically embodied in the local morphology through the essential values of the street, the street margin, city block, and local space configurations, and how these can be translated into typologies that satisfy changing community structures within high density morphologies that sustain cosmopolitan types of urban regime.

— A re-introduction of climatically suitable building and neighborhood component features such as natural shading, verandahs, and colonnaded street frontages to reduce heat gain and maintain low energy consumption.

— An urbanism of high adaptability, change, and flexibility as necessary measures of use and variety embedded in the complex framework of everyday life. Providing that there is a consistency in form and materials, diversity of buildings forms should provide for an urbanism of complementarity and balance, where likeness is tempered by difference, and where patterns of order arise out of complexity.

— Incremental regeneration of the public realm that opens up urban development possibilities while retaining cultural and intangible heritage. Without this, renewal processes become skewed toward perpetual redevelopment and undifferentiated urban quarters. Quite apart from necessary conservation and preservation policies, heritage tourism is now a major factor in local economies, and investment in the revitalization of older neighborhoods, landmark structures, indigenous areas, and older streets is a necessary part of a city-wide urban design strategy.

— It is necessary to ensure that ownership patterns, commercial, and servicing requirements do not dictate an overly course-grained structure of new urban layouts across the city, and older more fine-grained environments must be protected and reinforced wherever possible. In the process this produces an integrative street-based urbanism, where traffic and transport avenues are balanced by streets that prioritize a connective realm of pedestrian activity.

— Temporal transitions in the use of urban space, a mainstay of social and economic life in the Asian city, need to be respected as part of social and working processes that reflect a relationship between the passage of time and the programmatic change of uses throughout the day and evening. This generally involves different sets of users who inhabit public space, often quite intensively, at different times for different purposes, sometimes with a high degree of overlap.

— Historical markers need to be retained, if necessary, through adaptive re-use. Traditional typologies typical of older urban quarters, such as shophouses or *t'ang lau* tenements that define older urban quarters, open to sub-division and constant re-fitting, should be retained

The ethnic mix of Malacca is represented in the accumulated physical forms related to sacred spaces on Jalan Tukang Emas, representing a number of distinctive religious buildings dating back to the 16th century.

and upgraded. In the Asian city these have long been fundamental to both the process of street making, the absorption of high population densities, and intensive patterns of economic activity.

— Cheap, efficient, and non-polluting forms of public transport can cover both traditional and modern models. There need be no obvious conflict with the older established and cost-effective means of transport such as the pedicab or the trishaw that operate at a localized level in many South Asian cities, and mechanized transit systems. In these cases it is not necessary to modernize beyond prudent levels of economic investment and the public's ability to pay for transport services.

— Conflict between pedestrians and vehicles needs to be avoided as far as possible in order to incentivize pedestrian movement through improved comfort and access, particularly in condensed urban situations. This is being addressed in the new high-end city cores of the Hong Kong SAR, Tokyo, Singapore, and Shanghai through layered uses above stations and interchanges that in central commercial areas produce a vertical urbanism of connecting malls, bridges, and walkways. At another level it can be addressed through hierarchies of connectivity via street closures, elevated patterns of linkage, and the opening up of old waterways as recreational corridors.

— A respect for deeply held spiritual heritage with its reciprocity between different beliefs and customs, and the quality this exerts on the public realm through places that embody a relaxed co-existence between ceremonial and social gathering spaces.

CHAPTER 2

Back to the future: Toward a new asian urbanism

The diversity of Asian cities can be initially recognized in terms of their cultural traditions, their complex morphologies, and their different histories of intervention from the 16th century. However, with little in terms of historical unity, and an overall population density that is more than three times the world average, Asian urbanization and city building follows a consistent path. It can be conveniently defined by breaking it down into sub-regions that vary significantly, and with characteristics that are both embodied and expressed in the contemporary cities. The first known urban settlement was in the Mesopotamian region, followed by later growth along the Indus Valley and in the Chang'an-Xi'an region of the PRC around 1500 BCE. By the early 19th century only five percent of Asian territory was urbanized and even by the mid-20th century less than one-fifth of populations lived in cities.

In examining contemporary cities through the prism of urban design in the early 21st century when more than half of Asia's population now live in cities, we must accept that the Asian city is in constant transition. It now reflects a balance between urban cultures, sub-cultures, and new economic trajectories that inevitably respond to the dominant forces of globalization, where rapid development and modernizing interventions continue to signify changes to long-standing development patterns. While many Asian cities continue to embody a cityscape redolent of inescapable Western influences, they also display a more pragmatic vocabulary through a miscellany of physical and sensory values that underlie the urban design challenges during a seemingly continuing process of transformation.

Cities must transform themselves to keep in step with an ever-changing world, and this resilience has to be reflected in the urbanization process. This is no more so than in societies that

The Yu Yuan precinct—part of a shopping and entertainment complex of reconstructed buildings in the Ching style adjoining the Ming Dynasty Yu Yuan Gardens in Shanghai.

have been degraded by war, occupation, or civil chaos in the second half of the 20th century—Vietnam, Cambodia, Laos, and Korea—together with those shaking off the final remnants of colonization. The essential challenge has been in reconciling a new and necessary modernity with a lingering social culture, rooted in traditional Asian practices.

In part the inevitable consequences of the globalized economy is creating new drivers of growth, but also strategic augmentation through urban expansion. This process embraces intensified forms of residential development, specialized commercial centers, and technology parks that drive the momentum of the contemporary city while acting to restructure and reshape forms of capital investment. New spatial patterns are facilitated by tranches of urban expansion, redevelopment and suburbanization that have emerged as byproducts of both formal and informal development processes. All of these continue to impose different levels of impact on the creation of livable cities and the quality of life for their inhabitants.

Trengganu Street at the heart of Singapore's Chinatown creates a unified compositional character defined by three-story shophouses that demarcate bazaar areas and open shop frontages.

People's Square marks the central identity of Shanghai, housing among other buildings the Urban Planning Exhibition Centre.

The contemporary Asian city has many layers of meaning accumulated at different stages of growth, stemming from historical imprints, imposed land policies, industrialization, waves of migration, and distinctive patterns of development. It is therefore of crucial importance to understand the ramifications of urban design as representing the experience of the city in terms of actual use. This might well focus on certain aesthetic values but must also reflect the underlying values of urbanism. In most cities, there is no *tabula rasa* where unconstrained new development can take place, and urban design must take as its basis the active history of the area as a means of blending together physical and non-physical traces of past, embedded cultural values, and present elements as part of a new urban mosaic. In this sense the "locus" of collective memory and socio-cultural shifts hold a strong symbolic meaning in Asia and help to materialize a resource base on which to establish planning programs framed within the spirit and culture of the city.

In Asia's primate cities, the spatial overlap of built form creates virtually continuous patterns of density and commensurate population catchments for the alignment of commercial and community services. This does not necessarily knit communities together in a social sense, but makes related catchments effective from a functional and cost-effective perspective. Efficiency is induced in many situations by grid-like street patterns that provide a hierarchy of scale and order for different forms of transit including light rail, walking, and cycling. In new and extensively regenerated areas this can be further consolidated or extended through different types of street networks, from fine-grained pedestrian lanes to wider boulevards, each with designated street walls, widths, and setback requirements. Urban design codes for each of these need to regulate dimensions and specifications for such aspects as predominant street

Emerald Hill Road comprises two- and three-story terraced houses, providing a consistent mix of architectural features, stylistic embellishments and deep plan forms. The neighborhood was Singapore's first area conservation scheme, as a harmonious early housing enclave.

uses, pavement width, and tree planting, reinforced by points of focus for community facilities. Such planning measures coupled with transit-oriented development initiatives are also necessary to meet increasing air quality standards through reductions in automobile use.

The continuing process of transformation and change tends to provide for different degrees of co-existence and overlap. This frequently reflects dual economic structures where both contemporary and pre-industrial interconnected networks of small businesses operate virtually side by side. Planning processes leave open how urban regeneration should respond to situations where cultural boundaries are being steadily eroded through substantial population growth and the internationalization of business, finance, and technology.

It is necessary to assimilate and reinterpret the city language embodied in the local morphology—the essential values of the street, block, temple precinct, and monument—and how these can be incorporated as the drivers of new urban identities. There is a lack of clear methodological and stylistic models or prototypes that relate to the changing culture and configuration of city districts, so that mainstream architecture is still pre-occupied with buildings as objects rather than as part of the continuous urban fabric. Thus, new buildings contrast in an imbalanced co-existence with more traditional characteristics, because while they might broadly represent necessary economic and social modernizations that satisfy the changing requirements of the community, they provide little new or extended cultural definition to urban form. Traditions that remain and thrive relate to activity just as much as physical fabric. This includes an emphasis on the street and urban place for social rituals, festivals, ceremonial uses, market trading, and open eating areas, and the cultural use of small urban spaces and precincts rather than formal parks and recreation areas.

High building density and gridded street form established on early reclamation of the harbor edge is in Kowloon, Hong Kong SAR, exemplified by Sai Yeung Choi Street, Mong Kok.

The principle of transience might be said to represent a fundamental notion, embedded in most Asian societies, that there is a strong link between the spiritual and the human condition. This has undoubtedly been reinforced through several centuries of almost constant adaptation and change, so that cultural dimensions have become intrinsically associated with transition, heterogeneity, and pragmatic responses to prevailing problems.

Regeneration and urban design are interdependent. Oriol Bohigas who helped launch the transformation of Barcelona's city fabric in 1975 has stressed that the success of its revitalization program was essentially brought about through a series of one-off urban projects. District regeneration plans then became the sum of initiatives aimed at restoring a sense of activity and local identity, with new spaces opened up or remodeled by removing obsolete structures, and with public participation limited to the neighborhood level. This establishes the crucial transition between urbanism and processes of established urban design that make effective the overall scheme of intentions. Thus, regeneration can be carried out in an adaptive way providing continuity to established urban character.

This goes well beyond the normal conventions of urban grammar, blending the notions of monumental city form and visual address with an integral patchwork of multi-dimensional activity reflected in the compressed dynamics of surface texture but continually responsive to the changing requirements of its users. Such measures are essential if the Asian city is to maintain and reinforce the best of its urban characteristics—its diversity, drama, vitality, and eclectic mix of uses. It is equally important to equate these aspects with high-quality, sustainable places. Urban design must therefore be seen as a creative response to the challenge that this represents, and must reflect the complexity and identity of local neighborhoods, but within the framework of broad district planning and design strategies.

Lessons from Elsewhere

We might take a pause here to briefly examine the lessons, both salutary and beneficial, that might be learned from the evolution of American cities over the past century, as urban boundaries were expanded to contain growth through industrialization, just as new modes of transport opened up new development opportunities that came to represent an elusive relationship between city and suburb. This has some parallels with the expanding cities in Asia today where growth and change are taking place at an unprecedented pace, but also where cities face new and emerging challenges.

The first "street-car suburbs" in American cities were reliant on carriages pulled along metal rails. Concentrations of new building followed main street alignments. From the 1880s, electric trolley routes under the auspices of transport operating companies began to be

Church Street in Charleston terminates at St. Philip's Church, completed in the early 19th century, where the steeple form and height dictated the alignment of local streets.

A Market Hall terminates the vista along Market Street in Charleston, South Carolina, marking the original orthogonal grid layout and the proportionate relationship of streets and spaces.

associated with land speculation. Kenneth Jackson in *Crabgrass Frontier* notes that as the expanding beltline rail connections in America became the essential catalyst to servicing accessible land on the fringe of industrial cities, this led to rampant capital investment. Leo Marx observed in *The Machine in the Garden*, that the myth of the rural ideal fueled an escape from the older cities, where the domains of the working classes represented a degraded environment of overcrowded tenements and squalor. Periodic extension of the rail alignments to serve new tranches of suburban house construction, with little municipal control over zoning subdivisions, led to what became known as street-car suburbs.

By the end of the 19th century the residential suburb had become an indispensable part of the expanding American city. Commensurate with this, new municipalities and boroughs were incorporated in a wide radius around the urban fringe. Their primary purpose was to establish new transport connections and orchestrate public infrastructure, which for a time created an acceptable balance between cities and their inner suburbs.

The main catalyst for urban expansion however was the mass-production of the automobile, so that the early years of the 20th century became an era of relatively unrestricted urban growth. In 1921 the new Bureau of Public Roads began to plan a network of national interstate highways to connect all major cities. At around the same time a new national building code and model building ordinances were established to rationalize land use, and as city boundaries expanded, the distinction between urban and suburban areas became increasingly blurred.

The American League for Civic Improvement sought to instigate a strategy of social mix and housing diversity, while other groups concerned themselves with issues of overcrowding and public health. Possibly as a direct result of this, urban planning became increasingly utilitarian,

The American New Urbanism movement has relevance in attempting to overcome the crisis of place and the environmental cost of sprawl through the application of urban design principles, well in tune with earlier neighborhood models developed by Clarence Stein, Henry Wright, and Clarence Perry. Arguably its first and somewhat innocuous approach was the small town of Seaside, Florida, under the imaginative guidance of Andres Duany and Elizabeth Plater-Zyberk. This demonstrated aspects of design diversity, urban structure, pedestrian scale, and allocation of a public realm that has continued to be applied and refined at a metropolitan scale.

prioritizing functional order and regulation over more aesthetic and urban design considerations. *The Architect's Handbook of Civic Art*, was published in 1922, setting out standards for architecturally defined boulevards, prominent alignments, civic set pieces, and parkland, as a progressive force for moral authority and humanitarian ideals. This might be described as a watershed in American urbanism. High-rise construction met the immediate demands of urban real estate markets, characterized by the rapid spatial transformation of America's largest cities.

All of this set the stage for comprehensive planning of expanding metropolitan regions instigated by the American City Planning Institute, enthusiastically adopted by Clarance Perry through his notion of the "neighborhood unit." Perry's ideas were extended by Clarence Stein and Henry Wright in their plan for Radburn in New Jersey, based on a connective structure of greenways. However, what became known as "cluster zoning" succeeded only in inducing rigid demarcation between different uses, further compromising opportunities for neighborhood community development, but proving to be a convenient tool for speculation in land.

In the immediate post-World War Two period the Urban Renewal Act of 1948 ushered in a period of intense urban clearance and redevelopment that underscored the prominence of the high-speed urban highway as a key armature of movement and connectivity, while marking the predominance of private vehicle movement over coherent neighborhood design. The rigid emphasis on highways at the expense of investment in mass transit lines ignored the fact that traffic generation has a tendency to expand well beyond what is necessary to alleviate existing congestion, and simply facilitates additional growth in private car ownership. This proved to be the critical factor in consolidating the new age of the automobile, and the negative impact on suburban development that followed. It represents a salutary lesson to urban management of Asian cities as they continue to expand while responding to the pressing issue of climate change.

The result in America was an "Exurbia" that created a decentralized, inadequately planned, and low density counter-force to the central city, that prioritized the "here and now" through constant annexation of rural land over longer-term sustainability. Edward Soja has referred to this pattern of unstructured peripheral urbanization as *exopolis*—the simulated city full of "non-city-ness." In many cases this created lasting damage to natural ecosystems, overwhelming of drainage systems, impaired water quality, and destruction of natural habitats. Inability to coherently resolve the inner urban fringe model is sometimes referred to as the "missing middle" problem—the division is between the towers of the central city and the car-centric suburban detached residential situation. Low density car-dependent layouts technically accelerated sprawl and, inadvertently or otherwise, created a tenuous relationship between the achievement of good and energy efficient urban design, and a coalition of opportunistic bodies, which in many situations acted against the common good.

By the 1980s in the US it was estimated that around 60 percent of metropolitan populations, or 100 million people, lived in suburbs. On the outer fringe of cities so-called bedroom suburbs, characterized by Melvin Webber as "non-place urban realms," began to attract office and industrial parks and big box outlets that catapulted suburbia into the "edge cities," as described by Joel Garreau, introducing a new spatial dimension to outer metropolitan areas as the embryo of new business centers. It was not until the 1998 Transportation Equity Act for the 21st Century that intermodal surface transport was properly linked with environmental legislation and energy policy focused on new planning directions. By then almost 90 percent of all federal funds handed to states for transit went on road construction—a percentage that still exists in 2022.

The private automobile has shaped the development of urban environment and new development patterns for over 100 years, and its pathway through the last century has diverged from wide-eyed exhilaration and unprecedented convenience to become the agent of urban disruption and environmental tumult. The rate of private car ownership in the US continues to trend upward, with 91 percent of households having access to at least one vehicle. In Asia around 80 percent of households own a car in Japan, South Korea, and Malaysia; 50 percent in Thailand; and 17 percent in the PRC. Other countries have household car ownership of somewhere between 2 and 6 percent.

The allure of the city has not disappeared, however, and in examining a new Asian urbanism we need to utilize its social and cultural power to create urban communities that are not dependent on the private automobile. Cities will continue to be the engines of economic growth and social progress, but they must also creatively deploy technologies that make them more livable in terms of their urban quality. This includes sensing capabilities, energy efficiency, waste recycling, tree planting, and greenways to create comfortable microclimates. The technological revolution offers significant opportunities to regenerate the natural environment through the use of intelligent systems to eliminate waste, reduce greenhouse gas emissions, utilize satellite monitoring data, and improve recycling and higher levels of asset utilization, turning waste capture into assets. The question is how to go about it.

Motivating a New Urbanism Approach for Asian Cities

I used to be acquainted with the chairman of a construction company who once, in the aftermath of a typhoon, phoned his building manager to enquire what the damage had been. "The buildings are fine," he was told, "but the architecture got blown away." I think of that sometimes when looking at planning concepts optimistically assembled to impress clients, full of instantly mature landscape, a multiplicity of activity, and general bric-a-brac aimed partly at disguising the blandness of the layout or routinely fulfilling a supposedly catch-all clause in a set of lease conditions. This is not of course to denigrate the essential process of urban design, but to emphasise that this must be concerned with the entire range of forces that subscribe to the physical make-up of an urban area, including its subsequent care and management.

It was inevitable that at some stage there would be an urban "eureka moment" in terms of what it takes to produce good urbanism at the neighborhood scale. Like most such realizations, it would be both simple and, with a little consideration and research, self-evident that the crisis of place and community was increasingly out of step with new work environments in an age of advancing technology, and the drive toward resolving problems of climate change and achieving livable cities. Inherent in the nurturing of a recalibrated urban design approach to replace the misplaced values of the recent past was an acknowledgment that planning, at whatever scale, had to be community based. In doing so it began to unashamedly borrow from an informal vernacular compendium of past attributes, that in a non-standard and unpretentious way had been dedicated to urban comfort, interaction, and convenience while dealing with latter-day planning realities.

The advent of a New Urbanism, wherever it has been applied, has had surprising repercussions on urban design approaches by asserting the primacy of the public realm, made up of many eclectic parts and features within an architecturally consistent assembly. It emphasizes the neighborhood, the district and the corridor as being fundamental organizing elements of the planning and design process, where urban design responsibility can then be articulated by the street, the block and the building, with a focus on the public realm. The street is what Peter Calthorpe has called the "armature of urbanism," which structures the urban form itself. Its strong overall identity, some way removed from the land-extensive post-war examples, is attuned to the incidental ways in which older neighborhood communities could assimilate a stylistic consistency of "fit" but with an underlying ascertain of complexity and diversity rather than repetition and sameness. It arguably coalesces around well-established place making references according to contextual associations and aims to achieve a consistent vocabulary of elements that establish identity.

The end result is aimed at fostering a finely orchestrated grouping of buildings, spaces, and places, goes some way in creating a responsive urbanism, partly the result of participation procedures through purposeful charrettes that produce an articulated environment of variety, but with an overall consistency in full compliance with established urban design codes. Development control is at the heart of this in order to safeguard health and safety, where unrestricted design interpretation has recourse to carefully crafted, form-based codes as a modern reflection of older cultural traditions and an essential part of 21st-century smart-city thinking.

The Principle of the Urban Transect

A New Asian Urbanism in itself emphasizes the importance of a coordinated approach to planning and urbanization, together with a unification of land use and transportation that is more strategic than the conventional zoning and regulatory approach. The Rural to Urban Transect Concept conceived by Andreas Duany and Elizath Plater-Zyberk provides a means of classifying development, open space, and transit requirements. It seeks to address concerns for a more sustainable approach that is needed to resolve crucial issues facing cities and suburban development in the 21st century. It is based on a spatial distribution of interconnected natural and spatial elements distributed across a geographic region as a continuum from "rural" to "urban," although this applies to a theoretically greenfield situation where an orderly hierarchy of planned density zones can be applied. The so-called "transect" approach acknowledges that the rural setting will have the lowest intensity of use, and the sequence of zones up to the urban core will provide for a gradation in density. The broad intention is that within the various zones development

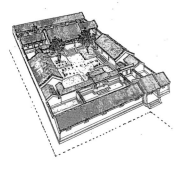
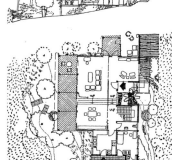
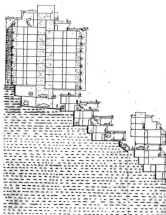

OUTER RURAL TERRITORY
· Imposed Development Restrictions
· Preservation of Natural Landscape and Ecosystem along with isolated Historic Features

INNER RURAL DISTRICT
· Imposed Development Restrictions
· Preservation of Indigenous Village Structures and Cultural Landscapes

SUB-URBAN DISTRICT
· Low Density
· Predominantly Residential and Urban Village Groups
· Planned Residential Neighbourhood Growth within Landscape Setting

URBAN FRINGE ZONE
· Low-Medium Density Residential
· Low Density Commercial
· Planned Urban and Development Inserts with Access to Transit Alignment

The Asian Urban Transect

types and built densities will be guided by planning conditions according to transection codes or design parameters.

In Asia, however, much city building in mixed-use urban quarters is less associated with greenfield situations but with an intensification of new uses at increased densities across existing central districts and urban fringe areas through redevelopment and infill. New high-density business districts and residential estates must fit within changing land and zoning values. This calls for a more flexible approach but with strict planning controls, where integrated solutions must be responsive to existing uses, extended development patterns, historically important urban quarters, older street morphologies, and prevailing transit alignments. All of these are subject to additional principles and policies so that the urban design direction must be directed to overall livability, environmental protection, a high degree of housing choice and compact, and walkable neighborhoods. It must also reflect opportunities for new modes of clean and efficient public transit as the widespread use of private automobiles is gradually reduced in central city neighborhoods.

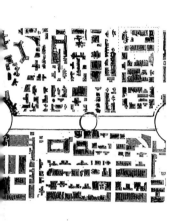

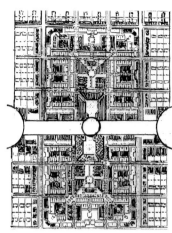

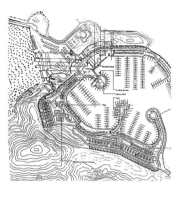

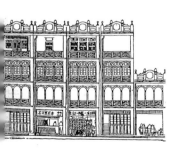

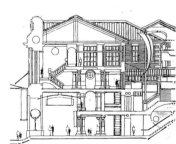

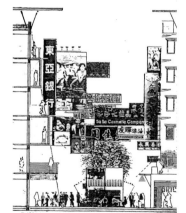

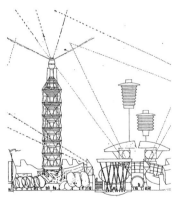

URBAN NEIGHBOURHOOD ZONE
· Low-Medium Density Residential
· Low Density Commercial
· Urban Regeneration with Preservation of Established Core Areas and District Centres
· Government, Institution and Community Uses

CENTRAL BUSINESS ZONE
· High Density Commercial and Mixed Use
· Commercial Intensification with Preservation of Heritage and Cultural Features
· Government, Institution and Community Uses

SPECIAL PRESERVATION ZONE
· Designated Conservation Area
· Preservation of Cultural Heritage Areas with Distinctive Plan, subject to Special Area Plan

SPECIAL DESTINATION DISTRICT
· Low Density Recreation and Leisure Area
· Waterfront Upgrading for Leisure and Recreation Uses, subject to Special Regeneration Plan

In addition, constantly refined technology offers new patterns of communication and information transfer that are being incorporated in new smart development and transit models.

Successful urban design demands a primary acknowledgment of the public realm—that is to say, the organization of space is just as important as the design of buildings that define or enclose it. The charter set out under the auspices of the American Congress for the New Urbanism, founded in 1993, advocates the restructuring of public policy and development practices to support diversity in use and population mix; pedestrian movement and transit integration; and public spaces framed by an architecture that celebrates local history, climate, ecology, and good building practice. This extends to historic preservation, safe streets, green building, and sustainable development, and its essentially simple but insightful approach represents a force for change in the urban design priorities given to metropolitan neighborhoods. In an urban regeneration situation the approach can accommodate higher gross densities and use less land within environmentally friendly urban quarters, through retrofitting.

The question is can we see a parallel here for a not dissimilar New Urbanism in Asian cities. A successful approach in Asia must draw on a range of contexts and critiques, bringing them together with a common focus that straddles diverse practices and disciplines, and of course two central ones—the community and the political economy. How this focus is determined is reliant on many factors, notably the political will to evolve a responsive urbanism. This infers that we use the smart city agenda, linked to the essential agents in ensuring sustainability, in order to connect and reconcile our reservoir of knowledge in focusing on the urban challenges. It also means drawing on philosophical ideas, and, in part, relating these to best practice. Cities can only ultimately thrive by attracting private investment to bring about public gain, thereby creating a catalyst to which public agencies can subscribe through appropriate initiatives and controls. The city-building process must therefore reflect a multitude of continuous recalibrations that represent countless interests and values. While the urban design approach must occasionally counter questions as to its precise and legitimate role in shaping the physical and social public realm, it is as much a force for urban enquiry as it is for informing practice.

This requires comprehensive audits and evaluation of each urban context as a precursor to detailed planning. These enable us to construct a meaningful relationship between the city, its constituent neighborhood districts, urban fringe, and surrounding suburban and rural means. In this way we can ascertain necessary indicators that help us to comprehend underlying attributes of the city—its physical forms, spatial qualities, expressive characteristics, its mix of uses, and its essential urban grain. It must also identify aspects that, in their current form, have a negative impact on the public realm, and which might for example require regeneration rather than redevelopment. This should almost certainly include the strengthening of pedestrian links and urban matrices rather than highway separators and the strengthening of street frontages and urban places.

Sets of information need to be overlaid and weighted in terms of priorities between physical development and economic information about the overall robustness and capacity of individual parts of an area to change, and the implication of these factors for new development potential in terms of the general scale and massing of built elements. The audit itself is used to provide a basis for an urban design framework and development vocabulary that, in varying degrees, can delineate the frame of reference for planning. It should not be seen as in any way fixed or rigid, but as a means of encouraging an integrated approach to the public realm, and as a precursor to the preparation of urban design briefs and parameters for developers to follow. This implies two important considerations:

· Some degree of control over building form, set within the wider urban fabric; and
· The integration of formal design and environmental elements, which establish an underlying urban order, linking the built environment with a responsive planning structure.

While some of these principles are somewhat abstract in nature, they help to establish a basis for ordering the layout and provide opportunities for a variety of uses, some of them disparate, through maximizing benefits to the wider environment outside the limited development capacity of each individual site. They include aspects of visual and physical permeability, the tailoring of a robust pattern of public spaces to the desired range of uses, and the coupling of accessibility with a variety of elements that have the potential to maximize urban vitality.

These must be then equated with the conceptual analysis of viable site sizes for commercial, residential, and other forms of development, and the ways in which sites can be assembled in the form of "cells" to provide development flexibility, adequate servicing, coordinated retail patterns, and a strong environment framework. The various layout options and the variations in intensity of commercial and residential land uses tend to suggest ways in which the cells and their individual site components can be grouped to form a wider pattern of building forms, spaces, and circulation elements. This calls for a consistency between stylistic design typologies appropriate for the specific context in question. Actual dimensions of sites will of course also vary according to infrastructure and servicing constraints.

All aspects must be combined within a coordinated open space and landscape structure, providing a mix of formal, semi-formal, and predominantly passive facilities for circulation and recreation, associated with commercial and community uses. This serves to extend existing provision, create distinctive edges between development cells, and helps to maintain

The Plaza Santa Cruz represents the center of the Chinese commercial district of Binondo in Manila.

The street fabric of downtown Mumbai contains a cross-cultural mix of stylistic and decorative references.

important view corridors. Open spaces must also act as nodal points throughout the plan, associated with the continuous and directional movement system.

The secondary benefits of this approach are that certain ground rules are established with which both public and private participants are familiar. This also helps, in varying degrees, to tackle another issue strongly linked with urban planning in Asia where commercial considerations and rapid implementation criteria often hold away—that of how to plan large comprehensive developments in terms of three-dimensional design, with guidelines that are interpretive rather than prescriptive.

We must be concerned with the entire range of forces that subscribe to the physical make-up of Asian cities, including opportunities for subsequent care and management. On the assumption that the built environment will continue to be a more or less accurate register of our prevailing social values there is a need to direct the emphasis on urban design guidance from a pre-occupation with architectural standards, mechanical types of building control, or illustrations of visions that will never be built, to ways in which we can satisfy community concerns for environmental quality and to replicate, as far as possible, the inherent complexity and vibrancy of the city itself.

Shaping the Dimensions of the Expanding Asian City

An Asian New Urbanism must articulate an approach that is relevant at all scales and is largely appropriate to most urban and regional situations, primarily for its organizational methodology and the necessary consultative processes involved. This involves the framing of urban development and regeneration qualities into an articulate set of design and layout parameters for application at different scales, from regional development corridors to local neighborhoods. In applying these to different Asian contexts it is necessary to lay out logical associations, qualities, and connections in recognition of widely accepted social and even psychological needs that reflect the complexity of human lifestyles. These should initially stem from lessons learned from older and well-established settlements where these responsive aspects represent a natural outcome of competent building practice.

In order to deliver green and sustainable programs of growth, either as new or regenerative quarters, it is necessary to apply consistent urban design principles at a range of densities. A New Asian Urbanism must be concerned with both the parts and the whole—a simple but significant departure from patterns of endless repetition, regardless of scale and hierarchy. Older urban communities in Asian cities have evolved through a wide range of owners, architects, and builders, which embraced an overall sense of likeness tempered with difference through a limited palette of materials and construction techniques. This was coupled with a certain level of idiosyncrasy representative of personal choice and restrained only by established design precedents and building standards. To avoid fractured settlement patterns through incremental but unconnected growth, networks of space must be formative, establishing hierarchies of use and definition, and must be embedded within fixed physical boundaries while establishing a design dialogue with adjoining urban quarters and the natural habitat. These must be structured by coherent but diverse patterns of public space as part of connective circulation systems that support high levels of pedestrian movement and, where appropriate, non-motorized modes of transport.

City cores and suburbs present different but related geographies, so that the essential task is to make them more compatible and therefore more sustainable and resilient. The challenge is to bring about new and transformative urban interpretations that help to resolve associated problems in the urban domain. These include provision of affordable housing and choice of tenure, new financing regimes, an increase in public transit options, an improved and shared public realm. and a means to introduce greater urban resilience. This implies examining metropolitan regions as a whole using a range of performance and "quality of life" indicators, including governance, to map opportunity areas for intensification of underused land and redundant brownfield uses.

The focus must be broadly concerned with generating a mixed-use urbanism, while respecting the ecological framework and reducing automobile dependency, with an emphasis on cost-effective public transport and user-friendly pedestrian systems. Procedures can be assisted by producing tools for neighborhood planning attuned to the local context and sympathetic to the use of green building agendas. This raises obvious questions over the ability to meet pressing public interests and properly managed growth, over narrow and short-term objectives that serve primarily private interests. Planning for growth of the right kind, including meeting the overall goals of a localized urban design agenda, necessitates a city planning apparatus that relates policy making to land use control and preservation of natural resources.

One potential tool is a "transfer of development rights," not dissimilar to that used for conservation of important older buildings, where an allowable increase in floor area ratio can be transferred to an alternative site in order to retain one or more existing structures. This incentive-based procedure can also be used to preserve certain types of land in their natural state, while other sites can be amalgamated and consolidated for development as part of a planned growth strategy, which is itself dependent on agreed land resumption procedures and an equitable return to affected land owners. Planning itself must be sufficiently backed up by strong legislation that requires impact statements to identify both the positive and negative consequences of development.

The New Urban Neighborhood

The New Asian Urbanism must purposefully confront a situation where new settlements form a physically integrated part of the metropolis, while effective metro planning itself must resolve the despoiling delineation of "non-places" through patterns of assimilation and densification. Ultimately, an important issue is the status of new settlements in the regional or metropolitan hierarchy. The optimum population size for a relatively self-contained independent neighborhood or township is the essential building block of metropolitan growth in terms of coordinated social, commercial, and many other functions of daily life.

If we take the minimum size of an urban neighborhood or satellite community as being around 10,000 persons, with an average suburban household size of 2.6 persons, this suggests a requirement of at least 4,000 housing units, taking into account the overall demographic mix—far more than most private urban fringe or urban development laid out simply as housing tracts. Housing alternatives must form part of metropolitan policy to create an equitable balance that caters for real need across the board without benefitting one socio-economic sector over another. Strategic planning requires a regional framework of urban sectors within growth corridors serviced by public transit, which must be sufficiently robust to accommodate fluctuating development patterns. This must operate at all parts of the hierarchical scale, and should form interconnected parts of a system, requiring different levels of treatment depending on varying levels of use as an effective continuum from rural to urban within metropolitan regions.

Development in each zone should best be guided by appropriate design codes in relation to levels of built density and prevailing morphology to reflect planning and urban design objectives. The key factor in effecting change in terms of both the urban entity and in policies relating to it, is cooperation between all citizens through a process that incorporates interest groups and stakeholders as participants in the planning and design process itself. What matters more than refined aesthetic concerns is the relationship between the built environment and the social, economic, and environmental aspects of urban life with the overall objective of inducing livability. This reflects a deeper cultural agenda, absorbing a variety of morphologies, governing regimes, and degrees of intervention, replacement, and superimposition.

A people-centered process must capitalize on the given assets of an area and its potential in terms of use and identity, that reflect aspects of both tangible and intangible heritage. These should form part of a regeneration process, based on the way that streets work and how buildings and spaces are used. In this way neighborhoods can be stitched together without unduly disrupting established social and economic networks. It can also help communities create distinctive quarters through collaborative and purposeful public involvement, encouraging imagination and invention in addressing their essential uniqueness. The validity of this approach stems from social as well as physical ideas about generating livable neighborhoods built around symbolic public spaces. Spatial and cultural links between the past and future ecologies of the city can thereby embrace many different meanings and uses within compact areas. This includes the eradication of overcrowding and congestion that otherwise leave a legacy of deep economic and social disparities.

Smart Growth

Smart growth is much to do with the effective transfer of information and ideas, and there should be no disconnect between tradition and innovation, that is to say between an urbanism rooted in local conditions, and an intelligent fit with new technology at increased densities. Digital technologies increasingly impact the ways in which we live, work, and communicate, but also positively transform the human condition and community identity. It has inspired breakthroughs that build on and fuse together preceding ones that range from perpetually advancing mobile devices to artificial intelligence, automation, and quantum computing. These continue to shape new industrial trajectories and bring about paradigm shifts in the global economy. In this respect the virtual context is just as important as the physical one, but its validation is dependent on how the full impact of change can be adequately absorbed within social and economic systems, and genuinely empower the multitude of potential stakeholders.

A "smart" approach has to be geared to regional development strategies and equally sustainable neighborhood design, while dealing fairly with private property rights. Equally appropriate mechanisms should establish the legitimacy of government control over well planned and acceptable forms of development to which private bodies can subscribe. In the process this must balance public needs with private interests and social equity. Managed built expansion through the incorporation of Urban Growth Boundaries is a necessary means of limiting growth and ensuring the best utilization of infrastructure through maximizing land capacity. It is also the means to ensure that sustainability concerns are met together with the ingrained pathologies of safety and security. Added advantages are the integration of affordable housing, effective transit systems that equate with patterns of density, and the reinforcement of downtown uses.

The approach to the Zojo-Ji Temple in Tokyo is marked by a large torri-gate indicating its historic role as a way-station for pilgrims.

This includes a street and place-based structure, well situated public spaces, integrated civic and commercial uses, and an emphasis on walkability and conservation policies that draw on existing localized character. In some cases, appropriate urban qualities pre-exist, and the challenge then becomes their integration or protection within the new growth structure. However, the ultimate standard of success is the instigation of a revitalized public realm through design, planning, and development control geared to mixed-use communities.

Wherever possible, new growth areas should be assimilated within broad development corridors to support transit alignments at a regional scale, and the environmental framework and performance of individual neighborhoods. Over time these areas, designed as distinctive localities in themselves, should shape and be absorbed within extended regional growth structures, with comprehensive environmental protection measures adding to the preservation and diversity of the wider domain. Environmental management should form part of this process, while state-of-the-art methods for such aspects as wastewater reclamation and waste management programs can be put in place for short- and long-term implementation. Open space preservation is necessary to protect the environment and maintain its resources as part of the wider ecosystem. This includes wetlands, watersheds, forests, and habitat conservation.

Many of the practicable principles associated with New Urbanism theory are applicable at a somewhat higher density to Asian city neighborhoods, including opportunities for revitalization and historic preservation. In terms of suburban development a continuing and future challenge is its consolidation within regional growth trajectories while integrating strong neighborhood communities that shape more extensive and hierarchical patterns, as the rate of urbanization extends toward 70 percent of the Asian population.

At the heart of this is a new urban design of community, aiming not merely to shape human environments but to ensure their workability in achieving related social, economic, and environmental objectives. In many locations it is also necessary to pursue resilient strategies in

The old city of Intramuros in Manila was laid out by the Spanish according to the codified urbanisation ordinances of 1573, which consisted of a street grid with open plazas that served as places for congregation.

mitigating the impact of a new order of climatic challenges. An urbanism that puts community and public interests first must also embody an insistence on measures that place these above purely private ones.

Many Asian cities retain narrow street related neighborhoods that in part contributed to the past layout and consolidation of downtown areas. In contrast to costly redevelopment projects, an incremental strategy of revitalization combines a varying amount of "new build" development, with a legacy of intact urban fabric and older buildings of quality, a re-routing of existing transit systems and a "joined together" program of street and space upgrading. The way forward necessitates an involvement of both public and private bodies including local citizens groups, businesses, and those institutions involved with housing, city management, and rehabilitation. An important aspect of this is a specification of allowable uses, with certain street matrices designated for intensive pedestrian use focused on an identifiable central area, and others providing for predominantly vehicular and service needs. A further measure is the consolidation of the linear streetwall fabric to provide continuous active frontages, along with intimate public space insertions through the demolition of seriously dilapidated

Hama-Rikyu Garden, associated with the Imperial Family after the Meiji Restoration, is now a public venue in Tokyo.

buildings. Sites for new housing infill or conversion of large but redundant buildings can act as an energizing means to maximize the different social and economic needs of local populations. Opportunities can also be identified for future acquisition in order to weave institutional, educational ,and cultural buildings within downtown neighborhoods.

This acts to shape the integrity and mutuality of both the planning framework and the buildings, ensuring a symbiotic relationship between the two that can be translated into spatially consistent parts by different owners and designers. The major challenge is in the transition from low-density neighborhoods to a city scale and density, through ongoing retrofitting and urban regeneration models.

The Need for Urban Design Control

In order to ensure that urban design intentions, broadly signaled in preliminary planning studies, can be achieved in practice, it is necessary to formulate design parameter codes that meet given density capacities. These should by no means pre-determine architectural initiatives, but establish in three-dimensions the principles by which the physical components of the urban structure add up to more than the sum of the parts. Thus, a vocabulary of design criteria can be formulated based on an interplay between urban elements, while also creating opportunities for new and expressive inserts to happen by chance. The process of urban design needs to effectively cater for and even encourage this informal level of spontaneity and complexity.

It is necessary to strike a balance between being over-prescriptive, that is to say too rigid, and being too broad so that design codes become meaningless. Parameters should therefore be interpretive, prescribing no specific physical solutions but a responsive framework that acts as a creative springboard for design. Guidelines must be supplemented by interpretive imagery and modeling and help to generate development conditions that equate with establishing an urban order but also variety through design, disposition, and height clauses in lease conditions, building management mechanisms and urban service procedures. This shifts the emphasis on design control from a preoccupation with regulatory standards to community concerns for urban character associated with the public realm. It might extend, in central urban situations, to issues relating to the distribution of multi-level pedestrian connections, walkways, and concourses as part of an integrated and spatially unified whole. Design codes need to be comprehended by both private and public participants in the development process as an integral part of ongoing planning and urban management, in all its forms.

The generation of clear urban design criteria in terms of what is to be achieved represents an opportunity for some genuine public consultation aimed not so much at specifics but at establishing what sort of place and character people want. This would involve giving people the right sort of comprehensive information so that they can fully understand future spatial implications, the impact of infrastructure, and other investment. This might allow various professional, government, business, and community organizations who would not normally talk with each other to work and consult together in defining what can be achieved in urban design terms.

One of the benefits of this is not simply the encouragement of meaningful and goal-oriented public participation, but the vehicle it offers to rejuvenate the role of building professionals as being concerned with an obligation to the public outside the role of individual buildings, and for government and private bodies to reconcile their interests. In passing, it also provides an encouraging informal forum for different arms of government, that often have conflicting agendas, to realize certain common objectives that enable them to work toward a mutually desirable and recognized end-state.

New Transport Technologies

A critical factor in projecting a new Asian urbanism arises from continued accommodation of the private automobile, and the degree to which it can be properly integrated in urban planning, along with public transport in its various forms. In a new age of environmental awareness and livable urban environments, we are on the cusp of a new and innovative chapter on the automobile, as 10 countries have set targets for 100 percent electric vehicles or those that run on other clean means of power by 2040, in part to combat global warming. Germany, Denmark, Spain, Britain, France, and the Netherlands in Europe, together with the PRC and Korea in Asia have set official targets for an end to the use of fossil fuels. The United States has no federal policy, although a number of states have set their own goals. According to the International Energy Agency, the PRC accounts for more than 40 percent of electric vehicles sold in the world. At the same time, driverless or "robotic" vehicles are likely to become commercially viable in some jurisdictions before the mid-21st century.

Street escalator alignment between central and mid-levels, Hong Kong SAR.

App-orchestrated car sharing programs are already a fixture in some western cities, where vehicles can be pre-selected and reserved. There tends to be two groups: those with fixed locations within neighborhoods where a time slot is booked in advance and vehicles have to be returned to the same place; and "free" locations where vehicles can be picked up or left at any location, and rates apply in accordance with a time charge. Car-share schemes generally also apply only to electric vehicles, which is a further advantage. In major Western cities private car ownership is being reduced. In New York, 55 percent of households do not own cars and only 23 percent of commuters drive from suburb to city, as opposed to 57 percent who take the subway, rail, or buses, while the remainder walk, cycle, or use ferries. In the Hong Kong SAR only 34 percent of households own a car, although seven out of ten licensed vehicles are private cars. In Singapore the figure is roughly the same. This in itself creates opportunities for retrofitting street avenues to further enliven the circulation grid by introducing central promenades that act as the focus for streetscape renovation, where even narrow alleys can be upgraded to offer a choice of alternative and environmentally contrasting pedestrian routes.

Autonomous technologies could significantly reduce the costs of providing transit services. In Asian cities fully autonomous electric vehicles are projected to eventually provide passengers with high levels of service and increased safety, with shared transit vehicles operating at an operational cost as low as 10 percent of today's individually owned vehicles. The planning implications of this might include a requirement for new roadway design features such as narrower traffic lanes, dedicated highway lanes to facilitate "platooning," and signs designed to be read electronically. To facilitate vehicle sharing, curbs must provide for convenient passenger

The narrow *roji* of Kyoto.

loading and unloading, parking must be managed to increase turnover, and off-site parking must be equipped with electric charging stations.

Other technologies and mobility options might well introduce new planning opportunities in accordance with changing user preferences, data-enhanced product capabilities, and improved conditions for walking and cycling. However, certain aspects must be resolved between individual users and the achievement of community goals, including access to dispersed developments, integration of transit stations, dedicated lanes, vehicle programming, enforcement concerns, and climate considerations.

Louis Mumford's notion of the city as a symbol of collective unity, brings into focus the need for consolidation of community programs in relation to social urbanism and a change in city image and identity as part of visionary transformation strategies. In all situations this needs to be properly examined in spatial, social, and market-attractive terms. A New Asian Urbanism must effectively re-introduce the art of well-orchestrated place-making as a reflection of older and naturally evolving communities, and underscores the fact that urban design is arguably a coordinating activity set around an overall vision, which can all too easily devolve into bureaucratic channels geared to meeting quite different objectives. While zoning and design codes have their place, they require a good deal of consideration as to the needs of separate localities and must be applied with a degree of flexibility.

CHAPTER 3

The mutating city: Traditions in transition

From an immediate post-colonial period where embedded traditions were insinuated in modernizing interventions to meet rising aspirations, the rapid economic development of Asian cities in recent years has produced a forcefield that continues to induce unprecedented disruption to long-standing development patterns. Value systems also change and evolve. The non-governmental International Council of Monuments and Sites (ICOMOS) now accepts "intangible heritage" in Asia as having an equal, and possibly an even greater, cultural relevance than physical traces in transmitting authentic value.

Modern architecture and its post-modern phase are generally identified in many situations through the transition from colonial to national modes of government in the mid-20th century, with an invigorated economic agenda that since that time has encompassed public buildings, commercial districts, and dense residential enclaves. While some modes of international modernism continue to be imported from the West in various adaptive forms, certain urban contexts provide the setting for a revitalized identity, drawing on vernacular traditions as centers of social space. These might be said to have multiple design roots that in the right hands can be refined into contemporary cultural and historic references, embodying climatically suitable design responses and refined degrees of embellishment. Buildings must, however, serve contemporary needs suitable to their context.

UNESCO World Heritage extended conservation and preservation activities to Asia in the 1970s at almost precisely the same time that many of its cities were undergoing substantial advances in economic production and modernization. A reconciliation between these different forces, requires tangible and even symbolic forms of expression related to community identity.

The Singapore River has been at the heart of the city's development since 1819 as the commercial lifeline of the emerging entrepôt. It has evolved from working quaysides to the site of major public buildings, leisure, and activity zones, such as Boat Quay and Clarke Quay.

This in itself suggests something of a dilemma—should a city obliterate traces of alien colonial intervention, no matter the quality of its architectural residue, or retain and preserve it as a tangible part of its history that acts as a legitimate resource? The Hong Kong SAR has all but lost much of its reserve of 19th and early 20th-century urban buildings, sacrificed to the demands of development intensification and prolonged but questionable adherence to free market principles. Singapore on the other hand—an independent state since 1965—has retained and preserved buildings redolent of its colonial past, and presents them as an effective tourism resource and attraction that underscores its historical identity.

In some urban situations such as the old International Settlement and French Concession areas in Shanghai, western styles of architecture and urban design that represent a legacy redolent of foreign occupation, have such a tangible place in both the city's development history and drive toward nationalism, that it underscores the essential image of the central city. However, one politically inspired initiative in Shanghai after 1949 was to change the British and French street names to form a more neutral encoding of the urban landscape, east-west roads being named after Chinese cities, and north-south roads after provinces.

Hindu Temples establish a low-key but purposeful presence in Mumbai's urban neighborhoods, creating a strong relationship with the residential and working community.

At stake in Asia is the cultural value and understanding that might be put on places of historic character by local populations. This raises certain questions about the identity represented by elitist architecture in relation to vernacular development. It also introduces a situation where the forces of international tourism tend to regard a heritage listing as something that brings new identity and attraction to a location, but might also introduce a new realm of commodification that can threaten the prevailing sense of place.

Asian cities have traditionally sustained a framework for a multiplicity of urban uses, established development patterns and local identity, and there is a need to consolidate and re-establish the traditional sense of street vibrancy and range of uses that could help knit together regenerated urban districts. However, diversity is gradually being replaced by uniformity as large areas become subject to comprehensive development or redevelopment, and zoned for single-use purposes or single-tenure estates, while regulatory measures frequently reinforce a doctrine of "separation" for purposes of administration and management. Urban design concerns can be similarly dominated by procedures that prioritize efficiency and expediency of urban management. Mixed uses that signify urban identity and variety are now, in many quarters, deemed to be incompatible with large-scale commercial centers, and residential estates

are frequently inward-looking, geared toward the private rather than the public realm. The lesson to be learned from this is that a blanket application of type-cast solutions for large redevelopment areas will gradually produce an undifferentiated urban form.

World Heritage status brings with it certain responsibilities such as UNECSO-endorsed height limits for types of new development that might otherwise compromise the overall setting. Unsupervised restoration can strip away heritage character, but on the other hand enforcement can make restored areas almost too precious. Conservation is also subject to competing visions, with gentrification often in danger of removing the mellow patina of older fabric that is a necessary part of its attraction. While sensitive restoration adds value to heritage properties, revitalization must be both socially and economically relevant to the local population and to artisans themselves in order to preserve a sense of belonging and usefulness. This calls for complementary intervention, in particular for measures to control vehicular intrusion within the older street framework. The historic streetscapes of Singapore, Georgetown, Malacca, and Yangon, for example, rely in large part on their multicultural heritage and range of building types including ancestral temples and clan houses. This holds the key to wider regeneration through clear management plans, conservation guidelines, and an empowerment of local communities with a sense of ownership.

To recognize and retain at least some of these aspects requires careful economic restructuring, responsive lands mechanisms, and a sensitive approach to urban design. This should ideally reflect, at least in part, the characteristics of permeability and robustness associated with the traditional street environment that affects the degree to which people can use a given

Decorated Doorway, Mumbai.

place for different purposes. Wider forms of community need to be recognized as part of publicly sanctioned regeneration processes, in terms of molding and reinforcing city fabric, introducing aspects that provide city vitality and interest at street level, and helping to sustain the character of the city for locals and visitors alike.

A further factor is the sometimes-troubling correlation between cultural heritage and ethnicity. The term "Malay," for example, at least in terms of its official definition, encompasses criteria of religion, language, custom, and roots in Malaysia by way of birth. Gwynn Jenkins points out, in the context of Penang, that there are thus two definitions: one based on constitutional qualifications, the other on ethnic grounds where there are four main groups—"Malay," "Chinese," "Indian," and "Others," and where even these can be further broken down into Hokkien, Hakka, Tamil, and Sindhi. Precise identification of authentic heritage is therefore often rather open-ended. However, the memory of cities and their historical associations are increasingly important as urban populations become more affluent and concerned about aspects of the city that mark a genuine genius loci through social and cultural continuity.

An urban landscape of culturally and functionally identifiable forms can be assessed at different levels: first as architectural representations of tradition and invention, where intervention might have an impact on physical integrity; and second as functioning components of a particular community, imbued with memory, and the spiritual associations of use. Both of these need to be assimilated, not so much in terms of a cosmetic or "reproduced" identity, but

The Psar Thmei or "Grand Market" in Phnom Penh forms part of the French colonial urban planning framework designed by Ernest Hêbrard.

as a necessary acknowledgment of the intuitive values of "place" that is somehow expressive and integral to the language of the whole. This implies that the term "conservation" should not necessarily imply merely the retention of physical structures, but a moderation of the rate of economic change to accommodate a continuing and evolving system of activities.

Asian cities have largely absorbed and retained the coexistence of indigenous and transplanted architectural forms that represented the exigencies of occupying cultures. The urban structure of certain Indian cities such as Jaipur evolved from a mandala temple form based on a geometrical representation of the cosmos that gave rise to sacred enclosures. These evolved through the medieval period, that brought about irregular arrangements of streets with a central space or bazaar, around which were the most important public buildings. The gradual accretions of growth then led to the segregation of urban quarters according to types of occupation, marked at a later stage by western influences. The colonial period further articulated this system through administrative districts, military cantonments, and virtually self-contained civil stations, partially segregated on the basis of employment position and status, and separated from the more organic local areas by buffer zones.

In certain cities the residue of imposed forms has been preserved as part of an adopted ethnic identity and appropriated within its miscellaneous cultural heritage. The notion

The Hokkien Goddess of Mercy Temple in Georgetown, Penang, with its ornately decorated copings and ridges is dedicated to Kuan Yin. Its adjoining streets are lined with mobile stalls selling flowers and joss sticks, and offering fortune-telling services.

of "cultural identity" is, in practice, highly sensitive in situations of reinforced urban quarters, such as the distinctively rehabilitated and commercially orchestrated ethnic enclaves in Singapore. Perceptions of cultural identity can also be elusive in that the interpretation of "historic" city fabric and sense of place must also reflect modernizing development trajectories that can create a degree of friction or discord with the historic areas themselves. The active promotion of tourism and visitation brings with it the need to foster stewardship of cultural heritage in order to ensure authenticity. A viable means of safeguarding this without incongruity is to upgrade the public realm and enrich the "memory of place" through regeneration programs. By extending cultural heritage to include traditional events, celebrations, religious festivals and heritage trails, development pressures can be counteracted by business collaborations between different neighborhoods that further the evolution of localized identity, given the importance of tourism and visitation to the economic health of cities.

Successful conservation strategies must accommodate a range of influences outside any precisely articulated planning framework. At the same time this should create an economic momentum toward restoration of older structures as urban assets, embracing both tangible and intangible characteristics. This tends to succeed when there is a strong cultural identity,

Preparation for the Durga Puja Festival in Kolkata for which artists create elaborate images of Hindu deities.

for example where active ceremonies and rituals associated with temple, mosque, and church are not incompatible with the integration of new uses that cement modern urban lifestyles and where the street rhythm can accommodate the individual but less tangible requirements of ethnic enclaves. For example, in Penang's Little India, part of the daily cultural ritual is the mix of turmeric and sandalwood strewn on the space between the public street and the private building edge, often accompanied by decorative artwork, corresponding with building entrances, and the burning of camphor. In the Hong Kong SAR, certain festivals involve the burning of "paper money" and incense along the street edge. This sustains a communal way of life that is strongly influenced by spiritual heritage, and necessitates a reciprocity between different interests and customs, which establishes a workable order out of apparent diversity, particularly where different ethnic cultures share the same environment. The enigmatic influences of feng shui, vaashtu shastra, or even the association of certain types of vegetation within the precincts of temples and mosques, establishes an ambiguous but symbolic identity, and requires wide community participation in any new planning initiatives.

The City as Text

Textual interpretation of cities is a means of signifying cultural change through nomenclature and iconography. In the post-colonial world, place name connotations of streets, parks, and highways with the names of European royalty as part of the colonial lexicon might justifiably be considered outmoded, but on the other hand might also personify a sense of history. They also provide cues to social mapping and ethnic groupings and establish an elusive engagement with the signification of place.

In the Chinese treaty port concession areas, street names redolent of the "unequal treaties" were quickly erased after 1949. In Shanghai, streets in the French Concession named after French revolutionary heroes and Paris boulevards such as Avenue Foch, Rue Lafayette, and Quai de France were politely changed to more neutral representation, as was the wide road between the International and the French Concession—Avenue Edward VII. The street names in the old city named after guild activities, such as Woodworkers Street or Pickled Melon Street were also phased out in more contemporary times.

In the reconstituted treaty ports new names generally accorded with cities and provinces. In Harbin, Russian street names quickly lost favor after 1946, so that Kitaiskaia Street—the central spine of hotels, department stores, and restaurants—became Zhong Yang Street, now refurbished as a "museum" street of old Russian buildings. The Hong Kong SAR retains the names of former governors, senior administrators, energetic figures in the field of public works and eminent Chinese businessmen in its street names, public buildings, and even country park trails.

An elaborate gateway indicates the entrance to the Chayamangkarama Buddhist temple in Burma Lane, Georgetown, reflecting early trading networks between Penang and Burma in the 19th century.

The ubiquitous "Victoria" is associated with road, memorial, and peak, having survived the political transition intact, even if her statue was removed to a more discreet park—still bearing her name—after 1997. In Yangon it is said that Lord Dalhousie, Governor-General of India, allocated street names mainly after British officers and commissioners, which happened to include Dalhousie Street. After independence in 1948, names were changed to leaders of the independence struggle and army generals. Fraser Street was changed to Anawrahta Road after the ancient founder of Pagan, while Fytche Square was changed to Mahabandoola Garden after the general who resisted the British during the first Anglo-Burmese War. In Malaysia, many Anglicized street names have been assigned indigenous equivalents, while in Singapore changes in street-naming policies were intended to assert an independence from its colonial identity.

The symbolic iconography of past regimes is frequently allied to a desirable image of present geographic identity that invokes a successful illusion of history and attainment. In all cases, new names are suitably neutral in connotation with few overtones. In Singapore, the non-Malay residents found the Malay vocabulary difficult to pronounce, and so re-naming was mainly restricted to single types of flora and fauna, while conversely certain Malaysian place names were rechristened, e.g., "Sentosa," meaning tranquility, replacing Pulau Blakang Mati for the new resort island. In turn, Chinese street names were simplified to avoid confusing transliterations. In the Jurong Industrial Estate, permutations of words suggesting "industry" such as Jalan Pesawat added to a linguistic realm that excluded ethnic associations. Bridges also represent dominant public objects on which their political instigator can append its name; for example the Cavenagh and Ord Bridges in Singapore are named for governors, and the Elgin Bridge paid colonial homage to the then Governor-General of India.

Since Malaysia's independence from Britain in 1957, Mountbatten Road in Kuala Lumpur became Jalan Tun Perak, and Province Wellesley in Penang became Seberang Perai. In Penang, street names not only reflect the far reaches of the British Empire such as Victoria Street and King Street, but also embody references to different ethnic groups and places of origin, such as Malay Street, Kampong Java, Bangkok Lane, Burmah Road, Chulia Street and Armenian Street that make up a series of urban villages, comprising an assimilation of different communities just as it reflects a fusion of indigenous forms and cultures that keep traditions alive. In Penang's Little India, for example, the street names connect with past occupations within the area. The Tamil name for King Street is *Padarukara Tharuva* or the Street of Boatmen; while *Kitengi Teru* along the quayside is known as the Street of Company Godowns.

Contested Space

Asian cities that evolved without a fully orchestrated program of civic set-pieces as unified physical foci for public life and activities, rely on spaces to provide a focus, for example a large area of urban parkland or public gathering space such as the Malayan Padang, or the Indian Maidan. In most cities the local precinct and street system represents a constant feature of all cities. Between these is a realm of incursion and overlap of uses that provide value to what are often fragmented or utilitarian spaces. Small trading spaces for example are often formalized only through pre-determined pitches and product specialization, and therefore have a heightened significance and value to an urban locality. However, the awkward relationship of social to economic space in the contemporary city underscores the tension between the often-different agendas of urban design in the public realm and the gradual commodification of public space. In general there is a low emphasis on public participation in the development and management of public space, outside the established or imposed administrative hierarchies, where government policies and priorities tend to outweigh most other aspects in the face of continually escalating urban land prices.

In order to guide the assembly of new buildings in Batavia (present-day Jakarta) the Dutch drew up urban design guidelines for street frontages so that they embodied front "stoops."

The Peranakan Mansion and Ancestral Hall built in 1893 forms a historic ensemble with the Chung Keng Kwee Temple in Georgetown, Penang.

Older street buildings with their periodic insertions offer a characteristic mix of superimposed styles and forms, Hong Kong SAR.

In the Hong Kong SAR, zoning plans regulate uses, and in correlation with the Buildings Ordinance dictates development value of all private sites through plot ratio designation. While this acts to regulate development, the resultant redevelopment momentum, built up over many decades, has effectively acted to erase the city's formative cultural identity, in many ways defamiliarizing the population from much of its past, and obliterating its collective memory. Massive land costs also have a clear bearing on the valuation of property on a square foot basis, technically outweighing its design value to the city. In large part this is because urban planning forms an integral part of city management and land use control procedures, through bureaucratic mechanisms that were established precisely for this purpose by colonial authorities during the post-war years of massive population growth and new town development. These measures continue to forge expedient and space-specific approaches to planning, with little respect for diversity, the offbeat or the idiosyncratic.

The Hong Kong Urban Renewal Authority has the authorization to initiate wide-scale land resumption and to partner with private developers who tender for construction rights. This tends to speed up the redevelopment process, although the focus of citizen engagement is largely limited to compensation paid to affected owners. The downside is firstly, an effective displacement of poor households from older neighborhoods, and secondly an orchestration of redevelopment to maximum allowable built densities with little or no improvement to the public realm itself.

A perspective on Asian urbanism and the perception of space requires an approach that searches for complementarity in terms of planning delineations, produced in the margins and interstices of state priorities, under which the populations can impose its own shades of meaning and understanding. Abstraction defies compartmentalism and instead seeks to adjust to different levels in the urban hierarchy and the constantly changing environment as a result of different influences. How space is used is at least equally important as how it is designed, and has a direct impact on place-making although there are many contested examples.

Gyeongbokgung Palace in Seoul constructed during the Joseon Dynasty was razed during the early Japanese occupation but has been restored to its original form.

Street food in the old part of Qingdao.

Rajadamnoen Avenue in Bangkok, commissioned by King Rama V and constructed in the 19th century as a ceremonial and processional route, links the Royal Field adjoining the Grand Palace with the Royal Plaza associated with Dusit Palace to the north. The original avenue served to extend the old city beyond its encircling walls and remains as the primary throughfare in the Thai capital. More recently it has served as a convenient setting for political rallies, justifying its informal nomenclature as a "corridor of power." The avenue therefore represents a paradoxical mix of royal authority and a physical depiction of civil contestation.

Seoul was laid out during the Chosun dynasty according to strict feng shui principles, which embodied a traditional respect for the sustainable configuration of mountains and water. Japanese colonization from 1910 introduced a politically inspired monumentalism as part of a modernizing agenda that was recalibrated only after the country's liberation in 1945, followed by the urban ravages of the Korean War. The reconstitution of the Gwanghwamun as a prominent cultural space associated with Gyeongbokgung Palace began a revival of traditional Korean culture, even as architectural modernism was transforming the face of the city in the 1970s, accompanied by an economy oriented around high-technology. However, the resilience of inner-city neighborhoods, based on a connective network of streets, also exerts an interwoven system of regeneration and renovation, including older hanok neighborhoods that blend commercial development with older refurbished urban quarters. The Insadong, Bukchon, and Seochon preservation districts have helped to create a momentum for restoration that has extended to older streets and water courses. These urban design initiatives contribute to an elusive combination of cultural tradition and cutting-edge technology that forms part of a South Korean branding process, and promotes a cross-sectional cultural construct that extends its Asian identity to music, art, and film.

Public Space v. Consumer Space

The history of cities as a coalescence of different urban neighborhoods is often characterized by spaces that signify local identity and nurture community life. Public space intervention must meet an overall civic vision while reflecting social needs, with adaptable space that encourages a diversity of uses. This has traditionally provided opportunities for passive recreational activities and local amenities such as weekly markets and festivals that generate interaction, but also fragmentation of these spaces in terms of appropriation by particular interest groups.

Retail environments have become an important part of city economies, at both ends of the market spectrum. The urban shopping mall tends to be associated with more affluent and high-density cities such as Singapore, The Hong Kong SAR, and Tokyo and has become a mainstay of urban centers with internalized environments, multi-use realms of retail, commercial,

Hong Kong SAR street café, Mongkok.

and residential uses that form part of transit nodes. This tends to divide city space into public, semi-public, and private zones, but also raises concerns about "placelessness" and an exclusionary re-ordering of many historic functions in the urban realm. Global chain stores have created a replicated and formulaic brand of urbanism operating across national boundaries that drives outlets progressively into commercial concentrations as part of highly choreographed and corporatized spaces shaped by market interests.

Open spaces in Asian cities have traditionally functioned as relatively organic activity and connective systems; that is to say they often operate in a largely informal way as layered networks, outside what is technically planned. Spaces, including street edges, create opportunities for an unofficial system of economic transaction and exchange that might cater for a mix of merchants and consumers. As the high built density of cities have a low ability to restructure or accommodate new public open space, linear forms tend to dominate, such as malls and sky streets, or quasi-spaces such as street markets, where strolling in crowded situations becomes a form of recreation. This is extended through time-sharing in certain streets that might be

closed to traffic during evening hours and then used as night markets and outdoor eating areas. Cities embrace or control this phenomenon in different ways. Most have a reasonable degree of tolerance to street vendors who traditionally operate without a license. In the Hong Kong SAR, where urban management is more circumspect, street markets are occupied by licensed hawkers and patrolled by uniformed officers, but with a loose fringe of adventurous mobile traders and cooked food operators. The informal sector and the varied entrepreneurial skills associated with it form part of an elusive labor market that is often necessary for economic survival. To an extent places and spaces need to be designed to cater for this situation, which means accepting the unpredictable and the indeterminate in recognition of the contribution this makes to the economic life of the city.

Technology enclaves have developed rapidly in Asian countries, supported by global organizations, progressively refined to accommodate "elite" communities that in turn attract large-scale economic migration from surrounding areas, but also introduce population pressure in the core cities. During the 1980s various cities in India, including Bangalore and Hyderabad with populations of 13 million and 10 million respectively, developed as centers of information technology that attracted an educated middle-class community of professionals with specialized skills. In Hyderabad an entirely new high-tech enclave has been developed on a 50-sq-km site to the west of the city with the gradual acquisition of land previously occupied by 17 established villages. Cyberabad is planned as the most advanced "Smart City" in India, but arguably at the expense of land that housed poorer communities where residents have largely lost both homes and livelihoods. The situation reflects an increasing polarization in Asian societies where much of the new wealth belongs to only a small fraction of the population. A similar situation of tenure insecurity to be found on the urban fringe of many Asian cities, where municipal planning policy tends to flounder in the face of both population and investment pressure. It is where the international information highway reaches a congested point of contestation.

In Singapore, Bangkok, Kuala Lumpur, Seoul, Penang, and Hanoi, specially demarcated outdoor areas are set aside for cooked food vendors under hygienic conditions that reflect an understanding of the underlying dynamics and interfaces affecting both the provider and the consumer. In Singapore, outdoor cooked food areas are imaginatively designed and well integrated. In Malaysian cities the *pasar malam* form a traditional means of equating temporary food stalls with local employment and social interaction, so that street vendors occupy space at a specifically agreed time, while the *pojang-macha* in Seoul operate in a similar way. In the Hong Kong SAR, the traditional *dai bai dongs* or "street cafes" are generally associated with night markets, and off-center locations.

A growing corporate landscape brought about by international investment in Asian cities has tended to deliver a concentration of new and often ambiguous spaces of questionable authenticity, related primarily to commercial undertakings. In some situations this produces a sequence of elevated connections between commercial and community uses, insinuated within a wider pedestrian movement framework and available on a 24-hour basis. This form of dedicated space, for use by the public but technically managed by private interests, is deemed to contribute a public gain that might be negotiated with a developer as part of the planning permission process, or in return for a bonus of floor area ratio value. In this way, the public is presumed to benefit through the provision of open space as an integral part of large-scale development at no actual cost to government, while developers maintain full control over its design and management. This also reflects the fact that many social and civic functions

that were historically conducted in the public realm can now, through modern communication devices, be undertaken from private space, including the "third places" of face-to-face communication—shared work spaces, coffee shops, cafes, and other facilities that facilitate social interaction. As Asian society becomes increasingly segregated and stratified according to wealth, education, and opportunity, and as cities compete for investment, quality of space comes to be associated with specific purposes and simple convenience, while enhancement of the public realm is left to government.

An important factor is to evolve a viable and community oriented mix of uses in relation to neighborhood fabric, that ensures a maximum of amenity and a minimum of conflict. Problems are most likely to arise in relation to the design and use of space in conjunction with urban gentrification and the requirements of different stakeholders. In practice it is the drive toward higher built densities that should make the integration of new spaces both viable and deliverable, with different degrees of public gain rooted in the history of a locality. In these situations public space both supports the wider urban environment and is, in return, supported by it.

In general, urban space in Asian cities are self-policed by the community, and conflicting uses can be accommodated while being continually shaped and reshaped in accordance with

The White Dagoba surmounts
the Qionghuadao Islet and
the Bridge of Eternal Peace
in Beihai Park, Beijing.

the aspirations and resources of its users. This enables market flexibility and diversity of functions, and rarely leads to severe levels of blight or abandonment, primarily because it is subject to a range of uses at different times of day. "In-between" space serve a special purpose in relation to a fine-grained system of incidental and ad hoc spaces, narrow connecting streets, and new public sites carved out of older urban fabric such as internalized courtyards, that can then form part a larger and more continuous public realm and activity matrix.

Broadway Mansions built in 1934 dominates the conjunction of the Bund and Suzhou Greek in Shanghai, forming a vertical termination at the northern end of the Waibaidu Iron Bridge constructed in 1907.

Invaded Space

Over the past 30 years Asian cities have become subject to what might be termed "invaded space," the most pervasive of which is the impact of private vehicles. Without a controlled hierarchy of use, traffic tends to seep into the fine-grained street systems and usurp both pedestrian space and comfort. New traffic arteries effectively sub-divide the urban realm into fragmented parts, frequently disassociating spaces from their existing catchments. This often impoverishes precisely the older area quarters that should present a distinctive historical identity, although in general the social function of open space is compromised rather than lost completely. However, invaded space has the effect of limiting the area dedicated to pedestrian functions and tends to result in a series of fragmented enclaves, where some parts remain vehicle-reliant environments. In addition, street parking encourages congestion and reduces opportunities for informal activities and exchange.

Reclaiming space from traffic is most likely to be successful in evolving a balance between public transport and a connective realm of pedestrian movement corridors and dedicated cycle paths, at a time when some cities have introduced measures to curb car use through traffic management, congestion charge zones and park-and-ride schemes. This has the added incentive of generating positive economic, social, and health benefits.

The interface between vehicles and pedestrians need not necessarily be incompatible, and some overlapping can be beneficial. Most major cities as well as incorporating vehicle-free precincts frequently have a "signature" street or boulevard that facilitates a relatively comfortable interface between vehicles and pedestrians. In this situation pavements must be sufficiently wide, edges robust, and continuity introduced through hard and soft landscape elements, with legibility reinforced through urban markers, in order to provide for interesting pavement life that captures the city identity and invests it with urban vigor.

The Burra Bazaar mixed-use area in Kolkata.

Over the past 25 years, private car ownership has grown at twice the rate of urban populations. Asian cities have a fraction of the road space available to Western cities, but with most metropolitan cities having mass-transit systems and mainline train stations. Advanced cities seek to solve worsening traffic congestion by providing different types of multi-occupant public transit, electronic tolls, and managing demand for road usage by means of road pricing, access restrictions, and experiments with the use of non-polluting autonomous transport systems. Rising car ownership has led to commensurate investment in road and highway infrastructure, designed to a scale capable of accommodating maximum traffic flows rather than regulating them, with inadequate consideration given to hierarchies of scale. Major highways bisect high-density development areas based on a functional orchestration of multi-carriageways along with central dividers and edge spaces, and with local roads chronically congested. In effect the utility of the urban grid has evolved into an expedient system of private auto-travel, anti-urban in its use, and increasingly outmoded in the digital age as a means of sustainable transit. In addition, a reliance on the private automobiles for urban use results in millions of square feet devoted to off-street parking, with the resulting congestion having a clear impact on susceptible microclimates.

Advances in new and clean mobility represent a model for future city regeneration and urban living. It is estimated that more than half of streets now devoted to private cars could become mixed-use public spaces through a recalibration of ecological and resilient urbanism, which in the process creates a greater emphasis on public transit, walking, and cycling. Urban mobility plans must therefore correlate with new forms of design and regeneration.

A future urban design model might involve a system of zoning for urban quarters based on "superblocks" made up of several street blocks that fit within street grid systems. These would form part of smart urban mobility plans that limit major traffic movement to an arterial system around groups of urban blocks. In this way, internal streets and spaces would form part of the local living environments, opening them up to multiple uses. While local traffic would be allowed to penetrate within the superblock assembly, between one half and two-thirds of streets could become "green" connecting streets with enhanced pedestrian mobility and a much less polluted overall environment. The peripheral street system would remain accessible from local streets and accommodate all public transit, with wide pavements and environmental improvements, reducing private car use and channeling public transit onto fewer transversal through routes. At the same time, the notion of street blocks in the form of human-scaled communities create opportunities for water capture, recycling, and thermal energy storage.

Loke Hall Kuala Lumpur constructed in 1903 before being converted to a hotel. In 1973 it was converted by the Malaysian Institute of Architects for use as a building center and secretariat.

Maintaining Cultural Identity

In many ways the Asian city has evolved an urbanism of high contrast but disjointed image. This stems from the post-modern situation that has generated a highly functional "international style" of tall and highly rationalized commercial and residential environments. These are often laid out in the form of self-contained enclaves, in juxtaposition with older patterns of development with the minimum of overlap. This tends to reflect the frequent co-existence of different economic and social systems and the perceptions associated with them—a duality of rich and poor; modernity and tradition; global and local; progressive and hidebound. In this context of unrelenting change and economic competition between cities, older street fabric can easily be perceived as an impediment to a progressive city image. If this position becomes sufficiently entrenched, the city growth model itself comes into question in situations where decisions have to be made between heritage conservation and extraction of value in the face of rising urban land costs and development expectations.

As indigenous forms disappear and heritage increasingly takes on contrived and commodified characteristics, cultural and functional identity imperceptibly merge. At the heart of this is the ways in which both tangible and intangible aspects that exemplify the distinctive characteristics associated with a particular city or locality, can be both preserved and properly integrated. Many Asian countries have successfully merged the cultural residue of historical, social, religious, and building traditions that have evolved over the centuries, with new settlement patterns, establishing a multitude of architectural styles.

There are several ways in which this can be legitimately approached in terms of urban design. The first is to prioritize the retention of distinctive urban streets and places based on existing morphologies, climatic constraints, and topography rather than zoning for dominant land uses. Second is through engendering a dynamic contrast between old and new, through

Revitalization of the old Central Police Station in Hong Kong SAR into a place for people.

Jalan Tuanku Abdul Rahman—the main route through the old city of Kuala Lumpur. A number of the old shophouse buildings were designed in neo-Classical and Art Deco styles between 1910 and the 1940s, and many of the older service retail shops still remain.

Religion in South Korea relates to both urbanism and symbolism spanning a range of spiritual beliefs that include Taoism, Buddhism, and Christianity, but also Animist beliefs and rituals related to the spirits of land, river, and harvests.

sophisticated technical application, elegant detailing, and permeable connections to offset the retained forms of a different era. Third is a sympathetic regeneration of older urban quarters including "native" or ethnic neighborhoods dispersed throughout the city, with a combination of incremental upgrading and retrofitted inserts within the older fabric, allowing these areas to retain their essential characteristics. And fourth is an upgrading and landscape restoration of existing urban ecologies such as canals, river courses, and stream beds as recreational and connective elements.

An underlying conundrum is that as cultural, social, and economic differences between societies are diminishing, globalization—or internationalism—is equated by many Asian governments, institutions, and developers, with Western industrialized city precedents so that planning and infrastructural elements emphasize axial boulevards, undifferentiated civic spaces, and a monumental emphasis on standard building forms. In established Western cities such elements have been introduced as formal interventions in older city fabric over several centuries as cities have experienced a retraction in older industries, often associated with harbor, port, and river frontage. In the process, obsolete but elegant buildings such as factories and warehouses have been subject to incremental regeneration and have effectively absorbed the past into the present. This is not to condemn the current globalizing ideology of Asian primate cities, but to direct it along appropriate and responsive channels to ensure that the accelerating process of growth and change in existing city quarters will add up to more than the sum of the parts, and enhance the stability of the community as a whole. With a high percentage of Asian populations now living in cities, it is also incumbent to ensure their sustainability far into the future.

In Singapore, the Urban Renewal Authority has made a quantum leap in terms of protecting and refurbishing older ethnic enclaves. In the Hong Kong SAR, rehabilitation of conserved buildings is largely left to non-government organizations or established charitable organizations. In Kuala Lumpur it was a coalition of professionals who began to act in the wake of wanton destruction of important older buildings in the 1980s that helped turn the development tide toward conservation. In Yangon it was the architectural institute leading the call for adaptive re-use of the many old colonial structures. In other situations it has come about through public programs of gentrification as an adjunct to tourism programs.

There is, in general, inadequate analysis of the long-term costs and benefits in the adaptive re-use of redundant buildings in public ownership. In many situations these can be used to meet the demand for small business growth, and the relationship of this to the underlying color and dynamism of older city quarters. In the main, existing plazas and parks represent a residue of Western city planning, where redevelopment or rehabilitation of colonial

The Bukchun Hanok community has been subject to a preservation program from 1990 situated around narrow hillside streets in Seoul.

buildings have been used for community purposes. In the Hong Kong SAR, for example, two of the largest urban parks in Kowloon and Hong Kong Island were formed from redundant military installations, while also absorbing some of the older structures as museums and galleries. Several recent projects in the Hong Kong SAR suggest such initiatives are gaining momentum, and include the conservation and conversion of the Central Police Station and Victoria Prison complex, which dates from 1864, to new community, commercial, and cultural uses; the transformation of old Police Married Quarters, built in 1951 on the site of the city's first public school, into a Centre for Creative Industries; the conversion of the Bauhaus-style Central Market into a Festival Market, and a private sector revitalization of a famous textile factory in Tsuen Wan as a museum and event spaces.

Kampong Gelam derived
its name from the Gelam trees
that grew around the area
of the Rocher Canal. It is
focused on the prominent
Masjid Sultan Mosque. The
current building replaced
the earlier mosque built in 1826
that was named after Sultan
Hussain Shah who allowed
the British to establish
Singapore Island as a settlement
under the treaty of 1819.

Land Ownership

The issue of land tenure is fundamental to both the socio-economic as well as the spatial dimensions of urban design and is an important aspect of urban planning procedures in the Asian city. It is also a contested one. Access to urban land is generally through social or family relations, squatting, administrative means such as public housing, and through the real estate market. The concept of private property and urbanization are inextricably linked, although the processes of land assembly and sub-division are relatively consistent, as rising land values act to propel the sub-division process, particularly when land is in short supply. In situations of urban growth the ownership of urban land in itself establishes a causal relationship with the evolving framework of social and economic structures.

Private land speculation inevitably leads to significant appreciation in land value, of which the greatest impacts are on housing availability and affordability, unless public housing is provided. Even in wealthy cities, poorer households tend to spend a disproportionate percentage of their income on rent. While a concentration of land ownership leads to high population densities in central urban situations, in many cases rapid urban growth and accompanying land pressures extend to outer urban fringe areas where lots are amalgamated to form large housing compounds, industrial estates, and shopping centers.

While the process of land speculation is clearly not identical in all situations, a quite consistent pattern emerges in rapidly growing Asian cities. As described by Evers and Korff, this involves a first wave of speculation in the inner fringe areas through the development of private middle-class housing, followed by a second wave of densification within and around the central business district with resulting population redistribution. Former low-income and inner-city inhabitants then tend to either become urban tenants in overcrowded older buildings through sub-letting or move to temporary settlements on the urban fringe where they compete with both suburban developers and rural-urban migrants, intensifying the competition for building land. In the process this tends to fuel a transition from agricultural to urban land use, although in some situations this can be interspersed with some agricultural intensification for production of cash crops. A growing urban elite is then concentrated in new high-rise enclaves within the city and in low-to-medium density suburban estates.

In most situations government itself is a significant land owner, so that land can be sold on a leasehold basis. In the Hong Kong SAR and Singapore large public housing estates, as part of new town programs, have been constructed for rental or sale to middle-income groups on land created through reclamation at strategic locations along the shoreline, or resumed from previous owners. In the case of the Hong Kong SAR, this goes back many decades, with significant income to government derived from land sales, and with lots throughout the city classified into marine, town, and suburban. The new town program that commenced in 1972 was largely reliant on large-scale formation of new land from shallow estuaries and bays around the coast of the New Territories in order to skirt around the problems of private land resumption. In Singapore approximately one quarter of the entire land area has been created through reclamation, commencing in the area now known as South Boat Quay as part of Raffles's 1822 plan, and recommencing in 1965 after independence.

A direct result of colonial intervention in the urbanization process was the registration of land, reflecting the simplistic notion of individual property rights in the city and native land rights in rural situations. However, in later periods of rapid economic development, customary land rights have frequently been overwhelmed by a recalibration of land tenure at the urban fringe, often with little statutory basis. Social relations and neighborhood organization in low-income communities offer some means to resist the forces of demolition and eviction associated with the impetus of economic change. Certain types of established community such as indigenous occupants of older villages or the Indonesian or Malaysian *kampungs* are based on cohesive social and family ties, so that compatibility creates patterns of conformity and cooperation, with close neighbor relations but not necessarily any sense of formal spatial

The prominent corner site of the Song Pu Foreign Company was built in 1909 and represents the largest Russian-built baroque-style building in Harbin and a landmark on its major avenue Zhongyang Street.

organization. In these and similar situations a key factor is to overcome disparities in access to business opportunities and urban production.

In Bangkok the pattern of land ownership is somewhat fragmented as a result of early land allocation to a noble elite, making public agencies and high-ranking officials the biggest land owners. Various ethnic quarters could be identified until the early 20th century – the Western trading quarter along the Chao Phraya River, the Sampheng and Yaonarat Chinese quarter, the Indian neighborhood along Phahurat Road, and the Malay quarter at Phya Thai. As the matrix of canals that crossed the city was largely reclaimed in the mid-20th century to form urban streets, this acted as a catalyst to the transformation of the older settlement patterns to form new commercial and shophouse avenues such as Sukhumvit Road with incidental residential development behind. With a rise in land values these urban corridors have in turn become redeveloped into high-rise alignments of offices, hotels, and apartment blocks, with smaller lanes or *sois* connecting a more fine-grained amalgam of residential lots set back from main streets, creating a mix of urban and semi-rural development.

The organization of most Korean walled cities emanated from their role as government administration centers, connected to rivers in order to facilitate the transportation of grain tax to the capital. As in the PRC, planning grids and location of key buildings were based on the Zhou Li planning model, but because of the mountainous topography streets followed a more organic layout. It was only during the later stages of the Joseon dynasty that cities began to be transformed into commercial centers. Seoul, as the capital of the dynasty, was laid out along wide roads that formed the city structure, and the narrow semi-private *golmaks* that characterized the small neighborhoods. The hanok house types represent adaptations of historic village models—the hanok maeuls—within a dense urban setting, that from 1910 came to partially reflect Japanese urban design influence.

Urban Migration and the Temporary Settlement Predicament

In China, from the inception of the modernization period, around 15 million rural inhabitants have moved to cities every year creating a situation familiar to other rapidly urbanizing and transforming economies. As traditional villages and brownfield areas around the urban fringe of cities become engulfed by urban development, older lifestyles and cultural traditions are eroded by new urban economies that then attract further tranches of migrants. The result is pockets of remodeled communities as a result of uncontrolled redevelopment and urban infill, making existing infrastructure inadequate, installation difficult, and livability increasingly constrained.

The riverine settlements or *Bangs* of Bangkok preserve the past water-related communities along the Klongs, used for floating markets and transportation. These are associated with the lower part of the Chaophraya River and its tributaries across the city's floodplain, in the form of north-south rivers along with an east-west canal system. These gave rise to floating habitations or *ruenphae* that included houseboats, rafts, and commercial craft, while the associated land-based settlements were built on stilts and accessed only from the water. As the traditional *bang* settlements were gradually reduced through reclamation of the canals, gradual urbanization and urban road networks replaced the canals as a means of transport. Specific networks associated with the narratives of the remaining floating world have been awarded UNESCO Awards for Cultural Heritage Conservation.

As continued urban infill encroaches on productive agricultural land, it gives rise to what has been termed desakota areas, where urban and rural uses exist in environmentally challenging proximity. These areas are situated outside peri-urban zones within commuting distance from the urban area, and are characterized by relatively high population density, multiple patterns of unregulated land-use, and declining agricultural productivity. This encourages a co-existence of piecemeal and separately located uses that are less than compatible, and also constrains the installation of necessary service structure along with the subsequent sustainability of economic growth. A planned urbanization process must therefore be balanced by two interrelated initiatives: the continued development of new satellite towns as part of a regional growth process that serves to attract investment and signify a need to accommodate new urban forms, technologies, and sustainable environments; and a more contentious hukou or household registration system that establishes territorial affiliation to control the "floating" population of rural to urban migrants.

The acute shortage of building land in cities inevitably necessitates increases in built and population density through redevelopment, including areas of informal settlement. In Mumbai for example the agglomeration of the migrant housing sector occupies 10 percent of the city's land area but houses around 75 percent of its residents. This includes the largest "temporary" housing area, Dharavi, in close proximity to the Bandra—Kurla business district. The area covers around 530 acres, divided into 80 diverse *nagars* or village-type neighborhoods, and is organized into occupational, religious, linguistic, and caste groups all accommodated in tiny rental structures. Settlements such as these combine both living and livelihood spaces, including cottage industry, that provide valuable benefits to the urban poor, but can also create zones of contestation that can constrain cost-effective attempts at rehabilitation. This challenges the orchestration of incremental building and infrastructure upgrading that should be beneficial to all, and falls well outside simplistic spatial scenarios and planning ideals.

The growth of large temporary settlements around the periphery of many rapidly growing cities is a reflection of the informal means by which low-income workers, including new migrant populations, are integrated into the urban labour market. This includes both occupation of public land, or rental of lots on private land, making tenants vulnerable to eviction through rising land values, although long-term leases can be negotiated under public auspices. In the

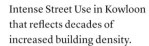

Intense Street Use in Kowloon that reflects decades of increased building density.

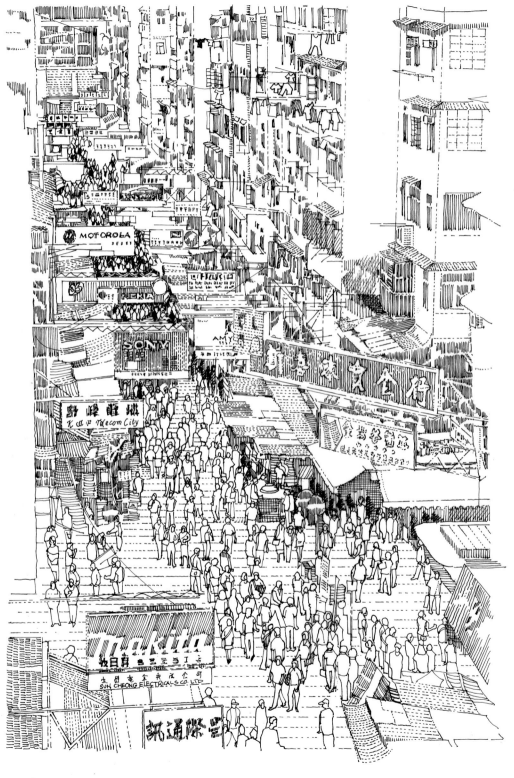

PRC's Guangdong Province older traditional villages have become absorbed within expanded urban frameworks and have accommodated much intensified forms of development taken up by migrant communities on a semi-permanent or informal basis.

While squatter areas are characterized by temporary buildings and a general lack of proper service infrastructure, a lingering problem is that of substandard tenement accommodation through subdivision. In the Hong Kong SAR, the inner-city neighborhoods make up around three million people, with extreme densities in older districts with an average of 130,000 persons per square kilometer. A recent study showed that about 72,000 households or 170,000 people are deemed to be poorly housed with a further 29,000 households living in other poor forms of accommodation such as cocklofts and unsheltered rooms attached to private quarters. Of those in what is classified as "poor condition" households living in single rooms or cubicles are the most common problem, with a high proportion of poorly housed people being elderly and single. While relatively recent immigrant families make up 8 percent of the Hong Kong SAR population, 26 percent of this category are living in housing of a low standard.

Dharavi in Mumbai is commonly known as Asia's largest slum that evolved from a small fishing community. It covers around 240 hectares of land, clustered and expanded by successive tranches of rural-to-urban migrants and their families. The area houses up to one million people in some 85 quarters or *nagers*, interfacing awkwardly with India's financial capital of Mumbai. It has come to symbolically represent an alternative self-built and informal urbanism set around a labyrinthine layout related to both housing, businesses, and social mechanisms, rooted in a necessary resilience to the urban surroundings of the city itself. It can also be described as the heart of a contested redevelopment project introduced in 2004 that pit state agencies and development interests over the future of the strategically located inner-city district adjacent to the financial center of Bandra-Kurta. It personifies both the land values of the city, its inequalities and market pressures, and a not untypical tension between top-down planning and activist resistance.

The broad area plan produced by the Maharashtra Housing and Area Development Authority was to sub-divide the area into five sectors and allocate each to a single developer, with little coordinated plans for resettlement of migrant workers. This continues to represent a complex and contested situation that challenges the various parties involved in recognizing its multi-layered spatial, social, and economic narratives, and the politics of transformative planning through responsive alliances. Such a strategy is intended to shape the urban landscape through bottom-up community driven imperatives that might respect its continual metamorphosis, and the use of space as a social product based on human need rather than an architectural response based on real estate values. In fact, some progress has been made through the interventions of cooperative housing societies to provide incremental and in situ renewal, to rehouse small numbers of households.

Dharavi signifies an elusive right to the city through a "new heterogeneous urbanism," made sustainable through gradual transformation that best responds to immediate needs through adaption over time, grounded in inclusive processes that respect urban diversity. In this way it becomes a meaningful recalibration of the urban design process, set around its use value as opposed to exchange value.

Large squatter areas are still a characteristic of Manila, Jakarta, Mumbai, Kolkata, Dhaka, Bangkok, and on the fringe of large cities in the PRC as a result of rural-to-urban migration. Within slum or squatter areas, social networks, and kinship play an important part in providing initial access to building lots and assistance with construction, with reciprocal ties and co-operation based on traditional cultural values but also on common economic situations that generate overlapping networks of interdependencies. In most cases this makes communal action relatively easy to organize and creates an effective means of representation in dealings with authorities.

CHAPTER 4

Metrofitting the city

Designing the Public Realm

The Asian city works both literally and figuratively in several dimensions, some of them formal, managed, and mechanistic, others more random and responsive to underlying activity patterns. For some users it is sufficient that the city simply functions in a convenient sense; for others it is important for the city to be perceived as reflecting its essential energy, typified and charged by change. The tension between these aspects produces the essential value of urban design in high density Asian cities and makes the idea of catalysis work. However, this should not imply change simply for its own sake, nor involve elements that are overly deterministic. It should rather extend the interactive process that contributes to the urban experience, and subsumes many design initiatives where the projected "end state" can be non-specific.

Cities need to embody distinctive places redolent of both their evolution and identity, despite planning systems that often tend to be based largely on utility and practicality that tends to generate sameness. Urban planning has itself become dominated to some extent by outdated regulatory frameworks and building ordinances that are largely intended to serve public health requirements. At the same time, the achievement of maximum development densities does not necessarily denote actual benefit to the public realm in terms of durable and sustainable configurations, but instead can easily pave the way for the incorporation of large-scale and independently orchestrated private uses.

Urban design does not demand a utopian vision, but rather the outcome of a series of interconnected processes within which many public and private participants collaborate to establish an urbanism responsive to both existing conditions and design opportunities. Similarly,

in most cases incorporated spaces that act as public "rooms" help to alleviate the building mass, and represent a range of identifiable reference points. These provide contrasting and complementary spatial elements associated with the street itself and are particularly effective where streets are narrow and irregular in length. Transition spaces also provide sensory active elements such as visually permeable frontages, inset entrances, and outside display or terrace areas.

Amalgam of old and new building styles in the core of the old city, Macau SAR.

Senate Square housing some of the oldest civic buildings in Macau SAR, including the Holy House of Mercy. It was closed to all traffic in 1994. The new pedestrian plaza forms a focus for local and tourist activity.

the public realm does not have to simply apply to formal layouts and urban aesthetics, with axial vistas and strategically positioned civic buildings, but to its everyday operation that satisfies and stimulates its cross-section of users. The most appreciated urban streets do not necessarily depend on great architecture but on a combination of attributes that achieve contrast, scale, sensory stimulation, and user comfort, where the assembly of component parts is always subject to change and adaptation. In part this requires a respect for historical street formation in shaping form and growth patterns with its many necessary inserts of amenities and public landmarks, but also its variable domain of businesses, places of entertainment, shopping, and restaurant outlets. Buildings themselves play an important part in orchestrating degrees of scale, ornateness, and even grandeur, but the underlying success is in the composite achievement of urban places where people want to visit and gather.

Place-making in the Asian city is an ongoing and often incidental people-centered process that capitalizes on the given assets of an area and its potential in terms of use and identity. In fact, the perception of a memorable and identifiable place can be somewhat metaphysical, having much to do with a combination of impression, association, and imagination. Its validity

stems from social as well as physical ideas built around both informal and symbolic public spaces. It can therefore be said that placemaking is primarily about making public spaces into living spaces, but ones that invite exploration and that can often represent a spatial and cultural link between the past and future ecologies of the city.

The Western concept of place-making or *genius loci* has its roots in the work of Kevin Lynch and Christian Norberg Schulz on the perceptual form of urban environments via mental mapping and "imageability" of city districts through such physical aspects as edges, paths, nodes, and landmarks based on the phenomenology of place. By means of structured interviews with members of the public a number of common elements relating to the cognitive "legibility" of urban environment can be identified that allows city quarters to be recognized and appreciated based on intrinsic urban character and meaning.

While this cognitive approach is quite appropriate to all urban design strategies, successful urban places in Asia must articulate a significant interface with the people who use them and to an extent dictate their functional priorities. Value to the community comes from establishing places that are memorable and reflect aspects of both tangible and intangible heritage. If these

A piazza cross, fronting the Espirito Santo Holy Spirit Church at Margao, Goa. These represented an adaptation of the Syrian crosses from Kerata to the south formed from stucco molding and based on a combination of Rococo church decoration and Hindu temple architecture.

do not already exist or have little to support their integration, then the public realm must form part of a robust regeneration process based on the way that streets work and how buildings and spaces are used. This helps to stitch together neighborhoods and establish points of focus without unduly disrupting established social and economic networks, and in the process helps communities to establish distinctive quarters through collaborative and purposeful public involvement, imagination, and invention. This might extend to the notion of defensible space, overseen through natural surveillance, and expressed through elements that communicate a visual relationship to the wider pedestrian realm.

Development strategies can best be developed around a clear and networked system of public spaces or "voids," which can act as urban design templates for building disposition that reflects the unpredictability of future design and development. In this way the spaces, monuments, and civic buildings continue to define the identity of a locality, with "joined together" architecture displaying an essential variety in individual interpretation of established urban design parameters. Such an approach provides a combination of fixes and flexibility that fosters circulation, encounter, and assembly without an overly imposed sameness of architectural treatment. Public spaces become arenas of activity and receptacles of values, open to adaptation at the behest of the community at large. This represents a means of utilizing the concept of informality, independent of aesthetics, that might best resolve urban problems associated with rapid development intensification that are not disconnected from economic competition among Asian cities. In the context of evolving capitalist economies such an approach calls for a responsive planning apparatus that must continually address a multitude of urban scales and challenges facing the city.

In this situation design itself is secondary to the urban setting, providing that its associated structure and amenities are sufficiently robust, allowing it to change and adapt over time. Successful places must also invite a level of spontaneity where design elements can be placed in conjunction with each other to foster informal levels of use and social interaction, daily, weekly, and seasonally. Urban management should therefore ensure that places have the capacity to respond effectively. This does not by any means rule out forms of activity that exploit the spatial framework in relation to their surroundings and add a sense of uniqueness to the setting.

In exploring the means to transcend functionalist practice and zoning provisions, there is a need to allow within this the capacity to embrace many different meanings and uses. These aggregated values can provide a compelling design language, but must ultimately be redolent of the social identity of the neighborhood. Place-making might therefore embrace some or all of the following:

- Retained or reinstated remnants of previous uses, creating an authentic identity related to memory of the city;
- A degree of transparency that can break down rigid distinctions between spaces and "edge" elements that define it;
- Unifying elements that combine a sequence of uses that engage with local conditions and natural features, and that facilitate civic engagement;
- Comfortable dimensions, for example the relationships between height and depth of enclosing or defining elements relative to adjoining streets or walkways;
- Tree planting, that introduces urban greening and induces climate protection;
- Place "branding" through a fusion of recognizable identity and association; and
- Capitalization of the creative energy of the community to transform underused spaces that might include such things as pop-up uses, performance spaces, and neighborhood exhibitions.

The newly redeveloped square of Masjid Jamek in Kuala Lumpur, characterized by an urban design that echoes that of the mosque. The central space shaded by tensile umbrellas acts as an extension of the prayer hall.

Regenerated pedestrian precinct in Kuala Lumpur.

The Concept of Place

The notion of identifiable place is in general constructed around lateral elements, cognitive association, intensive foci and point references. All of these can be associated with a sense of environmental harmony with an appealing and memorable disposition. Taken in isolation this is essentially concerned with achieving a sense of "balance," much as feng shui is said to be centered around the metaphysical aspects of environment concerning people's perception in relation to their surroundings. In Asia the successful urban place must therefore relate to a series of gambits that collectively consolidate a positive relationship of spaces and features. These can embody a strong association with activity pockets, pedestrian precincts, temple compounds, or waterfront destinations, and can extend to other local gathering places. The way in which we perceive phenomena as they are manifested in the subjective experience and habitation of the city captures references to the philosophical poetics of space discussed by Gaston Bachelard and Michel Foucault. Jane Jacobs notes similar "frames of reference" along with the urban design, social, and economic opportunities associated with dynamic urban environments.

Design approaches must straddle many different facets, and these can be deployed strategically to achieve different ends. Urban design mechanisms that have been successfully applied to place-making concepts according to particular circumstances in one jurisdiction, cannot necessarily be transferred to another. However, the process must be catalytic in nature so that the ongoing building dynamic itself is able to ignite changes that relate to various urban scales but are in all cases shaped by their association with the existing city. This then acts to stimulate revitalization of a particular place within its urban context, allowing for subsequent actions and outcomes that can enrich the overall city identity.

Place-making need not be dependent on formality or architectural aesthetics, although many parts of the Asian city are at least partially dependent on the presence of vernacular and heritage elements that embody a degree of idiosyncratic significance. This implies the capacity to absorb aspects of underlying character and diversity as part of an expressive and responsive urban environment, where voids in the city fabric become positively charged to fit within its figurative patterns. This tends to cross-reference a description of urban design, given by Colin Rowe: "simultaneously an appeal for order and disorder, for the simple and the complex, for the joint existence of permanent reference and random happening, of the private and the public, of innovation and tradition, of both the retrospective and the prophetic gesture."

A number of Asian cities are notable for their opening up of new urban places and spaces as part of long-term revitalization programs that entail a wide variety of small-, medium-, and large-scale projects. Their completion has formed the basis for more strategic enhancement initiatives bringing together representatives of relevant authorities, service providers, and other concerned parties and stakeholders as a prerequisite for making these accessible and widely known, and that can be extended to the design of street landscape, furniture, urban lighting, and signage.

In restoring a sense of activity and local identity, older spaces can be rehabilitated and re-modeled as neighborhood gathering places and promoted through historical and cultural references that help to foster a shared sense of identity. This promotes the image of a vibrant, multi-faceted urban environment, helping to regenerate the traditional aspects of Asian street life and connectedness between parts of the city. In this way place-making becomes socially relevant, engendering a sense of belonging, particularly if places take their character from the neighborhood. Such initiatives are by no means a panacea for urban decay, but act to propel the notion of a singularity of place determined by form, setting, and pre-existing relationships.

At the same time the 21st century emphasis on economic growth in Asia places a not coincidental relationship between this and the incorporation of spaces within private commercial complexes. High population densities make these accessible to large urban catchments as internally oriented destinations that encompass pedestrian malls, plazas, and atria subject to private surveillance. Homogenous precedents can be replicated by the same developers across the region as social and cultural differences gradually diminish. In the process the unique atmosphere and multiple identities of public space gradually make way for a materialistic culture at the cost of genuine public ownership and affiliation with specific geographies.

The place-making process in Asian cities should seek to bring about or reinforce both daytime and evening activity patterns that consolidate areas of intensive pedestrian use and absorb activities such as street processions and bazaars that contribute to the life of the public

The Phnom Penh Museum designed by George Grosher seen from the Foreign Correspondent's Club.

realm. Evening activities represent an inherent part of urban improvisation and casual use, establishing a sense of fit with normal daily functions. Traditionally this has come about in Asian cities through a combination of high urban residential densities, the availability of late-night public transport, and the small seasonal variation in the time at which darkness falls. Thus, the daytime to evening transition is marked by distinct changes in lighting, drama, and atmosphere. Because of the high level of pedestrian activity at night there is also natural surveillance and a feeling of security in the public realm. In a physical sense certain places and streets undergo a change in the articulation of character as new functions such as street markets, cooked food, and entertainment areas provide for new levels of diversity, and in this way the theater of commercial exchange becomes a theater of events. In large part this is due to the flexibility of older building fabric in accommodating a diversity of outlets and an intangible fusion of other uses conducive to casual activities including simply walking, sitting, and browsing. This can also be assisted by permeable fabric, open at all times as pedestrian thoroughfares, and best involves an incorporation of a range of ad-hoc textures that re-invigorate the city realm. The ultimate concern is for public well-being and the preservation of differences between urban places.

Reinforcement of Street Scale

Streets essentially represent the armatures of the city, and serve a range of functions. The traditional characteristic of most Asian streets is the informal context for localized social and business "transactions"—a changing and variable relationship between different uses and users, that co-exist in a successful expression of congruity and commonality. This accentuates the function of the street as a place of resident and commercial encounter, and as a meeting place for the local community living in accommodation alongside. It therefore represents a marketplace in a more traditional sense so that street-making can be reconciled with the ongoing forces of change. However, the uncompromising economic forces behind redevelopment, in whole or in part, too often threatens the street value itself, where single minded scenarios tend to remove or tidy away the superfluous through functional segregation, and in the process act to compartmentalize areas of activity, extracting its contrast and informality. At the same time a failure to reinvigorate the street frontage can lead to increasingly sterile enclaves within urban districts.

Distinctive "edge" activity
on the Sai Kong waterfront,
Hong Kong SAR.

Many Asian cities retain narrow street related neighborhoods that have, in part, contributed to the tight layout and physical character of present downtown areas. The urban neighborhood is the social focus of the Asian city, with several key dimensions in terms of its compact scale, its contribution to the activities associated with daily life, and its physical characteristics as places of encounter and transaction. It is, however, precisely these vernacular properties of organic placemaking and flexible occupation that are threatened by large-scale redevelopment, gentrification, and an accompanying splintering of established spatial networks, that John Friedman has termed "life spaces." In general these "urban villages" evolved over many years around matrices of narrow streets and lanes that can take a number of forms.

The assembly of small "dong" neighborhoods of Seochon in Seoul were originally inhabited by scholars employed at the nearby Gyeongbok Palace during the Joseon dynasty until 1910, and make up collections of traditional hanok structures spread around a series of narrow lanes, partly focused on the Tongin Market.

Primary pedestrian corridors permeate the high-density localities of Tokyo.

The Tokyo and Kyoto urban *roji* form old established networks within established residential neighborhoods. They represent matrices of fine-grained lanes that have been re-appropriated and gentrified in various forms for new and commodified uses that reflect their adaptive versatility in embracing changing social environments. The roji relate to an even more elusive even of place—*ma*, derived from an intuitive awareness or "consciousness" of both form and space that facilitates an engagement with the surroundings.

The *Sois* of Bangkok are named after past landowners, although as some of these have developed into major thoroughfares within hierarchical street patterns they are referred to by both name and number. These neighborhoods create semi-rural pockets of residential development, around which tightly packed communities have developed in contrast to the main city streets. Shophouses and villas co-exist with food outlets and small hotels, along with leisure and entertainment venues. Sois also act as communal corridors that link together well established and informally developed neighborhoods, acting as spaces of social connection and transaction.

The two-story townscape of Margao, Goa defined by colonnaded frontages, open balconies, and elaborate window openings.

In Hanoi the close-knit urban spaces and narrow streets known as *ngõ* establish an interaction between public and private realms, creating a constant vibrancy but also a sense of inclusivity and social conduct. It is where domestic activities mingle with a range of temporary uses and meeting spaces that create sites for the rituals of daily life.

The night markets on Raohe Street, Shilin, and Huaxi in Chinese Taipei represent an established culture of street trading, cooked food outlets and permanent shop frontages that define the street edge. The central division of market stalls creates a mutually supporting relationship between permanent and temporary uses that inter-relate with local temple precincts and intersect with connecting lanes in the adjoining neighborhoods.

Georgetown in Penang first attracted merchants as part of 18th-century trading routes, with an assembly that combines Jawi and Chinese Peranakan cultures with Western, Malay, and Indian influences within networks of distinctive streets and urban quarters that accommodate a mix of ethnicities and notable temple structures.

In contrast to costly redevelopment projects, an incremental strategy of urban regeneration can combine a legacy of intact urban fabric and older buildings of quality through a "joined together" program of street and space upgrading, and where appropriate a rerouting of existing transit systems. The key to this is an involvement of public and private bodies including local citizen groups, businesses, and those institutions involved with housing, city management, and urban renewal. An important focus is a specification of allowable uses, with certain street matrices designated for intensive pedestrian use focused on an identifiable central area, and others providing for predominantly vehicular and service needs. A further measure is the retrofitting of the linear street wall fabric to provide continuous active frontage along with new insertions via the demolition of seriously dilapidated or abandoned buildings. Conversion of older buildings with redundant uses tend to act as an energizing means to maximize different social and economic needs of local populations. Sites can also be identified for future acquisition in order to weave institutional, educational, and cultural buildings within downtown neighborhoods as their population intensity increases.

Pedestrian continuity and linkage are key factors. Neighborhoods should fit within the larger urban circulation framework through continuous "citypark walks," linking activity centers, public open space, and, where appropriate, regenerated waterfronts through one or more principal elements that act as city stages for activity—precincts, urban passages, plazas, and elevated connectors. In major urban centers multi-level spatial and movement frameworks have developed through an indeterminate but purposeful amalgamation of public, semi-public, and corporate alignments, where "public gain" might be negotiated with a private developer, but quite possibly in return for a bonus of allowable plot ratio value. These can be linked to internal atria and malls that form part of adjoining commercial complexes that create a notable degree of planning gain through public/private partnerships. In this situation regeneration becomes not an end in itself but a stimulus for a range of ongoing uses and mixed functions for the benefit of the wider community.

While the physical qualities of the street in terms of architectural design and consistency are important, the compositional qualities of traditional street design should not be ignored. In the older quarters of many Asian cities, older shophouse terraces together with colonnaded frontages continue to exert strong and consistent typologies that generate identifiable street forms with variable functional qualities. The older Chinee shophouse street made up of three- to four-story buildings is an excellent example of "rhyming urbanism." The design is expressed through simple elements that act as breaks in the facade that includes an arcaded ground level with balconies, shuttered window and door openings, and a defined cornice line above, which create breaks and shadow lines on the street facade, both horizontally and vertically. Each

The area around Xi Hai, 'Iou Hai, and Qian Hai lakes 1 Beijing incorporates old 1ansions, promenades, nd lakeside cafes.

individual structure within the street terrace can differ, both in terms of detail and the extent to which a complex organization of shapes, profiles, and textures procures a coherent state of balance. This is an almost inevitable result of style emanating from the use of appropriate building methods and materials. By way of contrast, taller and more intensively built structures tend to use podium elements to convey a blander version of street-edge continuity.

The Relationship of Urban Blocks to the Street Framework

Social and economic change in wealthy Asian cities has manifested itself in the physical transformation of the street in terms of the overall urban fabric. With development intensification in line with increased land values, streets increasingly tend to demarcate rather than service a public realm of social and economic interaction that sustains local communities and provide areas of special or unique character for visitors. This has had the effect of dividing rather than consolidating old established neighborhoods.

Narrow *roji* street through residential area, Tokyo.

At certain periods in history the integrity of street design was carried out in a purposeful and self-conscious way, with examples in some cities of elected officials being charged with responsibility for enforcing design criteria leading to a high degree of uniformity, only alleviated by differences in detailed design interpretation. In this situation the street is retained as the primary component of urbanism rather than the individual building. However, the insertion of primary roads within and through urban neighborhoods has disrupted and reversed the previously consistent form and scale of the urban street, where main traffic arteries have acted to usurp other urban uses. In the process the street as an expression of public life, where building disposition and neighborhood use were significant determinants of its character, has in many areas been largely compromised.

The agglomeration of small urban lots along major thoroughfares to assist their redevelopment to higher densities, has in many cases tended toward self-containment of private uses. In these situations the public realm, made up of many individual parts, has been usurped by the private realm through the accommodation of overly large parcels of property under single ownership. Activities that were previously laid out horizontally as legible street uses are increasingly stacked vertically in the form of commercial development nodes. With little overall urban design control and low site coverage, tall buildings often utilize only part of the site, with the remainder being devoted to parking. Although an internalized concentration of retail street environments in high-density cites reflect an intensity of activities based on levels of use. Continued integration of large volumes of people living adjacent to main streets and large working populations in adjoining business districts create an interaction of people and activities within the street matrix. No regulatory control or planning parameter can legitimately dictate the allocation of specific commercial-retail uses, which are permitted under somewhat flexible zoning categories, with both design and disposition largely determined by the developers of individual buildings. Urban design mechanisms and special lease or tender conditions should ensure continuity of active frontage across a defined matrix of streets that influence the pattern of spatial interaction, making this conducive to multiple levels of use.

The Ximen Mall—part of a connective pedestrian system that forms part of Chinese Taipei's street upgrading program.

activities offers the benefit of convenience, with open space located on private podium decks disconnected from the street, this does not in most cases provide the rich variations in urban experience that should occur within the public realm.

This brings into question the fundamental principle of how urban streets, as the prime components of urban areas, are conceptualized within the regeneration process in terms of shaping requirements for economic and social activities at the district level while creating livable urban localities. If we accept that the street is the primary medium of economic and social exchange, its spatial configuration and layout in dense and compact urban environments must be key catalysts for sensitive urban regeneration. In this way the street and its essential components come to represent the essential health and interactive characteristics of the urban neighborhood. This must simultaneously act as both a centripetal and centrifugal force to attract and disseminate activities, illuminating its intrinsic character and socio-cultural significance to the community it serves. At the same time streets must provide a sense of safety and a high level of pedestrian comfort and convenience for users.

A number of Asian cities have at least part of their urban form set around broad grid layouts, introduced into the original city-making process as an expedient means to structure new development and ensure a nominal degree of servicing. This encompasses a number of variables—street length, street width, and block dimensions—and provides an effective means of accommodating transport, energy, water, and sanitation infrastructure. The Tang dynasty Chinese capital Chang'an, with its orthogonal grid created a model for the 8th-century ancient

Japanese cities of Kyoto and Nara. Other examples of gridded urban environments in Asia include Beijing in China, North Jakarta in Indonesia, Subang Jaya in Malaysia, Islamabad and Karachi in Pakistan, the older part of Singapore, a number of Portuguese planned settlements in the Philippines, and Ho Chi Minh City in Vietnam.

Older areas laid out as matrices of shophouses or similar low-rise terraces have either survived as conserved and upgraded entities, or been substantially reshaped within new neighborhood layout formats. This has allowed characteristic urban quarters to evolve and absorb both public and private initiatives within a tight networking of street blocks defined by joined-together buildings, creating urban compositions of public frontage, together with semi-public and private spaces.

Colonial city planning in the 19th and early 20th centuries incorporated older quarters within expanded city boundaries, so that in many cases the "old city," often walled, occupied a separately defined entity from the new city of administration and commerce. Increasingly, however, both urban design and architecture became instruments of separation between communities focused more on individual privacy rather than the primacy of the public realm.

Over the course of the 20th century, city building in Asian cities was further formalized by imposed means of planning control, zoning, and building regulations that indirectly predicated sameness in both appearance and use. With the advent of motorized transport, street grids took on more of a hierarchical and asymmetric form, with larger amounts of land devoted to streets, and block dimensions that dictated the frequency of intersections. From the mid-century these were resolutely combined in high-rise estates and mega-commercial centers that have in many cases had the effect of rationalizing the urban design process in ways that isolate city quarters rather than drawing on their interdependence. As urban land costs in major cities continue to escalate, to the extent that public land sales in some cases generate a high proportion of city income, land use decisions and subsequent development control mechanisms have steadily become geared to the maximization of building densities despite the evident urban consequences whereby older and characteristic low-rise fabric is put at risk of redevelopment.

For both public and private development the urban and "design" must be interactive. Consistent design parameters are essential to ensure that private development is sympathetic to the overall urban framework. At the same time, architectural design must, at an increasing scale, establish a designed level of fit and a strong correspondence with more placemaking requirements. This can still distinguish the street character of older neighborhoods in the cities of East Asia, including the port cities of southern China that continue to express a street-related disposition based on a configuration of sections that integrate set-backs and arcaded frontages, along with informal shifts in scale.

The Raohe Night Market,
Chinese Taipei.

The Boyyoke Aung San Market
in Yangon comprises a series
of interconnected arcades,
colonnaded streets,
and pedestrian precincts.

The old merchant city in Hanoi,
known as the thirty-six streets
and guilds quarter of specialized
crafts, dating back to the twelfth
century.

In re-orchestrating the street morphology as part of the urban regeneration process a number of conditions can be considered in combination. Street edges in district centers must be physically continuous as far as possible, dedicated to publicly accessible uses, both horizontally and vertically. Integrative design interventions must also aim at maximizing pedestrian permeability as part of integrated initiatives such as the integration of continuous colonnaded frontages at ground level. Fine-grained mid-block passages or "skinny streets" can act as connecting arcades between parallel urban streets can increase permeability and contrast in binding together urban localities. These can form animated nodal points at their intersection and act to supplement and extend the pedestrian route matrix beyond the street frontages, designed and inserted in contrasting ways. The benefits include breaking up oversized volumes, establishing contrasting means of pedestrian circulation, and increasing available options for pedestrian flow.

The narrow walkway structure creates extensive patterns of connectivity within and through the old city fabric of Shanghai.

Street blocks or terraces, in one form or another, make up the fabric that defines the public realm of older Asian cities. In this sense their shape and regularity can be either formal or irregular, in response to the prevailing context and features. In new street block configurations such arrangements can accommodate semi-private or community uses, and where appropriate allow for the integration of below-grade parking and servicing. Individual sites can be of different widths with the outer faces defining the active character of the public street walls, where a variety of individual building inserts is informally regulated by an underlying design language. In this way patterns of order can be realized out of complex urban forms, and is why we refer to the "weight," "strength," or "symbolism" of building features. This does not necessarily equate with a symmetrical appearance, but aims for a situation where likeness is tempered by complementarity. It is these subtle variations in the street wall that produce a sense of both familiarity and novelty, articulated by the design rhythms of built frontages, openings, and cornice lines, that are visually appealing and in line with older street fabric. This can be achieved through the application of design parameters that complement building codes and provide individual designers with sufficient flexibility to interpret these in different ways within a coordinated whole.

The grid of streets that form the heart of Georgetown, Penang was laid out in the 18th century and reflected the make-up of the population with streets allocated to different groups on the basis of ethnicity and kinship.

An important aspect of this is the resulting building configuration in relation to applied floor area ratio and site coverage, set out in building and planning regulations. Six-story street blocks with intersections at around 150 meters, relatively low plot ratios and high site coverage, can satisfy virtually the same development density as a series of isolated tall blocks on large sites but with low building coverage, which leaves a residue of empty spaces, often used as ground-level carparks. Design parameters therefore need to incorporate envelope guidelines that equate development and layout conditions of scale and function appropriate to street and block-making requirements to safeguard the quality of the public realm. Different developers, designers, and users in combination are able to establish a covenant that satisfies individual interests and contributes to the orchestration of street buildings with architectural ingredients in common that achieve both consistency and diversity. It is also important that buildings are designed to facilitate their potential for long-term rehabilitation and reuse.

Livability is a term widely used in the context of sustainable planning, but as a concept it has much to do with social interaction. The cultural interpretation of this in older urban quarters tends to focus on streets that experience low traffic volumes and high levels of walkability. In other words, there is an interrelationship between subjective and objective values

that introduce performance dimensions in terms of environmental quality, amenity, and individual well-being. There is therefore a clear interface between livability, street pattern, scale, and traffic conditions, where positive social indicators tend to correlate inversely with traffic volume. With redevelopment programs motivated by pre-set floor area ratios to maximize built densities, this calls for both a recalibration of traffic and transport planning, and both its existing and potential means of travel focused on autonomous "clean" modes that priorities both health and sustainability.

Revitalization of City Spaces

While there has been a determined focus on urban revitalization, there are few references that set out urban values in terms of both design and social objectives, and the determination of creative planning and design conditions to achieve them. Physical qualities clearly need to be balanced by the means to realize public and community values, as well as the ability to meet economic performance criteria. Socio-economic considerations require certain critical factors to be addressed as a means to establish "fit" and settings for urban activities, and as a basis for creative architectural solutions at the smaller scale. This requires a conceptual approach that establishes initial values, and from these certain physical qualities can be derived. These can then be translated into urban design conditions to be met by all participants in the urban design process. This includes the following:

· Pavement widening to facilitate the ability to walk safely at varying paces;

· A continuity of active mixed uses at ground level;

· Periodic setbacks of built fabric to incorporate forecourts;

· Incorporation of visual landmarks and design features;

· Variety and diversity of streetscape elements;

· Street landscape and furniture for physical comfort;

· A measure of contrast, permeability, and route alternatives at ground level;

· The incorporation of green walls and other types of planting;

· Facade relief through incidental details and surface texture in relation to pedestrian circulation levels;

· Incorporation of signage within urban centers that provides for color, complexity, and light quality;

· Provision of lighting that allows street facades, structure, and details to stand out in a way that might not be visible during day time; and

· Climatic protection from seasonal heavy rain and direct sunlight in summer through canopies, arcades, and street trees that introduce a filtering of light and shadows, and serve as visual buffers.

Singapore's fire-foot ways act as both climate protected circulation and display areas, forming a physical transition between public and private street realms.

The urban street matrix requires planning reconciliation at a district level so that it becomes possible to delineate a hierarchy of movement channels of various types and scales, complemented by other initiatives such as pavement widening with integral street planting and furniture. This can be combined with efforts to resolve traffic problems, with commensurate reductions in energy consumption, noise, and air pollution.

Shophouse Street, Xiamen.

The Red House built as a public retail market and now serving as an arts venue in Chinese Taipei.

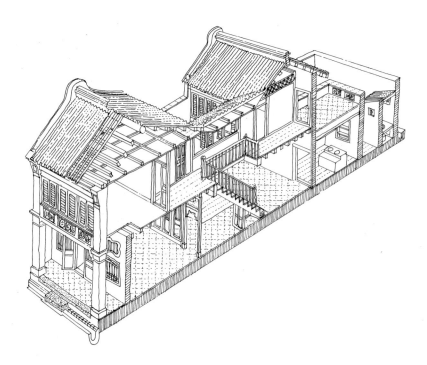

Shophouse Design and the Street Making Tradition

The degree to which urbanization is unified by older commercial and residential models repre-sents a cultural link with the past, with at least some affinity to traditional values. Shophouses in Canton, Xiamen, Malaysia, Singapore, Penang, and Melaka embody a social as well as an economic dimension, representing a situation that is still predominant, and where family and business life are closely related. The shophouse, as a generic component of street formation, can be said to have originated in Southern China, and spread to Asian port cities through mar-itime trade. From the late 18th century the shophouse was a basic component of city growth, with a simple form of one to two stories, and extended to Hong Kong and other cities in ways that varied in terms of architectural style, volume, and climatic features. While the colder northern climate produced variants with a narrow frontage and generally short depth, the southern version tended to integrate a deeper plan form with an open courtyard to assist venti-lation, and generally subscribes to a north-south orientation.

The Chinese exodus to southern destinations in Asia introduced building traditions dating back to the Song dynasty. More formal relations were established in the 15th century when members of a Ming court retinue to Malacca intermarried with local Malays to create the be-ginning of a "Straits-born Chinese" culture. With the Portuguese arrival in Malacca in 1511, and their new trading links with China, many thousands of Chinese moved to the growing city

Typical shophouse along the Avenida de Almeida Ribeiro, Macau SAR.

through the next 250 years of Portuguese and Dutch rule. However, dwindling trade trajectories were reflected in a decline in the Chinese population, and it was not until 1786 when the British East India Company took possession of Penang, and again after 1842 following the foreign concessions within the Chinese treaty ports, that trading ties were reinforced. The many internal upheavals in China were catalysts for many Chinese to emigrate in large numbers to escape their economic predicament and to take up business opportunities in the new Asian colonial settlements.

The Singapore shophouse, while technically reflecting a Chinese typology that developed virtually simultaneously in various port cities, evolved in both stylistic and ornate terms to embody an almost unique combination of Chinese details and European neo-classical and decorative references. There were several reasons for this, the primary one being the rapidly developing coastal settlements in the 18th and 19th centuries as competing Western nations developed Asian trading routes that became bases for trade in and around the South China Sea. European settlers introduced aspects of grand design that were prevalent in Western cities including classical orders, Palladian motifs, baroque, neo-classical, and later art-deco elements that combined to create a new architectural realm.

Through the involvement of builders, carpenters, and compradors, these details were passed across strict typological boundaries, and also across regional borders to insinuate themselves through an adaptive integration within the most prevalent of building prototypes—the new Chinese commercial enclaves. The migration of traders from southern China, in particular from Amoy, Foochow, and Canton, was associated with the continued development of trading links. They brought with them new stylistic innovations to such outposts as Singapore and the Philippines that then intermingled with local skills in carpentry and masonry to evolve new typologies and decorative additions. In some cases these were then reintroduced to Chinese cities in a culturally extended and cosmopolitan form by returnees, for example to the streets of Amoy and the villas of Gulangyu. This in turn led to the early 20th-century *Lingnan* vernacular practices in Southern China that embodied Western styles and decorative additions.

Modern time-specific values need not replicate traditional forms, but can draw on a compositional vocabulary of relevant cultural dimensions, proportions, and responses to climatic conditions through devices such as verandas, colonnaded terraces, welcoming thresholds, and shaded courtyards. These are what the Malaysian architect Ken Yeang has termed "inventive transformations"—an informed and knowledgeable distillation of crucial elements that have a "signature" role in framing inclusive urban environments.

Migrant settlers tended to bring with them both design and building traditions, modified to fit climatic and contextual situations, but also responsive to prevailing foreign influences and

available materials. In tropical situations, colonnaded structures and verandahs functioned as transitional spaces that regulated the relationship between internal and external space. The grid layouts allowed for shophouse depths of several times the width, with internal airwells and service lanes at the rear. Each floor could be sub-divided into semi-private compartments through partitions to increase the capacity to sub-let spaces to new immigrants.

Between 1840 and 1900 the style evolved to reflect a more decorated facade with carved doorways, distinctive gable ends, and terracotta roof tiles. In response to the tropical climate louvred shutters were used to protect openings on the upper stories, with airwells introduced for ventilation. The later and more eclectic models were influenced by Western styles and decorative devices reflecting British colonial influences. "Late Straits" period shophouses were often highly decorated with projecting columns, arches, plaster relief, embossed tiles, and ceramic air-vents. An art-deco style followed the European design trend in the 1930s with geometrically designed facades and plaster wall finishes replacing the earlier decoration. Designs were even further simplified from the 1950s reflecting modernist influences together with the availability of new building materials and construction techniques. Shophouses were constructed mainly by Chinese builders and craftsmen, so that in many parts of Asia they have come to be regarded as a predominantly Chinese building type with a common heritage,

Theater built in 1911 forming
part of an elegant street block
along Longsheng Xiang, Dalian.

Hong Kong SAR shophouse
group on Hollywood Road.

Hanoi shophouse.

hophouse interior, Malacca.

typical Peranakan property on
Jeeren Street, Malacca blends
Chinese style with European
aroque, Dutch features,
nd Palladian references.

adapted to suit local environmental and economic conditions. In this way a combination of labor resources and business access fueled city development programs.

Cultural diversity in older Southeast Asian cities has tended to combine various ethnic neighborhoods with long-standing social heterogeneity, distinctive urban design characteristics, spacious layouts for western residents under colonial regimes, and dense concentrations of urban terraces. These came to represent the dominant older typologies and characteristic heritage quarters as the post-industrial city changed its economic emphasis.

The "bamboo barrel houses" in Canton were designed with a long plan form and narrow frontage, the frontal part serving as the shop and the rear part residential, while the upper story could be used either for residential or storage. A narrow lane divided units that were largely laid out in parallel street blocks, so that servicing could be carried out from the rear. A similar type can also be found in the old city of Hanoi where they are known as "tube" houses, reflecting the long plan form that might extend to 60 meters, divided by courtyards to introduce light and ventilation. In the late 19th century, certain shophouse streets in Canton faced the waterways that permeated the Liwan area of the city. The transport of mineral ores and jade depended on these, and the orientation of shophouses facilitated and enhanced both the

South Back Street—a major axis through the "Three Lanes and Seven Alleys" area of Fuzhou that represents a mix of urban renewal and regeneration initiatives. The alleys take their names from the city's rich literary and musical associations with past dynasties

delivery and emerging business systems. These later became centers of visitor interest, including the Yuan Sheung and Hua Lin jade markets, and as water channels became filled in for road formation strong retail edges were established alongside new transport corridors.

Low-rise three- to four-story Chinese tenement structures in Hong Kong constructed after 1842 were known as *t'ang-lou* where the internal walls were separated from the structural fabric to allow for flexible sub-division. The width of around 12 feet was determined according to the span of available timber, although timber floors and pitched roofs gradually gave way to concrete structures and flat roofs. Families operated a ground-level business, lived on the first floor, and often let out sub-divided spaces above to Chinese relatives from the home province. This allowed Chinese city quarters to absorb high population densities and intense patterns of economic activity. The open colonnaded arcade at ground level was a southern European design feature probably introduced by the Portuguese in Penang, Malacca, and the Macao SAR. It was later transferred to shophouse street designs in the Hong Kong SAR, and the Chinese Treaty Ports such as Canton, Swatow, and Amoy. Its most widespread use was in Singapore during the early 20th century, where the five-foot way as a generic feature was formed by an overhanging upper story, designed to project over the pavement and supported by pillars, created a colonnaded public circulation space at ground level, separated by a granite step from the

The Gu Yi Street area of modern Tianjin extends back to the Yuan Dynasty. It now acts as a regenerated shophouse and street market area, integrated with converted older buildings and temples.

adjoining roadway. This characterized large parts of the city, acting as both a social and commercial threshold, and offering untold opportunities for hawker activities.

What makes the shophouse stand out from other indigenous Asian residential types is its relationship to the process of city-making through a consistency of form but with a variety of interpretations, including aesthetic treatment. The redevelopment of Singapore's Orchard Road, from a shophouse avenue made up of small lots to a high-rise commercial and hotel spine in the 1970s, creates a contrasting template to the older row houses and narrow roadways of Emerald Hill, and the inter-linked shophouses that have been converted into cafes and bars.

Shophouse streets and clusters still maintain a low-density and predominantly "green" presence in many rapidly regenerating Asian cities. As city cores change their identity and mass through new business structures, fragmented older quarters take on what has been described as a "bazaar economy" where commercial transactions relate to the street framework of shops and mobile vendors, including street markets independent of the central location. These older and more flexible quarters have strong social and cultural ties, as well as persistent but relatively informal trading patterns that are responsive to facets of change, but are also vulnerable to officially sanctioned urban management policies.

CHAPTER 5

Regeneration as value added

While the urban structure of most Asian cities is quite legible with a generally hierarchical network of streets and centers, their high-density agglomerations embody a diffuse and generally non-hierarchical narrative made up of different layers superimposed on older frameworks, which contrast but do not necessarily conflict. The notion of co-existence suggests an approach to urban regeneration that might combine an underlying pattern and necessary spatial organization, with a more abstract, piecemeal, and incremental three-dimensional structure, at a time when cities are experiencing rapid urban change and strong pressure for physical reconstruction. The key to attaining sustainability is an approach that involves an amalgam of participants—local authorities, developers, investors, and other stakeholders that should reflect the current tools and metrics used by public, private, and non-government sectors, and how these can contribute to the implementation of social stability according to prevailing community agendas.

The terms renewal, regeneration, and redevelopment are often used in an interchangeable way, but in effect mean different things. Renewal goes on all the time to a lesser or greater extent of its own volition, unless there are prevailing reasons such as conservation of heritage buildings. It can best be described as the physical change stemming from prevailing economic forces—that is to say it is normally motivated when the actual building on a site is worth less than the land it is sitting on. As land in developing Asian cities steadily increases in value, so redevelopment has in practice become a fact of life and puts both urban heritage and the memory of the city at risk.

edestrian Street
the rejuvenated heritage
arter of Nanjing.

An orthodox urban renewal procedure under these circumstances is insufficient in itself to cater for the complex situations that prevails in many Asian cities, which calls for a more regenerative approach reflecting an amalgam of measures necessary, in varying degrees and at various scales, to resolve a range of problems in the urban domain and ensure its lasting improvement and livability. In the Hong Kong SAR, for example, all land in the city is zoned and sites have a development value according to their plot ratio designation under the Buildings Ordinance, and means that all relatively low-rise sites are vulnerable to either private or institutionally orchestrated redevelopment, which is in itself alien to normally recognized city building objectives.

St. Michael's Cathedral completed in 1934 in Qingdao in a refined Romanesque design in close proximity to the older Missionary Society and Franciscan Convent buildings.

Urban regeneration is a continuous interventionist process aimed at resolving particular sets of problems and requirements under at least six themes that must deal with physical, environmental, economic, socio-political, housing/health, and employment/education. The interplay between these, together with a balanced response to a detailed analysis of prevailing conditions, is what defines successful urban design, but is also important as a crucial element in strategic planning, taking into account external influences and characteristics. The relative importance of these in serving the collective interests of society can be expected to change over time creating new demands in certain areas but also ensuring that change is beneficial in bringing about overall improvement.

An important aspect of this is to contain urban growth through selected urban regeneration and densification while ensuring both the protection of neighborhood structure, co-ordination of essential public uses, and containment of urban sprawl. The overriding outcome in terms of operational objectives and policy implementation must be a gradual reshaping with regard to both existing and forthcoming technological change, in line with new construction at higher densities to achieve environmentally sustainable development. It must also ensure participation by all stakeholders who have a legitimate interest in the regeneration procedures and can assist in mobilizing collective effort under an effective management process. Residents of individual neighborhoods require a clearly delineated power to protect and reinforce their underlying character, but this must be in line with the future needs of the city as a whole and its ability to effectively conserve and integrate a range of historical references and destinations. In many situations there is no single cause for apparent urban problems, as these can reflect local and city-wide issues, and even the outcome of political and global processes.

According to the World Economic Forum, over 50 percent of Asia's 4.5 billion residents will live in cities by 2026, with 60 percent of these living in megacities, where growth is driven largely by rural-to-urban migration. In Southern China this has led to the phenomenon of "urban villages," previously situated within the agricultural fringe, but now absorbed within

Jalan Petaling, part of the Chinese shophouse quarter of Kuala Lumpur, now revitalized as a street bazaar.

Jalan Petaling, part of the Chinese shophouse quarter of Kuala Lumpur, now revitalized as a street bazaar.

the urban fabric, which have evolved into packed high-density conurbations to house migrant families. The fastest rate of urban population growth is now occurring in regions of South and Southeast Asian cities in India, Pakistan, Bangladesh, Indonesia, Thailand, Vietnam, and the Philippines where urban infrastructure is often less than adequate.

Urban regeneration, wherever it occurs, requires a comprehensive and integrated vision aimed at achieving lasting improvement to both the private and public realms, with an effective interface between them. It is best implemented through small one-off projects that are meaningful to the community and consolidate local identity. The complexity of Asian cities coupled with their high land values, indicate that improvements need to be carried out in an adaptive way to provide for both continuity of urban character and community gain. One of the most pertinent aspects is that successful regeneration must have a long-term strategic purpose and should represent all stakeholders who have a legitimate interest in the city—it should therefore be carried out slowly and strategically.

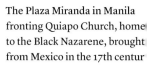

The Plaza Miranda in Manila
fronting Quiapo Church, home
to the Black Nazarene, brought
from Mexico in the 17th centur

The public sector role must consider overall benefits that extend well beyond a reconciliation of regulatory boundaries and procedures. The transition from a redevelopment approach toward a more focused urban regeneration one, needs to reflect a means to tackle problems associated with long-term urban betterment. It must therefore simultaneously relate to physical fabric, social structures, the economic base, and environmental conditions. This calls for integrated strategies that deal with the resolution of problems in a balanced, comprehensive, and positive manner, and ensure that programs of implementation make a positive contribution to the city as a whole. An important aspect of this is where the orchestrating authority acts as an advocate and enabler rather than an instrument of control—this implies a need for community participation in all large-scale regeneration initiatives.

ernacular market spaces n Tokyo are often ntegrated with high-density onglomerations where the relationship between buildings, ngineering structures, nd street activities are both uid and impermanent. hese form labyrinthine hopping and restaurant nvironments, often located eneath elevated structures ch as railway alignments.

In many Asian cities the "pull" of low-density suburbs as a refuge from the crowded city has been reoriented in many cases by the "push" factor—people moving to medium- and high-density enclave estates within new town or satellite communities on the city outskirts, within easy commuting distance of central business districts by public transport. These are exclusionary only in the sense that estates are built by private developers for the more affluent or by government for public rental housing—effectively producing a recolonizing impact. This does not necessarily erode the traditionally strong patterns of kinship and social cohesion associated with Asian communities, nor does it reflect an absence of adequate social and institutional facilities. There are also few negative issues with regard to ethnic dimensions of integration. New towns built over the past 40 years in the Hong Kong SAR, Singapore, and Seoul have, for the most part, created improved environments as planned rather than infill places. The physical obsolescence of urban buildings and outdated infrastructure associated with older parts of the city can be dealt with as part of wider property-led regeneration and restructuring scenarios, with pedestrianization initiatives that contribute to economic, social, and environmental benefit.

In cities that have historic centers or important heritage structures, regeneration has to center around physical revitalization, improvement, and upgrading exercises, commensurate with livability agendas and ways to encourage public participation. This type of project is intended to produce an enhanced city image with direct, indirect, and induced impacts through increased cultural and symbolic values. It therefore suggests a focus on regeneration initiatives and pilot projects that can contribute to the improved economic functioning of urban areas and their associated city regions. These include environmental action linked to economic goals including refurbishment of heritage buildings, revitalization of historic centers, urban design integration, traffic management, pedestrian connectivity, and promotion of cultural activities associated with the older city fabric as a focus for new business development.

The Upper Mall or Shahrah-e-Quaid-e-Azam in Lahore showcases a range of imperial buildings, built in 1851 in a mix of Anglo-Mughal styles.

In general, regeneration needs to equate with economic progress, increasing affluence, pro-active policies to overcome housing need, and other aspects geared toward city betterment. It must therefore represent a continuous process of urban improvement rather than a "once-and-for-all" solution. In this sense urban management must encompass a deliberately broad strategy that relates to physical intervention, social action, and strategic action associated with other policy fields. This is not to downplay the importance of local concerns and the need to deal with diverse local issues and needs, but to contextualize them. In discussing social and community aspects the main issues are: the precise definition of community in the context of an identified regeneration area and its actual or potential catchment; the special needs of the community and those of other important stakeholder groups; the provisions necessary to meet these needs; the development of shared goals to promote the improvement of economic, social, and environmental conditions; the establishment of effective community partnerships; and capacity-building with communities, stakeholders, and local authorities.

ty Hall and Cathedral,
Chi Minh City.

It is best to allow for a wide definition of regeneration based on a variety of perceptions, attributes, relationships, attachments, and sense of belonging to the community, as the conception of the term community associated with a specific place, district, or density can vary substantially and engenders powerful emotive connotations derived from social and place-based identity. Vibrant communities also form civil associations that establish supportive relationships producing a sense of togetherness that is not necessarily defined by neat physical boundaries.

With an ageing population there is also an increasing demand for health care, community support, adequate social provisions, the means to overcome deprivation and exclusion, and a pleasant walking and passive recreational environment. This in turn enhances the capacity of localities to provide for locally responsive services, and to ensure that as far as possible all sectors of the population are properly represented. Communities can then be empowered through the most effective form of ownership initiatives as a central strategy of neighborhood regeneration and the means to achieve public-private partnerships.

Sustaining Diversity

Diversity and mutuality, particularly in a business sense, have traditionally been the means by which society is sustained. With the accent strongly on private enterprise, this has led to an intricate and diverse mix of uses and organizations inhabiting the older urban buildings, many of which have operated outside the formal structure of rigid land use zoning. The physical framework of joined-together blocks, almost infinitely flexible despite their older physical fabric, has provided inner urban districts throughout Asia with a congenial blend of frontages, retail competition, and constant activity. These establish a variety of design interpretations within a fine-grained street matrix, where the high concentration of people and unique sets of social and economic characteristics have allowed businesses to flourish.

Aspects of design that affect where people can go and what they can see requires a high level of permeability that facilitates a choice of access and circulation routes. In The Hong Kong SAR, the condensed street matrix, together with a continuing demand for retail uses, signifies a potential for permeability in three dimensions rather than two, utilizing elevated walkways, malls, and atria with strong vertical as well as horizontal connections, and which in some cases extend below ground to MTR concourses and interchanges. In this way vertical segregation of people and vehicles helps to maintain circulation flow and also caters to multi-level retail distribution and other activities. At the same time, however, vertically stacked commercial complexes with large floor plates can also act to privatize the public realm with an accompanying range of commercial priorities and prohibitions.

It is necessary to introduce some visionary thinking into the renewal process, taking into account experience elsewhere. As Jane Jacobs stressed in *The Death and Life of Great American Cities*, the destruction of diversity is often caused by success, not by failure. Diversity emerges because of economic opportunity and attraction, and certain uses develop at the expense of others. A simplistic zoning system, in effect acts to freeze economic conditions and priorities where they stand at any one point in time. One of Jacobs's concerns was to emphasize the importance of an underlying city culture derived from both physical fabric and human activities, both spatial and temporal. As she stated, sameness needs to be zoned out or, in effect, differences zoned in, and change, as and when it occurs, should not be overwhelmingly of one kind. This also implies that urban regeneration should be a slow rather than a breakneck process, and arguably this applies more specifically to Asian cities rather more than to Western ones.

Dante Plaza, Tianjin, China, forms part of a villa group built between 1908 and 1916, and formally known as Piazza Regina Elena.

The Challenge of Obsolescence

Obsolescence can be described as the imbalance between the prevailing standard of building accommodation and the basic requirements of its occupants. This relates to a number of Asian cities but to the Hong Kong SAR, in particular, where older parts of the urban area continue to suffer from the legacy of a low standard of construction dating from the 1950s and 1960s, together with poor maintenance and lack of management in older high-rise urban buildings. It is also inextricably linked with the role played by changes in the political economy, and the importance to government in retaining high land prices. Redevelopment to higher development ratios has therefore taken precedence over rehabilitation and regeneration as a means of combatting obsolescence. This was in part expedited by an accelerated social housing program that took form in the 1960s. In this sense the intention was to provide improved living conditions for low-income urban dwellers, while enhancing the economic base of the city as a whole. However, the compensation and redevelopment approach related to low-rise buildings tended to be carried out in a piecemeal manner, while taller buildings in multiple ownership made land assembly difficult.

In the Hong Kong SAR, under a government controlled "positive non-interventionist" economic policy, the proceeds of land sales have always been used to sustain its development functions. Reclamation of land from the sea, free of private land-holding constraints, has therefore continued as the dominant means of facilitating urban growth, while land resumption must be for a defined public purpose. However, a high land price policy has, up to the present time, continued to generate a bias toward a property market fueled by speculative interests. In 2022, as prices have continued to soar, the Hong Kong SAR's biggest developers in what is the world's most expensive housing market continue to build predominantly micro-units or "nano-flats"

The Plaza Santa Cruz represents the center of the Chinese commercial district of Binando Manila.

to meet the dictates of affordability. At the same time the territory is characterized by increasing areas of extreme land-use density on the 23 percent of its total land area designated for urban development.

Necessary urban improvements must overcome not only the poor condition of older housing, but the decay of local infrastructure, and the low provision of open space and community facilities on a per capita basis, and must at the same time aim at overall betterment of the public realm. While the physical dimension of the urban renewal process is formidable, the overall achievement of urban regenerations in the Hong Kong SAR, has been destabilized through the difficulty associated with resolving compensation levels together with the high cost of urban land necessary to facilitate profitable redevelopment. In order to redevelop existing blocks, developers must show that buildings are in a dilapidated state and not economically viable for refurbishment under a "Compulsory Sale for Redevelopment Ordinance,"

Street market of religious offerings associated with Quiapo Church, Manila. Informal street vending of one kind or another represents an important role in the economy of many cities, and accounts for a significant percentage of employment opportunities as part of their socio-economic fabric. The situation reflects an increasing polarization in Asian societies where much of the new wealth belongs to only a small fraction of the population. Street vendors operate outside the normal priorities of urban planning that tend to focus more on static configurations rather than mobile impermanence. Both male and female vendors occupy public spaces, streets, and other popular gathering areas, operating during daytime and evening hours, and frequently become embroiled in conflict with authorities or subject to illegal or "enforced" levies. Street vending is, however, an established entry point into the urban economy for self-employed low-income families, with little or no education.

sakusa Kannon, named after
he Buddhist Goddess of Mercy,
ave rise to the Senso-ji Temple,
he most important place
f Buddhist worship in Tokyo.

with surveying and structural engineering reports prepared and filed in the Lands Tribunal. However, this has become a means to replace old and relatively low-rise tenements, that have been allowed to deteriorate by their owners, in order to maximize redevelopment values, with no consideration given to the importance of comparative urban design benefits and mixed use to the wider community.

The top-down "financial viability" approach adopted by the Hong Kong SAR's Urban Renewal Authority severely limits a robust basis for long-term value-added regeneration. Private units are unaffordable to a large sector of the population except in the form of micro units, and the waiting period for public housing is six years, despite the existence of around 800,000 public rental flats in the territory.

It has been shown that urban design, in meeting the many challenges of obsolescence, produces specific economic, environmental, and social value, with commensurate benefits to a range of stakeholders. A report by the UK Commission for Architecture and the Built Environment Department of the Environment, Transport, and the Regions in 2001 states that this includes an improved return on investment, a reduction in whole-life costs, and a regeneration dividend based on creating a forceful district image and landmark status; responding to public expectation; equating high density with user comfort and connectivity; and creating opportunities for retrofitting.

The main aim of regeneration should embody a compact fit with high quality mixed-use developments, within a process that is more effective and sustainable than a piecemeal approach. This should be subject to an urban design code setting out community and architectural parameters incorporated within development briefs following the involvement of local interests and key stakeholders, while avoiding unnecessary prescription. It should be possible in this way to articulate requirements in terms of scale, treatment of the public realm, connectivity, movement, and related factors that encourage all-round gain, promote walkable neighborhoods, and encourage social integration. It must also effectively restore run downs areas and amenities to beneficial public use, and in the process boost community pride through an enhanced civic image.

Urban rehabilitation must be regarded as a key part of the community-oriented regeneration process, with distinct phases of policy development related to making up housing deficiency, improvement of existing conditions, and neighborhood upgrading, but also to ensure tenure diversification and community expectations. Successful programs involving community-based associations generally involve a calculated mix of rehabilitation and new build, with some tenure diversification in the context of projected demographic change.

A strategic approach relates to the goal of creating lasting and comprehensive solutions, not merely in response to urban problems, but for wider benefits in terms of achieving urban design value. This means that the orchestrators of urban planning and renewal must advance their agenda toward regeneration, and must move toward becoming a strategic facilitator of urban policy intervention that can guide associated programs of action. This will not only help in the planning and implementation of individual built projects but can also assist the adoption of wider objectives, for example improving the pedestrian experience, installing and reinforcing district systems of connectivity, re-establishing street and place character, and satisfying the visitor experience. This implies strategic resource commitments as part of the delivery capability. All this adds up to the need for regeneration to operate across the boundaries that act to divide economic and organizational objectives from environmental and urban design concerns.

For urban regeneration to be successful in practice, solutions must be sustainable—that is to say the process should take on an enabling role, with an emphasis on safeguarding the interests of future generations, ensuring the equitable distribution of costs and benefits, and emphasizing the promotion of economic activities that enhance environmental quality. This accords with the policy priorities defined by the Organisation for Economic Cooperation and Development (OECD), and reflects an inescapable fact—that the future will be predominantly urban.

…nposed height restrictions
…low for scaled-down
…edestrian precincts to the east
…f the Palace Museum in Beijing.

A Sustainable Approach to Urban Regeneration

Urban regeneration must be focused around centers of activity and other aspects that need to impart district identity. In the better examples the benefits of new service sector activities extends to the local population. However, the rates at which older parts of the urban areas associated with Asian cities are being incrementally redeveloped, often outpaces the ability to integrate strategic urban design interventions that might revitalize at a wider level. While these areas might be subject to cyclical economic downturns, an emphasis on visitor and tourist facilities and the function of urban neighborhoods as dynamic meeting places where activities overlap provides a hedge against this.

The problems facing sustainable regeneration are partly those of perception. A carte blanche approach dictated more by financial imperatives than the need to equate a balance between producers and consumers of property allows for little discrimination in the planning process and even less opportunity for genuine urban betterment. This calls for a more sensitive approach to property led urban revitalization that reflects local conditions, targeted at the long-term transformation and betterment of the environmental qualities inherent in the location. This is not necessarily setting out a case for public subsidy, but for more inspired public intervention, where programs of animation act to enervate the regeneration process and provide a

The Sule Pagoda in Yangon marks the centrifugal point of the city plan. The pagoda dates back 2,000 years and it is said that a relic of Gautama Buddha is enshrined within it.

basis for a series of "cultural industries," such as small studios, as well as arts and performance venues. Commensurate with this, legal measures must be introduced that require all buildings to be periodically inspected, in order to prevent them falling into a state of deterioration.

The regeneration process must provide added value over and above property value itself, in order to incentivize private development while signaling new ways to conceptualize the nature of the process. Different districts can, for example, display distinct variations in levels of deprivation that cannot be solved simply through a one-dimensional approach to renewal, and might call for a more diverse mix of ownership and tenure conditions.

Networks of relationships in both a business and community sense should form a basis for dynamic local regeneration. This should, in practice, satisfy several conditions, by means of flagship projects to encourage the interest of the commercial sector; small scale projects—including those that might encourage start-up operations—aimed at encouraging a localized level of investment, capable of generating multiplier effects, and local synergy that encourages interaction and cooperation; integration of a diverse range of uses including leisure and recreational amenities that might in turn attract other uses and generate vitality; a culturally inspired approach in order to create a distinct image and a quality of locale to encourage wider neighborhood revitalization; and different tenure patterns involving private and public owners who might, in some cases, form partnerships.

A suitable supply of commercial and industrial property is necessary for growth of enterprises and to provide assets, but there must also be some scope for adaptation and upgrading. Many small manufacturing concerns with low profitability are sensitive to rent costs but relatively impervious to building or environment conditions. Improvement might not prove an impediment to their performance but redevelopment with higher rents or enforced relocation might well drive them out of business. This is clearly also dependent on other preconditions such as a generally buoyant economy and robust export markets.

Urban regeneration, constituted under whatever auspices, must take on a visionary role with regard to the city. In particular, community and culturally oriented projects need to be identified that will energize the renewal process around a series of locales to create places of unique identity and interest within core districts. It has to be recognized that some up-front public investment is necessary to create both the right environmental conditions and "attractions" that might then act as a catalyst for a range of private initiatives, including opportunities for relatively small-scale developers and operators.

District identity can be improved by bringing about a better perception of neighborhood on the part of established communities through physical improvements, including environmental and amenity betterment of the external environment, sympathetic to the existing social, physical, and economic character. This also helps to encourage community participation in area-based initiatives by residents.

An evaluation of directly measurable outputs in relation to urban renewal policy in Asian cities tends to emphasize the difficulties encountered in the renewal process in steering a course through innumerable obstacles and constraints, almost from start to finish. This inevitably results in two potential weaknesses: first, a tendency to equate efficiency of the process with effectiveness of the product; and second, a frequent absence of attempts to gauge the overall lasting consequences to the wider environment and body of users, over and above the development of new buildings and infrastructure. The real contribution of urban regeneration must be measured in added value to the urban districts involved. That is to say, it must be more than can be expressed in terms of carefully sanctioned and approved deliverables, and must also be measured in terms of its contribution to the social and economic life of the community at large.

Most Asian cities are subject to a constant process of population growth as a result of economic development, with policies constantly re-focusing and adjusting to urban change, employment trends, and technical innovations. This requires new modes of urban governance, management, and policy instruments, as cities increasingly search for innovative ways to compete for investment and visitation.

Placemaking is a vital aspect of regenerated urban areas and has as much to do with image and promotion as it does with reinforcement and revival. The introduction of new sectors and activities, as part of positive interventionist strategies, can help to transform older parts of cities through both development of brownfield sites and upgrading. The challenges that are likely to confront an urban regeneration approach are:

Kampung Bugis originally represented a multi-ethnic neighborhood of Bugis, Chinese, Indian, and Malay traders in Singapore. From the 1920s, Bugis Street evolved as a "red light" and nighttime entertainment district. Intervention came in the form of a plan for the wider Kaltang area around the Kallan basin and river, along with conservation and environment improvement initiatives.

The Drum Taower in Ningbo— one of the oldest surviving city gates dating back to the T'ang Dynasty.

- the adoption of goals that reflect necessary aspirations for green and sustainable development;
- the need to resolve questions of economic polarization and social justice that secure economic progress and reduce exclusion. This underscores the need to work with and alongside communities rather than simple imposition of development solutions;
- the need to introduce procedures and processes that, however difficult and time-consuming, will benefit the city and its population in the medium-to-long-term through better integrated regeneration initiatives;
- the desirability of providing more satisfactory spatial and social solutions that will raise the identity, image, and connective frameworks within neighborhoods;
- the determination of resource requirements to address shortfalls as part of schemes or projects;
- the provision of utility and service infrastructure in ways that minimize penetration of vehicular traffic and improve environmental quality and safety of the public realm;
- the development of institutional mechanisms for the incorporation of community-based inputs as part of extended urban governance programs; and
- a spatial mandate and field of action that avoids a standardized approach, instead tailoring resources to meet the needs of individual areas within an integrative district-wide context, based on reinforcement of streets and distinctive places.

The added value that comes with this should:

- improve and sustain the character and sense of place of older urban quarters;
- retain the unique mix of uses, urban diversity, and features through which these quarters are identified;
- retain, within reason, the local residential and business community;
- improve the quality of the area for residents and visitors;
- establish sustainable social, economic, and environmental solutions in balance with the needs of the city as a whole;
- preserve the heritage of the area as far as possible including its intangible heritage;
- cultivate cultural capital and pluralism;
- create a reasonably flexible framework for adaptation and change—a common characteristic of older areas, which explains their traditional mix of uses;
- provide affordable accommodation for existing and potential users to meet specific community and economic goals;
- resolve, either directly or indirectly, the poor housing conditions for the seriously disadvantaged, and facilitate ageing in place.

Integrated pathway
and promenade alongside
the Singapore River.

A Cultural Approach to Urban Restructuring

One potential means to invigorate the regeneration process with more of a community-oriented agenda is through culturally based initiatives that reflect age and income profiles of the neighborhood population together with changing patterns of leisure and consumption activities. This can encourage a demand for new types of urban facility, consumer services, and visitation, and indicates that cultural investment should be concerned with an emphasis on a city district's traditions, history, and uniqueness.

Over the past 15 years, a number of cities have launched innovative urban cultural strategies that have redefined the boundaries between traditional elitist concepts and popular culture. This provides for an evolution of cultural infrastructure from museums and theatres to buildings and spaces with wider public uses. To a large extent these have been related to urban restructuring policies and include:

- the need for flagship projects to launch urban regeneration programs;
- encouragement of local communities to participate in cultural activities through workshops and new media sectors;
- design and integration of public spaces for multiple uses and activities, both formal and informal;

Revitalization of Telok Ayer
Market, Singapore.

- encouragement of events, concerts, and festivals in different districts that could be held in public areas such as parks and waterfronts that generate a high level of activity and lead to local economic investment;
- making traditional institutions such as museums more user friendly and open to private participation;
- some devolution of spending on arts to local organizations together with business sponsorship; and
- provision of new and "different" facilities to attract youth activities.

These policies, in something of a symbiotic way, both generate and reflect changing social and ethnic values based on cultural populism, often brought together by new "cultural intermediaries" in the arts, and through media, video, film, and computer technology. These have also gone hand in hand with a type of urban re-imaging, with private investment inducing an entrepreneurial approach to arts-led coalitions representing various interests, often with different goals and interests. Mellow texture and traditional urban references help to inform the sense of history and natural evolution of the locality. The primary goal is the creation of a comfortable and coherent environment, pleasurable for pedestrians and comprehensible to visitors.

Connecting with the Community

Community involvement requires measures to involve local people in identifying issues, needs, and solutions. This can take the form of multi-professional team approaches through charrettes; community education in terms of developing a critical awareness; technical aid and expertise particularly related to planning, design, and business or legal matters; and the development of particular community skills in order to encourage initiatives toward the built environment and local economy.

Such enabling roles as "enterprise partnerships" between public and private bodies help to establish the feasibility of projects in terms of bringing about genuine regeneration, enabling major players to participate in terms of both resources and expertise. It can also bring together people, including professionals, the voluntary sector, representatives of public bodies, and members of the community who have common interests and can invigorate the process with design ideas. There is a responsibility to articulate other priorities that have a wider bearing on the face of the city itself that might involve initiating urban design workshops at an early stage in the planning process. This can help to identify key issues as part of an urban improvement process and assist business, environmental, and community organizations to work together in realizing certain common objectives reflecting an obligation to the community. This represents an opportunity for genuine public consultation aimed not so much at specifics but at establishing what sort of place and character people want, with detailed agendas for business, recreation, and culture that should act to inform the process itself.

From the mid-20th century comprehensive redevelopment programs in Asia have been responsible for major shifts in population involving different degrees of dislocation. Overly expedient development processes have, in many Asian cities, been driven primarily by the priorities and values associated with engineering infrastructure and highways, and in terms of urban renewal programs implemented by both the public and private development sectors. As the emphasis shifts to the physical and economic regeneration of the city, it is increasingly clear that planning and large-scale urban renewal initiatives should no longer be applied through top-down processes but need to be carefully constructed through an interactive process that is more responsive to community needs and aspirations. The "principle of subsidiary" must be adopted that supports the concept of action related to the smallest neighborhoods. This should enable those who might be potentially affected by development to contribute to the process in some way. It also needs to be acknowledged that in every community there exists a wealth of knowledge, energy, and creativity into which to tap. This entails networks of bodies—public, private, and voluntary—who share some common concern, and who work together on initiatives for the good of the city and the community.

Urban design is essentially an interdisciplinary activity and, even within extremely high-density cities with high land values, there is a need to reflect increasing levels of planning concern through working forums whereby specialists, interested parties, and key stakeholders—together with the priorities and insights these represent—can be introduced into mainstream planning and decision making. Within this process, Urban Design Assistance Teams might have a significant role to play in teasing out issues and using design devices to stimulate visionary solutions derived from process planning sessions, action planning events, interactive exhibitions, and formal consultations. A fundamental objective of this process is to ensure an increase in the sense of community belonging, responsibility, and civic pride directed toward improving the overall quality of life. The challenge is to transfer the techniques to the mainstream planning process as a result of inter-disciplinary and community liaison. The principal components of livability are public gain from planning and development; personal well-being derived from housing, healthcare, education, and security; and environmental protection in terms of ecological safeguarding, adequate environmental infrastructure, and resilience.

In terms of community participation the benefits are likely to be commensurate with the inputs. In other words the fostering of community participation and representation will help to improve the regeneration process itself and enable better facilitation by authorities and

The old Kuala Lumpur Railway Station constructed in 1892 with its domed towers, minarets, and Moorish fenestration. It now houses a miscellaneous collection of restaurants, and the station hotel.

professional representatives i.e. those who experience change and those who help to bring it about. The approach should be to ensure maximum involvement by the key players according to clearly stated aims. Sufficient resources need to be allocated and specialists should assist in facilitating community involvement and training. This is particularly important as there needs to be a careful 'balancing' role in Asian cities to reconcile the views of different stakeholders geared to improving the living standards and quality of life for the community.

In the Asian region there are a number of major issues that need to be addressed through community planning and long-term commitments with regard to funding and resources. These are:

- Technical and professional support, together with resources to develop local capabilities. This includes area-based initiatives on a self-help basis that can become self-sustaining and build up social capital. In fact, most communities are exceptionally buoyant and relatively self-sufficient in economic and social terms, although in many cases there is clearly an overriding need for improved housing conditions and welfare.

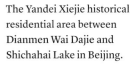
The Yandei Xiejie historical residential area between Dianmen Wai Dajie and Shichahai Lake in Beijing.

- Certain sectors within the community are likely to have special needs, for example the poor, elderly, and recent immigrants who are, in different degrees, alienated from the mainstream of social and economic life. These require special provision within regeneration processes.
- Local communities are generally focused around mixed-use neighborhoods but subject to different levels of obsolescence and environmental change, whereas new development provides few real community benefits. To overcome this, strategic partnerships should involve the community in an integrated process that can promote a sense of trust and confidence. This can also be assisted by building a "coalition of stakeholders" that can develop this shared vision.
- An important aspect is the mandate that individuals or representative bodies possess, and the amount of information that is disseminated to a community and its various stakeholders. In this sense the greater the degree of knowledge and interest, the more time that can be spent on creative action. Where voluntary bodies share a common concern, representatives will normally be elected through community planning forums.
- The empowerment of communities is subject to a clear political questions in situations where truly elective processes are undeveloped, and District Advisory Committees could be involved in responsive neighborhood-based community initiatives that primarily reflect social, economic, and cultural concerns. The essential aspect is to facilitate community ownership of activities and actions that affect them. As these become progressively more sophisticated, empowered communities can then form part of more mainstream activities.
- The creation of a partnership approach to regeneration is intended to evolve into a situation where local communities can work together as equal partners with other public and private agencies in the design and delivery of regeneration programs that can achieve action-oriented initiatives from below.

Pilot projects in Asian cities clearly indicate that local communities, whatever their size, can ably identify economic, social, and environmental problems and opportunities through community-based planning initiatives, providing that these can be properly organized with the support of public and private sector agencies and programs. This entails networks of bodies—public, private, and voluntary—who share some a common concern and who work together on common initiatives for the good of the city and the community.

The broad objectives are to achieve a vision for the city and its various parts based on public awareness that cannot be obtained in any other way. This provides a mechanism to identify complex development issues, foster broad agreements among different interest groups, and act as a catalyst for action. Innovations to the planning process need to be introduced carefully, so as to build up a consensus before actually submitting firm plans to the spectrum of bodies charged with their approval. This in turn can assist and possibly instigate local rejuvenation and revitalization with a sense of purpose. The UK Urban Design Group has distinguished three aspects: general principles, specific methods, and overall processes. General principles can apply to virtually all situations while methods can involve activities, events, and types of organization. The process itself must take into account local circumstances, conditions, and resources, but its effectiveness will depend largely on the way it is integrated within the overall planning and development context.

This process is not without problems and potential conflicts in the context of political priorities and urban governance. As citizens in Asia demand greater participation in the decision-making structure that surrounds planning, they also demand greater accountability from government bodies. Requests for comments on planning proposals that might impact tens of thousands of people must be based on the premise of who is listening. Ongoing community involvement in city-building has introduced a need to develop effective ways of engaging stakeholders along with capacity building so that participants from different backgrounds and from different parts of the city can learn from each other. This introduces fresh models of decision-making that are necessary for open city governance and sustainable development.

In the Asian context, four relevant themes can be identified: the refocusing of urban renewal to urban regeneration, that is to say a marked change in emphasis from physical development to the wider perspective of social well-being, environmental care, and economic inter-dependencies; an increasing devolution of central and institutional power, in whole or in part to a local level of responsibility; a reconciliation between market factors and community welfare; and a focus on betterment of the public realm.

In terms of community planning it is important that the benefits are commensurate with the inputs. Fostering of community participation and representation should help to improve

Stylized pictorial representation in Tokyo's changing and regenerated quarters such as Shinjuku carry a symbolic connection with what they convey that allows component parts to be constantly re-assembled in an abstract iconography of patterns and combinations that is both descriptive and iconic. This is spatially represented by a complex and additive texture of parts and symbols with little compositional geometry.

the continuing regeneration process itself and enable better facilitation by authorities and professional representatives—those who experience change and those who help to bring it about. The approach should be to ensure maximum involvement by the key players according to clearly stated aims. Sufficient resources need to be allocated and specialists should assist in facilitating community involvement and training. This requires a careful balancing role to reconcile the views of different stakeholders, geared to improving the living standards and quality of life for the community, together with a common "language of interests" based on a mutual understanding of prevailing issues and processes.

A fundamental objective of this process is to ensure and extend a sense of community belonging, responsibility, and civic pride as part of a "Better City" program directed toward improving the overall quality of life. While the accepted urban design process can come up with a wealth of ideas, the challenge is to transfer the techniques to the mainstream planning process as a result of inter-disciplinary and community liaison. This provides a mechanism to identify complex development issues and goals, foster a consensus among different interest groups, and act as a catalyst for action. It is therefore necessary to make the process itself less abstract and distant in the minds of the community, and instead to place their concerns firmly on the main regeneration agenda.

Regeneration Principles and Values

Urban Design Principles	Sustainable Values		
	Economic	Social	Environmental
Character	Design solution capable of place-marketing, corporate imaging, and performance values to capitalize on local regeneration agenda.	Local contextual value and sense of place, sense of recognition and belonging; encourages development mix.	Low energy consumption; ecological and landscape values commensurate with place making potential.
Continuity and Enclosure	Continuous frontages interfacing with public realm, with good rental / capital values and take-up rates.	Defensible space and low crime rates; good accessibility and increased vitality; sense of community.	Clearly defined and well connected public open space and robust edges; capacity for energy-saving strategies.
Quality of Public Realm	Benefit for place-marketing; health and satisfaction of community and workforce; corporate imaging; marketing of city for tourism; and opportunity for project participation.	Appropriateness for levels of use by all members of society; ability to absorb change from daytime to evening uses; encourage sense of community.	Reduced pollution; overall greening; shade and shelter; ecologically supportive; provides effective precedents and examples.
Ease of Movement	Benefits of accessibility gives competitive marketing edge and reduces travel costs for workforce and visitors and improves overall building approach at ground and elevated levels.	Good accessibility between home, workplace, and recreational amenities; reinforces use of facilities and open spaces that are easy to move through.	Reduced energy consumption and increased environmental experience through easy travel modes; encourage walking as an activity; encourages landscape design along movement corridors.
Legibility	Place-marketing through image-making potential and ease of recognition.	Identity and civic pride through inclusiveness, recognizable routes, intersections, and landmarks.	Icon building can deliver energy efficiency and strong ecological image.
Adaptability	Ease of response to change and flexibility maximizes take-up rates and rental / capital value.	Responsiveness to changes in local employment, social and investment patterns; sustains existing residential and employment mix.	Reduced construction waste emanating from redevelopment; reduced resource / land consumption.

Temple Street in Singapore's Chinatown facing South Bridge Road. In Singapore, the shophouse style evolved to combine a blend of Chinese, Malay, Indian, and European features including carved doorways, stucco motifs, glazed tilework, fluted pilasters, and full-length shuttered windows.

Diversity	Mix of compatible developments work together to create viable places that respond to local needs and encourages visitor spending.	Place vitality, variety, and public choice; sustains existing community uses and business population.	Ecologically supportive environment; individual uses can share energy sources; minimizes wholesale redevelopment.
Richness	Identification helps market recognition, welfare identification with place, and corporate imaging.	Local identity and civic pride with built development; strong community associations; visual interest.	Environmental and ecological richness associated with overall environment; encourages long-life buildings.
Identity	Place-making through distinction image helps building take-up and rental levels.	Place identity provides sense of belonging and pride on the part of residents and businesses.	Landscape acts to provide green image and reduces environmental damage.
Durability	Longer useful life of buildings; cost effective use of materials, finishes, etc.; incorporation of energy-efficient structures reduces on-going costs.	Enriches the city through new sustainable building typologies; better preventive maintenance and better management of buildings.	Reduces construction waste; initiates advances in energy-efficient construction technology.

CHAPTER 6

Planning with the past

Planning with the past signifies a relationship between heritage fabric, time, and identity, and their effective correspondence with political and economic factors that include the contemporary interface with the priorities of global capital. In an examination of Asian cities this must cautiously confront a pre-eminent issue of precisely whose heritage is under debate, and the level of contestation associated with it.

Urban design and conservation are, to a large extent, two sides of the same coin. Their roots can be traced to the need to make cities richer through inscribing historic buildings and quarters into the fabric of contemporary urban environment. In this way they can become the cultural and economic components that invigorate the regeneration process through a successful relationship between preservation and sustainability. In Asian cities the urban design process needs to cope with the effects of untrammeled development in recent years, while it must also come to terms with the failure of much of this to create coherent places. Historic environments define our sense of place, memory, and identity, while an understanding of heritage underscores urban values and aesthetic appreciation. The concern is not so much confined to the preservation of old buildings, but the extent to which new development can be framed by historic or vernacular forms and spaces that can provide a foundation for informed innovation.

Lewis Mumford in *The City in History* noted that to lay a new foundation for urban life we must understand the historic nature of the city. The existence of cultural heritage introduces varying degrees of policy response in terms of the relationship between planning, land value, and urban design. To some, historic structures, sites, and monuments evoke nostalgia and memorable permanence, while to others they are simply an impediment to progress. Opinions

elhi Gate Bazaar in the Walled
ty of Lahore.

might vary on aesthetic value, but this does not by any means represent merely an elitist notion. The essential value of heritage buildings and monuments comes from "urban landmark" identity and place-based memory that must be the hallmarks of heritage preservation policy. In virtually all Asian countries this follows UNESCO practice codes that establish a platform for management of historic buildings and occasionally more extensive conurbations. In some situations, however, this might be a contested one, that raises issues of reuse, cultural identity, and city memory. In particular, the preservation of both vernacular and colonial built heritage can be challenging in some postcolonial and multi-cultural cities where political self-determination remains linked with iconic spatial references from another era.

The notion of historic preservation in relation to urban design is that it must impart value to the community. A mix of cultural, aesthetic, architectural, and contextual values can help to give present meaning to an inheritance from the past and should also have at least some economic potential. The promotion of heritage tourism is important from the perspective of enhancing the competitiveness of cities as visitor destinations. This is part of an overall direction to diversify the product range and enhance the variety of experiences the city has to offer. Such an approach is fine as far as it goes, but there is sometimes a thin line between the preservation and upgrading of older environments, and a replication of character through a pastiche of history. In the case of private properties having statutory declared preservation status,

property rights might, in certain circumstances, be compensated through the transfer of development air-rights. This represents a question of equity and fairness, so that conservation of historic buildings is seen in the same way as sites made available in the urban area for communal welfare.

"Preservation" and "conservation" both refer to the protection of cultural heritage, but conservation has a somewhat extended meaning. While it encompasses the intention to maintain and preserve, it also involves management of its sometimes-problematic function in the contemporary urban realm that is necessarily focused on a new international modernity. This is further extended by the welcome introduction of "intangible cultural heritage" by the International Council on Monuments and Sites (ICOMOS) in 2003.

In the older parts of Asian cities, the variety of streetscape and the contrasts and complexity associated with it have always produced intensively used local environments, with points of incidental interest or distinguishing features keyed into the pedestrian movement system, helping to make the city "legible" to residents and visitors alike. The underlying objective of urban rejuvenation must therefore be to increase the variety and contrast of experiences that users can enjoy and allow them to impose an intelligible order on the environmental structure, which, in itself, contributes to a sense of place. In an introduction to Camillo Sitte's book *The Art of Building Cities*, Eliel Saarinen writes that "the building must be an integral part of an environment of such organic town pattern as is expressive of contemporary conditions and no other conditions. With this comes the comprehensible qualities of community at a neighborhood level."

Regeneration implies a form of continuity with the past and demands some acknowledgment that even the newest development is, at least to some extent, determined by the form and footprints of its antecedents. The conventional conservation approach is geared to site-specific protection and refurbishment but there is also a need to understand this conceptionally through the components and interstices of the urban context. The issue of colonial-built heritage raises the question of precisely what identity is being preserved—that of public place, national ideology, or historical reference. A further issue is the degree to which preservation and conservation is appropriated to either programs of "nation building," or marketing efforts to attract tourism and global capital. The issue is confounded in some situations by the association of settlement with an abstract ideology of social organization. Many cities were typically divided into distinctive quarters of administration, business, residential, and institutional, with their architecture and urban "landscapes of power" reflecting both differences and commonalities in terms of how they were used but also how they were understood.

Changing geopolitical factors and the attraction of global capital bring with them an almost inevitable privatization of public space, which has the effect of excluding local sections of the population in a not dissimilar way to the colonizing process itself. In these situations preservation might therefore be said to be part of the decolonization process itself in the face of privately owned and land-extensive assets that have been available for redevelopment, such as central sites and waterfront utilities.

As many listed or "declared" buildings in Asian cities are likely to have been previously occupied by government or institutional users whose space and operational requirements have changed, there can be problems in finding alternative uses for these. This is partly because quite onerous financial and other conditions are frequently attached to restoration, and approval is necessary before any work can be carried out. There often exists no mechanisms to introduce

commercial considerations into this process, and listed buildings are therefore left vacant until such time as new uses are identified and public funds made available for conversion.

Because of these factors, many historic buildings have tended to ultimately fall into disrepair or are demolished to facilitate redevelopment at higher densities, along with new engineering infrastructure. Not all historic buildings can be reincarnated into new cultural uses, and there is a need to consider their revitalization as functioning parts of the city. This places an emphasis on achieving a balance between architectural quality and financial incentive. Both conservation and urban design share an ideological basis through the betterment of the public realm, but also necessitates a sustainable approach, matched by new visions for urban regeneration that must be design led. The revitalization of older areas through intelligible regeneration of the city fabric becomes an instrument of this approach, where one century's idiosyncratic grouping of building forms might be transformed into the next century's landmark destination.

It is necessary to distinguish between functional and physical preservation, although both are closely related. Functional conservation involves the purposeful retention of uses to achieve social aims, for example, the retention of a resident population in a central historic area that might otherwise be subject to the inexorable process of economic change, where higher value uses displace lower ones. Physical improvements might therefore have to be made to accommodate these, possibly involving public subsidies. Physical conservation on the other hand involves the simple retention and upgrading of buildings that embody sufficient historical and architectural merit. Where these are in private ownership, varying degrees of building control can be exerted over conversion and adaptation, but the process would normally be subject to some kind of functional gentrification according to its use value and wider

The older part of Fuzhou represents a neighborhood of narrow streets and mixed uses with a mix of stylistic references.

zoning controls. In this situation there also needs to be careful development programming to ensure the building's integration within the inherent mixed-use attractions of its associated urban neighborhood. Buildings under public ownership are, in theory, easier to deal with as they are not normally subject to strict market conditions but should be responsive to the wider economic picture that might relate to city culture and tourism.

Heritage as Part of Nation Building

The cultural heritage discourse in Asian cities is frequently out-of-step with prevailing political-economic situations, but also with less than effective urban renewal legislation, generally introduced to legitimize expedient courses of action on the part of both official bodies and private parties. In this sense land and buildings are treated as commodities, where redevelopment masquerades as renewal, and regeneration takes the form of gentrification at the expense of displaced communities. Place identity therefore becomes associated with sites of contestation.

Stamford Raffles, the founder of Singapore, then a melting pot of immigrants and traders, prepared a preliminary plan in 1822 that allocated separate urban quarters to six ethnic groups that formed part of a maritime network: European, Chinese, Malays, Indians (or Chulias), Arabs, and Bugis immigrants from Sulawesi in Indonesia. In practice there was considerable

…he style and decoration
…sociated with the older streets
…Swatow that blend formal
…mposition with a random
…nse of personalization.

overlap, but also a more subtle division between different Chinese ethnic groups—Peranakan, Cantonese, and Hokkien. This marked the beginning of a genuinely multi-cultural heritage and multi-ethnic cityscape that absorbed differences in terms of race, language, and religion as an integral part of the new community. While this designation has since been simplified in terms of commonalities, multi-cultural heritage values have become integrated into the various historic ethnic enclaves that preserve their different identities in a spatial and artistic sense. This has acted to retain a multitude of local characteristics including traditional trades and retail outlets, along with new businesses. To an extent the conserved and upgraded ethnic neighborhoods represent a somewhat sanitized recalibration of historical process, but is symbolic of co-existence and multi-ethnic ideology as part of a hybrid cosmopolitan imagery.

Penang, now a Malaysian State, was a central part of the "Straits Settlements" along with Singapore and Malacca, formed in 1826 and strategically located on the main British trading route between China and India. The process of Malay-centered nation-building is directed toward an Islamic-oriented Malaysian nationhood derived from the pre-colonial Malacca Sultanate, although the city itself has a cosmopolitan heritage that includes Portuguese, Dutch, and British, whose building styles have been well preserved. The Penang Heritage Trust was founded in 1986 and continues to play an important role in heritage preservation in George Town, which, along with Malacca, achieved World Heritage status in 2008. In a similar way

The Jamae Mosque in Singapore constructed in 1895 for Chulia Muslins from the Coromandel Coast of India.

separation of clan associations
and temples at the junction
of Church Street and King Street,
Georgetown, Penang.

to Singapore, Penang was established by the British in 1786 as a port city whose cosmopolitan demographics were shaped through interaction between migrants from East, South, and Southeast Asia. Certain streets were named after ethnic groups that settled there rather than being deliberately designated as separate settlement areas, while others were named after prominent personages representative of the British Empire, including Queen Victoria. Traditional kampong quarters were, however, identified according to their individual features.

The strategic plan for Penang is an ambitious assembly of industry, business, culture, and heritage tourism, with a strong international development agenda centered on George Town. The World Heritage designation therefore reflects both tangible and intangible heritage that equates with a long history of multi-culturalism, and a diverse residue of influences from their roles as colonial port cities. These have, over the years, experienced a coalition of contested political interests, elusively reflected by multi-lingual street signs that denote cosmopolitan places of encounter, deeply embedded in their morphologies.

In both Singapore and the Hong Kong SAR, the centers of colonial administration, supreme courts, prominent institutions, and cathedrals, together with civic spaces and monuments related to the British Empire continue to be used for much the same purposes. In a similar way former colonial administration and military establishments have been converted to politically neutral museums or libraries as educational centers in the post-colonial era. Singapore's major civic space, the Padang, was where colonial state activities took place. In the 1950s it became the site of social protests, but is now utilized for the annual National Day Parade, which tends to reproduce both its ceremonial and hierarchical past.

Since its departure from the Confederation of Malaysian States in 1965, the ideology of the People's Action Party in Singapore was top-down government. Lily Kong and Brenda Yeoh have neatly summarized the ramifications of this as "survival, discipline, and pragmatism." The heritage preservation policy commenced in 1971, and the Urban Redevelopment Authority designated a number of historic districts that represented the national's multiculturalism and multiracialism. Conservation is under the responsibility of the National Heritage Board, which also covers heritage education as part of a nation-building agenda. Within the designated historic districts, such as "Chinatown," "Little India," and "Kampong Glam," the older urban quarters have been retained and restored, paradoxically but sympathetically underscoring the notion of segregated ethic enclaves, but within a multi-cultural ideology attractive to visitors. In secondary settlements some modification of structures is permitted under controls that are intended to preserve the older building envelopes.

The Hong Kong SAR, not unlike Singapore, commenced its modern existence as a maritime city, where its trading affiliations embraced an array of ethnic groups. Apart from Europeans this included Americans, Baghdadi Jews, Indian Muslims, Hindus, Sikhs, and Parsees who commanded individual trading networks, and whose most prominent members contributed to both business and charitable bodies.

In the Hong Kong SAR, the Antiquities and Monuments Office was only established in 1976, and although historic buildings are graded, their fate rests with a government appointed board. Under the Antiquities and Monuments Ordinance, a group of buildings can be declared as monuments in their entirety if these form part of a coherent organizational complex. However, under a system geared to upholding free-market priorities, protection can by no means be guaranteed. This is intended to retain historical character by maintaining the existing diversity of buildings, grouped around pre-existing courtyards in and around the Central area that have become the foci of intense urban activity, reinforcing these spaces as a strongly differentiated part of their surrounding urban fabric, in order to establish city-wide landmarks.

In older parts of the Hong Kong SAR's urban area an unofficial collaboration between public and private sectors, aided by redevelopment programs as part of officially sanctioned urban renewal processes and empowered through the Land Resumption Ordinance, has extended private pro-business interests at the expense of an improved public realm, distinguished landmark structures, and properly conceived urban design. This has continued to accelerate the growth of preservation movements and popular discourse around the issues of collective memory and place attachment on the part of the public. Heritage trails in the Hong Kong SAR are perhaps unique in marking historical associations with scarcely any remaining physical itineraries or buildings to demarcate them.

It was not until 2007 that a Conservation Policy was introduced for the Hong Kong SAR, along with a roadmap as to how this could be carried out through revitalization as well as preservation, in order to maximize economic and social benefits. This suggested an emphasis on adaptive reuse and led to selected government-owned industrial, institutional, and military heritage buildings being repurposed for new uses. At the same time, the intention was to highlight the significance of historic urban places while retaining their essential character.

In 2007, as a result of a judicial review, the Hong Kong SAR government was prevented from carrying out further reclamation around its central harbor apart from situations of "overriding public need," which did not simply involve capital accumulation. The preservation of monuments from the colonial era became viewed as unpatriotic and at odds with the government's vision. The central axis from the harborfront Queen's Pier that marked the civic entrance to the city, was reconfigured as a predominantly commercial-related corridor. The part-occupation of the central public waterfront for military use physically emphasized a new sovereignty. On another level, the appropriation of central open spaces at weekends by foreign domestic helpers in the Hong Kong SAR, contests the general order of public space, but also reflects its inclusiveness and "right to the city."

The World Bank has supported a number of cultural heritage projects in the PRC, promoting conservation in historic cities from the early 1990s, but has also assisting in the achievement of economic and social development. The first phase involved sites in Zhejiang, Lioning, and Yunnan that were in need of immediate action due to natural disasters; the second three projects in Sichuan, Chongqing, and Shanghai emphasised cultural heritage; and the remainder addressed heritage conservation as part of large urban management projects for historic cities that included strengthening urban planning skills in Xi'an, Gansu, Guizhou, Yunnan, and Shandong.

India has established a system of sustainable planning and urban renewal focused on heritage areas and precincts under the Ministry of Urban Development. Projects have been carried out under various categories of institutional infrastructure, revitalization, urban planning, and stakeholder participation. This is based on utilizing heritage resources as assets that embody culture and tradition. The Master Plan for Delhi in 2021 focused on conservation of built heritage while the city of Jaipur in Rajasthan has prepared a Heritage Management Plan. Initiatives in Pondicherry integrate conservation proposals as part of an economic rejuvenation strategy. These and other initiatives recognize the significance of community engagement and awareness programs in order to equate local needs with both knowledge and resources.

A "Compendium of Good Practice" has been produced by the National Institute of Urban Affairs according to established criteria as a resource for municipalities following the UNESCO heritage management recommendations related to historic urban landscapes. Various UNESCO initiatives have also focused on heritage-based tourism as a vehicle for protection of local cultural heritage. This is not restricted to buildings, as mountain railways have been added to the UNESCO World Heritage List. Under the Institutional and Infrastructure category one of the major initiatives was the Walled City of Ahmedabad undertaken in partnership with the Archaeological Survey of India through a revitalization plan carried out in 1995 to integrate heritage into the master plan of the city, including a heritage walk. In Hyderabad, Special Area Projects have included urban design and environmental guidelines. Under the Urban Renewal category two major projects are the Jaipur Heritage Management Plan for the historic walled city, including its bazaar revitalization, and the 1991 Mumbai Heritage Conservation and Regulation documentation, the first to be carried out in India.

Revitalization of urban heritage in India involves the needs to address urban problems arising from traffic congestion, environmental degradation, and urban expansion. In Pondicherry the Asia Urbs Project was undertaken by the Municipality to enhance economic development and environmental management through heritage preservation initiatives

including the bazaar revitalization and street façade restoration. The Muziris Heritage Project in Kerala focuses on rejuvenating traditional industries that go back to the spice trade between Southeast Asia, Africa, and Europe. Heritage protection involved the preparation of a Conservation Plan for the entire region, aimed at protection of ancient buildings and monuments, infrastructure works, and academic exchanges.

An example of mobilization of the community in Indian heritage projects together with skills training is the Nizamuddin Urban Renewal Initiative in Delhi, which carried out regional mapping of heritage structures. It includes the World Heritage Site situated in one of Delhi's oldest settlement areas with ancient Sufi shrines and the Humayun's Tomb complex. Planned interventions through community engagement have included sanitation and health programs, with measures that are managed by the residents themselves. Awareness programs are carried out by the Heritage Education and Communication Services through citizens forums, with target groups that include teachers, students, and professionals. This represents a special campaign group under the Indian National Trust for Art and Cultural Heritage that also supports school publications and media programs.

Revitalization of Historic Urban Quarters through Preservation

Preservation of protected heritage buildings in older world cities has long been perceived as necessary in maintaining their architectural and cultural legacy. This has broadened into area-based urban regeneration initiatives that include defined "conservation areas" where the overall character must be preserved and enhanced. In the UK this was brought about by the Civic Amenities Act of 1967, and in the USA by the National Historic Preservation Act of 1966. This designation, while conferring statutory protection, provides an open-ended commitment to renovation, maintenance, and general rehabilitation of all listed structures. Privately owned buildings can continue to house any normally permitted uses, but there is an obvious limit to the range of uses to which public buildings can be put. It is not sufficient to simply list buildings that might then stand empty because of the restrictive conditions that are put on them. Thus, in addition to the qualities of cityscape, consideration has to be given to the area's capacity for active uses and overall management. This must respect the unique character of the area and its potential to invigorate the locality, with new uses identified for the historic buildings and street activities that help to animate the external environment. In this sense revitalization could well be undertaken through public-private sector partnerships.

In many Asian countries the rapid change from individual historic building protection to area conservation must evolve according to a greater concern for economic revitalization and enhancement, and must be seen as an integral component of the urban planning process, with

The character of Senate Square in Macau SAR continues into S. Domingo Square where the baroque-style church forms a prominent face to the public plaza.

on-going implications for overall land use and infrastructure. As a result, resourceful growth management policies must generate levels of investment necessary to open up areas that are in a rundown state. This is frequently related to the wider realm of tourism development that brings with it an economic momentum through certain types of investment for which cities in the same region often compete.

The actual process of revitalization can be brought about through any number of committed stakeholders, including major land owners, public agencies, local amenity, or business groups. In general, the more successful examples benefit from proper stewardship and the establishment of management corporations. These have served to transform older parts of Asian cities over the past 30 years, often playing a major role in restoring run down areas to economic health as identifiable centers of visitation. In these situations transactional businesses are

The Bulto Bristo Paul Medicine
House on Shobhabazar Street,
Kolkata.

Mansions to the north
of Dalhousie Square, Kolkata,
built by merchants linked
to the East India Company.

encouraged that provide interaction with people in terms of urban places, markets, restaurants, cafés, and places of entertainment. The primary challenge is not merely the adaptive reuse of older buildings but the reclamation of abandoned space or previously inaccessible areas for public use. The successful basis of such initiatives are their diverse uses, mix of building types and tenures, and the capacity to encourage pedestrian-friendly activities.

The notion of preservation and conservation has moved on from something that was largely concerned with preserving the past for its own sake, to something that is increasingly perceived as representing unique and previously underestimated attractions in prominent locations. In these situations economic change has left a residue of buildings that, while being run down, have substantial character. These might include older industrial, port, godown, dockyard, and

hrist Church built by
e Dutch in the 18th century
commemorate the centenary
their occupation of Malacca,
as later consecrated as an
nglican Church by the British.

wholesale market structures. Many such areas have been associated with redundant buildings sitting within disused waterfront sites of various kinds on the central fringe of cities, with an existing low urban value but enormous future potential, harnessing private resources to convert established characteristic structures with easy public access.

Heritage preservation in South Korea is aimed at cultivating cultural heritage under a number of categories, with nine UNESCO World Heritage Sites. It is administered under the country's Cultural Heritage Administration, whose legal framework was established in 1962 to explore intangible cultural properties with the objective of safeguarding folk and artistic traditions. Historic sites include fortresses, tombs, and temples.

Seoul's Management Plan for its downtown area led to proposals to purchase the traditional hanok housing and restore these to preserve the historic urban quarter of Bukchon along with streetscape enhancement. The area itself was home to high-ranking officials of the 600-year-old Joseon dynasty. During the Japanese annexation, large plots of land were purchased by developers who constructed traditional hanoks in the 1920s along narrow streets on steep slopes running toward the south. Protective measures were introduced in 1983 when the area was designated as a preservation area, along with restrictions on construction to regulate development and maintain the landscape setting. In 1999 the Urban Planning Council introduced new preservation guidelines as part of a Downtown Management Plan, which included proposals to revitalize the area with public subsidies for repair or remodeling of almost 1,000 hanoks, with some used for museums, workshops, and guesthouses. The project was

The Bukchun Hanok communi[ty]
to the north of the royal palace
in Seoul served as a village
for aristocratic households
dating back 600 years to the
Joseon Dynasty.

The Tung Lai Bank Tianjin
was founded in 1918, designed
in a neo-classical style but with
Chinese-patterned capitals.
Above the corner entrance
is a distinctive circular tower
that is said to resemble the
Temple of Heaven in Beijing.
The converted building is now
the Tianjin Science Museum.

awarded a UNESCO Asia-Pacific Heritage Award in 2009. The Bukchon Cultural Forum was established in 2001 to explore further ways to protect the historical environment of the area, while the cultural center offers lectures on its architecture. In 2009 Seoul expanded the scope of hanok preservation across the city to areas adjacent to the Unhyeongung Palace and Gyeongbokgung Palace.

In Chinese Taipei preservation programs of historic urban landscape upgrading commenced in the 1970s, with preservation of a number of old street areas in Lukang and Anping. The former is the second largest city on the island, but the first to establish an urban conservation area that became a model for street preservation from the 1980s. The Cultural Heritage Preservation Act promulgated in 1982 produced a legal basis for historic landscapes following a period of almost uncontrolled redevelopment. This was amended six times up to 2011 in order to incorporate various aspects stemming from international preservation principles to equity compensation issues and public participation. Cultural heritage was divided into various categories that included antiquities, monuments, and folk art based partly on Japan's Living National Treasure Systems and with reference to European and American legislation.

One of the first preservation projects included the continuing program of upgrading along the Dinhua Street area of Chinese Taipei that contains a large number of restored shophouses and established trades within its matrix of narrow streets. It forms part of the Dadaocheng Historic Area Plan associated with the Danshuei River, which evolved as a market area in the mid-nineteenth century through new immigrant communities and merchant guilds. An Environmental Improvement Plan in 1995 extended urban regeneration initiatives to an integrated landscape strategy for the city that entails the revitalization of old waterways linked with the mountain areas that surround the city. During the Qing dynasty Western trading companies were established in this part of Chinese Taipei, with neo-Baroque and Art-Deco details. The upgrading process has been carried out by the City Government Urban Regeneration Office that has allowed owners to transfer redevelopment rights to other sites. The Dalongtang and Wanhua neighborhoods comprise the oldest settlement areas in the city.

The area around the Bao-an Temple and the Confucius Temple opens up to the Bopiliao Historic Area that forms part of the Tansui district in Chinese Taipei. The restoration program from 2004 has focused on blocks of arcaded Qing dynasty streets with the reuse of original construction materials to assist reconnections with the adjoining buildings. The area also houses a heritage and culture education center, galleries, and exhibition areas, together with spaces for creative industries that have triggered improvements in the surrounding area. The reconstructed area now forms a connection with the Longshan Temple and streets of medicinal shops that date from the mid-eighteenth century.

Tight massing of buildings
define a street-based shopping
district in Beijing.

In Japan a system of preservation districts for groups of traditional buildings was introduced in 1975 which enables municipalities to develop plans under their preservation ordinance. The Agency for Cultural Affairs provide guidance to municipalities and provide financial support for restoration, facade enhancement, and installation of facilities for disaster prevention.

Cultural heritage has long been protected in Japan, but the official "proclamation" began after the Meiji restoration in 1871. This was aimed at the protection and repair of shrines and temples in Kyoto and Nara, with funds provided by the government. A law for the preservation of historic sites and monuments was passed in 1919, and the enactment of the Law for the Protection of Cultural Properties was introduced in 1950. This comprised three categories:

tangible properties, cultural and historic sites, and intangible properties. The law relating to preservation of ancient national capitals was revised in 1975 to protect groups of designated traditional building, and in 1992 Japan ratified UNESCO designations with various national sites added to the World Heritage List. In order to extend this process to heritage districts, a further act covering improvement of designated historic urban landscape was passed in 2008, although local action varies from city to city, based on an evaluation of social, economic, and cultural benefit on the part of stakeholders.

In Tokyo the metropolitan government integrated the cultural heritage system into the urban planning process. This has become known as the Specified Block System to protect urban heritage from the pressure of redevelopment. Heritage-led regeneration was put into practice in 1999, with financial support for conservation efforts, with the capacity for floor area reallocation from designated heritage blocks to neighboring blocks, creating a mechanism for both protection and development intensification. Operational guidelines have subsequently been revised a number of times to incorporate conservation policy into the framework of urban redevelopment strategies.

New Urban Values and Economic Benefits

The potential to re-use and refurbish old buildings of historical merit reflects a growing appreciation of urban values and an enjoyment of city pursuits on the part of increasingly discerning communities. This has its roots in cultural and environmental factors that have come to the fore in recent years, in Asia as much as anywhere else, and include a growing concern for the environment, a greater will to list buildings of heritage value as part of sustainable development strategies, and related community and social concerns. Such an approach also reflects the existence of quarters that are identifiable because of their overlapping functional, social, and economic interaction, along with networking characteristics. They might include particular trades or products, and functionally related business inter-reliance such as Chinese medicine, clothing or antiques, that are recognized for their common identifying character embodied in activities that produce a collective image of contrast and vitality.

In neighborhood areas bereft of intrinsically beautiful old buildings, the scarcity value itself and the sense of continuity with the past, together with the aesthetic diversity and difference in scale inherent in this, should be sufficient enough reason to preserve older buildings whenever possible, in order to make the public realm more interesting. There is also great virtue in providing for a diverse range of spaces and tenure conditions that allow economically marginal but socially important activities to take place, particularly in juxtaposition with nearby business areas.

Historic buildings wherever they occur have a scarcity value, but to attract investment it is necessary to enhance economic value to the community. In appropriate circumstances this should also attract commercial users who perceive this scarcity as a potential economic benefit. The alternative is to attract private capital to extend the useful life of historical buildings and turn around the slow process of obsolescence by using identifiable historic features to accentuate opportunities for a sustained level of investment.

The social value of historic buildings is relatively intangible and therefore difficult to quantify. Thus, the revitalization of older quarters should involve both the physical regeneration of urban fabric along with spaces that genuinely contribute to the vitality of the public realm in an authentic sense. To some extent functional restructuring of a sufficiently large listed building, or group of buildings, might enable different kinds of spaces to be created through a supply of unique accommodation to meet latent requirements. Similarly functional diversification can help to broaden the mix of uses within a district, increasing its economic base and generating greater levels of use without necessarily displacing existing residents and businesses.

Paradoxically, planning blight itself can sometimes be a catalyst to breathing new life into an area, as a fall in values of rents and short leases can attract a range of activities wthat could

The Lingnan architecture of Southern China helps with the ordering of the street realm, providing visual identity to both the individual building and the street. This allows for differences in form, texture, and decoration, adopting a vernacular tradition that acts to unify the street through strong visual correspondence between its parts as a setting for everyday use.

Historical shophouse area between Nanjing West Road and Minquan West Road, Chinese Taipei.

not exist elsewhere, and thereby act to trigger revitalization. This might involve the production of a detailed mixed-use plan that includes active ground-level amenities and facilities for the area, suitable to its socio-economic status and catchment of users. In this way the essential qualities of the local culture can be both traditional and contemporary, incorporated as an integral part of the local economy, with activities growing and developing at their own pace and with mutual support.

In both cultural and economic terms, the process requires that contemporary needs are satisfied, and this can essentially reflect two different scenarios. The first is a situation where the city itself, or large areas within it, represent an important historic inheritance, where the planning issues relate to preservation of unique buildings, and the associated integration of necessary tourist infrastructure to cater for a radically changed economic and social base. The second relates more to cities built up over the past 200 years through industrialization, where new attractions can be created through physical regeneration of run-down or redundant urban landscapes, that in themselves promote the idea of placemaking and in turn attract new forms of investment.

The regenerated Wanhua area in Chinese Taipei around the Bao'an Temple and the Bopiliao area.

This puts the focus of visitation where it belongs—onto the city itself and the consolidation of its physical and economic infrastructure. For tourism to play a realistic role in heritage revitalization the totality and distinctiveness of the visitor experience needs to be considered. In a compact city the concentration of activities into urban districts allows for a greater degree of perception, focus, and usability, even if individual heritage buildings do not generate visitation in themselves. Higher spending thresholds associated with genuine historic quarters can be important in generating spin-off to other aspects of the economy such as hotels, transport, and retailing.

yokawa Inari Tokyo
a combined temple and shrine
dicated to the Buddhist
isters who protected
e ancient doctrines. Inari
e fox deity and the messenger
Ebisu, the god of commerce.

Managing the Process of Change

While it might be said that societies prevent disintegration by constructing formidable political institutions, the contribution and impact that private development decisions make to the public realm is probably the single most important factor that affects urban design in cities where we routinely attempt to reconcile private enterprise with public interests.

Historically, buildings were expected to form a dialogue with the "grain" of the urban fabric, and this applied equally to housing as to major public buildings. From the mid-20th century, however, growth trajectories in Asian primate cities have been largely determined by the exigencies of zoning plans, providing a framework not so much for expressive local environments but for large scale city management, expedient site sales procedures and traffic policies. In new development areas this has made it difficult to reinforce a sense of district or even local identity through the integration of pedestrian streets, informal urban spaces, and points of cultural or activity foci. It is in fact precisely these elements that should help knit together older areas and stimulate private investment, not only in quality buildings, but as part of a coordinated urban framework. Instead, older mixed-use areas continue to be replaced by predominantly single-use complexes that often turn their backs on the public realm, rather than integrate robust urban elements that might produce effective and enjoyable urban places and enable a variety of activities to co-exist for the benefit of the wider community.

It is important not to make the regeneration process too prescriptive, tidy, and easy to manage. Real urban areas are not like that—they are often visually complex and imbued with a variety of features, informal realms of use, and experiential attributes that denote character. Sweeping away all obsolescent building fabric is an insufficient enough objective in its own right. The process of urban design needs to cater for and even encourage this informal level of complexity, but must at the same time ensure a fundamental order, essential linkages, and continuity of both open space and built elements. This extends the urban tradition of intense street use and visual interest, animated by the retention of elements that are evocative of the local culture, for example street and night markets that act as distinctive visitor associations and attractions, even if these are only held at certain times of the week.

Change or modification to a historic environment must be properly and appropriately managed to ensure economically active uses while preserving character. There is a subtle but pertinent difference between preservation and rehabilitation that tends to exert some degree of planning tension—the first is concerned with protection, and the limitation of change; the second with accommodating necessary change brought about through economic circumstances. Thus, conflicts can arise within a revitalization approach that must be geared to accommodating new, economically viable uses. At the same time the design challenge is to reconcile the restoration of physical fabric through a process of intervention that maintains, rather than skews, historical continuity.

The former Central University in Nanjing, now Southeast University, contains a number of neo-classical-styled buildings from the 1920s including the assembly hall that forms a central feature at the end of the entrance drive, lined with London Plane trees.

In terms of rehabilitation, restoration priority must be given to buildings that continue to serve their original purpose, for example the use of an ancestral hall, a religious structure, or an active shophouse street. When this is not practicable and other uses are proposed, restoration can be considered on a case-by-case basis. However, this largely depends on whether the proposed use fits within the social and economic fabric and whether significant alteration works might affect the existing character of building fabric.

The preferred means of protection is through an established Antiquities Advisory Authority that represents a statutory body with members specializing in local heritage, archaeology, and history, and able to advise on matters related to preservation and conservation of heritage. The restoration or any alterations and modifications of declared monuments must be duly approved by the authority that serves as a mechanism to control the alterations of declared monuments. Ad hoc specialist groups can then be formed by the Board, with appointed committees to handle specific issues.

Managing change must be about responding to contemporary needs. The emphasis should therefore be on explicit principles and typologies based on the underlying significance of form, structure, and architectural syntax of each area rather than on prescriptive treatment that can lead to pastiche and imitation. In this sense the first step needs to be general repair and clean-up operations to remove signs of neglect followed by initiatives to upgrade or restore the area's economic infrastructure in order to infuse life and stimulate vitality. Streetscapes of special interest warrant a comprehensive reinforcement approach that establishes an explicit

The Molenvliet Canal along what is now Jalan Gajah Mada in Jakarta was the most fashionable avenue in 18th-century Batavia lined with mansions built by Dutch merchants.

The Lahore Museum was designed by John Lockwood Kipling and Bai Ram Singh, completed in 1890 in an expressive Anglo-Mughal sty[le] in red brick that complement[s] the adjacent National college [of] Arts and Punjah University H[all]

The Sun Yat-sen Museum
located in Kom Tong Hall
in Hong Kong SAR, following
preparation work undertaken
by the Hong Kong SAR Museum
of History. It was opened
in 2006 to commemorate the
140th anniversary of Sun's birth.

framework for local revitalization initiatives that respect its intrinsic character. This in itself has little to do with redesign, but rather with an overall mix of responsive uses and spatial continuity of defining elements. Urban quarters that contain historic buildings of unique character can, in certain instances, be extended through local street upgrading/restoration schemes with appropriate architectural typologies extending to streetscape improvement, with special street furniture, signage, paving surfaces, incidental seating, and new planting.

This does not diminish the need to bring the past into the present through economic initiatives and to reflect prevailing cultural values. Older areas are almost always characterized by a fine grain of streets and blocks or plot divisions that need to be preserved, both to maintain the smaller sizes and identity of individual buildings, and to enhance overall permeability. As older buildings of character have both place-making and place-defining qualities, the most robust and enduring historic areas tend to embody a loose fit between form and function in line with contemporary uses. This might, in most cases, involve less emphasis on the integrity

The Taman Falahilla town square area of Old Batavia in Jakarta has been restored and the old Dutch colonial buildings converted into museums. The Jakarta City Museum with its central cupula was formerly the Stadhuis or City Hall, completed in 1710

of restoration detail, and more on the retention of essential character. Thus, buildings should be repaired or restored in line with the authenticity of the older fabric, including its various accretions that reflect the patina of history and allusion of time. This can be adjusted or extended in ways that reflect the new functions in order to display an overall conceptual unity. In the case of infill or integration of new buildings through selected demolition, the aims should be to achieve both spatial and aesthetic harmony, fuse together aspects of continuity, containment, and enclosure, and enhance legibility through landmark elements that might animate urban places and vistas.

In China the preservation of built heritage associated with older foreign "treaty port" municipalities is not to deny its questionable past associations but the means to absorb their essential multicultural identities and complex histories within what are now international cities. Buildings continue to be used for a multitude of purposes and as an expressive means of articulating and diversifying urban space that engages with their urban histories. This avoids having to make necessary distinctions and instead delegates past stylistic insertions as part of an architectural evolution that connects with the contemporary city through patterns of spatial fit.

The lilong housing neighborhoods in Shanghai formed a spatially dominant part of the international settlement. The term is derived from *li* or neighborhood, *long* or lane, and *tang* or interior space. Their design combines the Western notion of tightly packed terraces that might have been associated with 19th-century Western industrial cities, but with an overall consistency of form, detail, and texture. This creates an ephemeral cultural symbolism related to former foreign enclaves as part of a social and spatial setting with strong cultural overtones. It is reflected in the modern reinvention of Shanghai, with its hybrid amalgam of Chinese and Western architecture that continues to be expressed through its remaining lilong housing found in the topology of its Zhabei, Nanshi, and Jingan districts. Three-story brick-built terraces are severed by wide central paths and secondary side lanes with single or shared entrance courtyards. The elaborate gateways or *Shikumen* date from the 1880s with stylized Chinese ornamentation that extends decorative cornices, corbels, and identifiable ridgeline profiles. The layout creates a compact matrix of public and private spaces that represent a traditional characteristic of the Chinese dwelling as a private walled enclosure.

From the 1930s the lilong terraces began to include five-story apartment houses with service spaces to the rear and a consistent southern orientation that is still retained in new residential estates. The emerging 20th-century urban landscape became further conditioned by the changing social and economic fabric within the older settlement areas, and after 1949 became used as social housing to accommodate families who shared the limited facilities. From the 1980s many lilong groups were demolished to make way for higher-density residential typologies during the opening up period, but the remainder have continued to be rented or open for sale and have been subject to various levels of upgrading from the late 1990s. These now form part of the city's cultural capital as a response to its changing socio-economic structure, under which unique heritage buildings gain value through their scarcity in a central urban location. This implies a need to balance economic change with preservation of local lifestyles as far as possible.

Shanghai's urban traditions can be expressed through the early *lilong* or *longtang* residential terrace typology found in the Nanshi, Zhabei, and Jingan districts. Built in red or black brickwork, they are served by wide central paths and secondary side lanes with single or shared entrance courtyards. The elaborately carved stone gateways or "shikumen" date back to the 1880s.

CHAPTER 7

Dimensions of density in the Hong Kong SAR

The growth and development of the Hong Kong SAR, has, from its occupational inception in the mid-nineteenth century, reflected a process of constant transformation and adaptation in response to almost continuing development pressure. In its transition to a Special Administrative Region of China, Hong Kong sits at the southern end of a development corridor encompassing the Pearl River Delta Region, with nine cities in Guangdong Province including Guangzhou as its northern hub. This is, not withstanding the COVID epidemic, transforming the region into one of the world's most important economic and trading centers.

In 1841, when Hong Kong Island was first occupied by the British under the Treaty of Nanking, few places around the southern China coast seemed more inhospitable to building. The city was built along the northern foreshore of Hong Kong Island. The city was named *Victoria* in 1843, with a new central district alongside the harbor that became its political and economic base, accommodating trading houses and prominent public buildings. By 1847 the population had reached about 24,000 people and the beginning of a "central" infrastructure was in place. It was not until 1898 that the New Territories were leased for 99 years, effectively adding a further 90 percent of land, and providing a catalyst to the accelerated development of the Kowloon peninsula. A further impetus to development was the inauguration of the Kowloon-Canton Railway in 1910 with its terminus at Kowloon Point.

During the course of the late twentieth century, instruments of development policy were largely based on reconciling the aspirations of a growing and largely immigrant population with the often-critical shortfall of land and accommodation. In the earliest days of the city building process, the government laid down certain ground rules that, while being extended

and refined over the years, still influence the form of development—the use of land, sold at auction, as a significant source of government revenue. This, together with a generally laissez-faire economic system has had a significant impact on planning directions. Flexible land-use zoning and lack of real design control, apart from that imposed through building regulations, has long encouraged developers to meet short-term market forces rather than longer-term needs.

The first comprehensive piece of legislation that introduced controls over development in the city was the Public Health and Buildings Ordinance of 1903. Part III of the Ordinance had particular ramifications for planning minimum specifications for private streets; building heights; number of stories; and the right to regulate building types. It was complemented by a Lands Resumption Ordinance, which set out procedures for acquisition of land or buildings for public purposes. In fact, much early development was associated with harbor reclamations, carried out as and when required. This established the growth of the banking and financial services industry, fueled some 20 years later through rapid industrialization and urbanization, when tall blocks began to permeate the grid-like street patterns originally laid out for low-rise offices and warehouses.

In 1935 new legislation effectively separated control of buildings from public health factors. The new Buildings Ordinance allowed structures up to five stories, while reducing the minimum accommodation standards. That same year a Housing Commission reported that living space in older areas tended to be subdivided between several households, in part defeating the principal objectives of the Ordinance.

Immediately after the Second World War, the population expanded from 600,000 people in 1945 to 2.36 million. The old housing stock had been severely depleted by war damage, and squatting became virtually the only option, not just for new immigrants but for long-term residents who had lost their homes.

In 1946 the government appointed British planner Sir Patrick Abercrombie to prepare the first comprehensive plan for the urban area, covering the city of Victoria and Kowloon. However, planning priorities were redirected in 1953, after a massive fire in a large squatter settlement in Kowloon made 53,000 people homeless. It led directly to major government involvement in public housing through the establishment of a resettlement program, aimed at re-housing squatters, and using the cleared land for more intense development purposes, including housing estates.

The second major legislation passed in 1954 was the Housing Ordinance, which established a Housing Authority to provide low-income accommodation. It was also granted powers to develop land and carry out improvement of acquired older buildings. With the population increasing to 2.5 million, the Town Planning Ordinance that year directed that plans should be prepared for a number of areas outside the urban area. So began the official commencement of the Hong Kong SAR's New Towns Program.

The maximum building height was radically overhauled in 1955 to permit a greater land-use intensity. Simultaneously, the Landlord and Tenant Ordinance was also amended so that building owners could compensate tenants and apply for redevelopment to realize their site's full potential. The following year the amended Buildings Ordinance allowed much greater plot ratio potential in urban areas, and because a building's height was related to street width in the ratio of 2:1, it was possible in certain areas to redevelop a site with a plot ratio of up to 20 times the site area. This instigated the redevelopment of low-rise blocks into high-rise tenements, which by the 1960s had led to a transformation of the urban area by tall "mansion blocks."

Successive amendments to the Buildings Ordinance in response to development pressure, particularly during the 1960s, inevitably paved the way for the physical transformation of the Hong Kong SAR's urban area into a high-rise city, with every site falling within outline zoning plan categories which have both floor area ratio and site coverage implications. This has had a clear impact on urban texture. The redevelopment of early three-story shophouses and four-story t'ang lau terraces into six- to eight-story blocks was followed in turn by redevelopment of these into multi-story tenements, and even taller point blocks. A joined-up urbanism relied largely on a retrofitting of urban streets through several levels of podium development that sufficed to ensure continuity of valuable frontage.

New regulations were brought into force in 1965, which provided a sliding scale of plot ratios and site coverage, related to building height and type, which are still largely applicable. The maximum plot ratio for domestic properties was set at 10:1 and for non-domestic properties at 15:1. Ground coverage was set at 66.6 percent for domestic and 100 percent for non-domestic uses. Open space integration depended on the class of site and gross floor area could be increased in return for a donation of public open space or as a result of road widening. Speculative blocks continued to comply only with minimum regulations throughout the 1960s until new regulations enforced greater building standards and, through leases, limited building uses.

High levels of immigration amounting to around 60,000 persons per annum between 1979 and 1981 led to the expansion of older squatter settlements that still represented less than half the estimate of those deemed to be inadequately housed. The majority of the remainder lived in old private tenements, with early public housing estates providing only a very basic standard of accommodation.

Transformation of the Hong Kong SAR into a High-rise City

While the Hong Kong SAR is associated with hyper-density development less than one quarter of its land area is actually built on. While this theoretically allows easy access to open space and enables country parks to be protected from development, the result is that buildable land

The central city form represents a constant process of redevelopment and urban adaptation, but also a convergence of social and traditional expression.

The imposition of building regulations that specify plot ratio limits to all sites has for many years presented a reduction in the life-cycle of much low-rise urban property, as site value increases at a greater rate than the buildings situated on it, creating a process of constant redevelopment to maximize permitted densities.

has been made to represent a scarce commodity and therefore an expensive one. The combination of land-use zoning and plot ratio conditions, together with the inherent flexibility of the planning system has propelled the urban land market on the basis that "ideal" patterns of land utilization must equate with the activity that generates the greatest return.

Castells et al., have argued that because virtually all land in the Hong Kong SAR was only leased to development interests, and because private interests have been well represented on the government's own decision-making bodies, decisions regarding development have always been made to the mutual advantage of both parties. However, the high financial return to government from land sales has been exacerbated by two other factors: first, the premium extracted by government through up-zoning of permitted land use to enable more valuable high-density development; and second, the mortgage policy of banks in extending favorable conditions to purchasers of new property, thereby encouraging almost constant redevelopment.

The city's gradual transformation into a high-density city therefore needs to be seen not only in terms of the constant pressure on scarce land area, but on the workings of a sophisticated financial model to which land-use zoning and lands mechanisms have contributed significantly. The result has been an increasingly undifferentiated urban form. Succeeding generations of buildings in the densely urbanized part of the city that are zoned to provide for the highest gross floor area values, have been invariably circumscribed in a largely ad hoc way, according to the environmental footsteps of their predecessors.

Accretions of constant change
and superimpositions reflect
random personalisation
and informal levels of use.

The first housing program in the early 1970s related housing demand to minimum accommodation and affordability standards. However, by 1980 housing demand and supply had begun to reflect a shift toward a greater consideration of the dynamics of the housing market. Under the 1987 Long Term Housing Strategy, the Housing Authority was reorganized with a large degree of autonomy, with the objective of increasing homeownership through public provision rather than through the private sector. Until today, approximately 2.1 million people, or around 29.7 percent of the population, have been accommodated in public rental housing, while a further 1.2 million people, or around 17.8 percent of the population, live in subsidized-sale flats.

The built-up area per person in the Hong Kong SAR (excluding large areas of open space, harbors and airports) is only around 28 square meters per person. This compares with 25 sq m per person in Mumbai; 35 sq m in Shanghai; and 145 sq m in Beijing. In addition, Hong Kong accommodates around two-thirds of its population within a 10-kilometer radius of its urban core, which is abnormally high and greatly exceeds that of other metropolitan areas with a much greater amount of built-up land per capita. This level of population density close to the urban center has contributed to a strong sense of urbanity through its traditional land-use mix, but has also changed the inherent nature of the inner urban districts, largely in response to the Hong Kong SAR's transition to a service economy over the past 30 years.

The insertion of elevated pedestrian routes establishes a three-dimensional form of cityscape.

The government effectively holds sway over both land supply and housing in several ways. First, it controls the land sales program and can regulate the land allocated for housing; second, it controls land use through zoning, and changes of use through lease modification; third, it controls the public housing program under the auspices of the Long Term Housing Strategy; and fourth, the right to resume land for public purposes. The full-blown public housing program, established hand-in-hand with the new town program, has become a key aspect of the current housing policy, effectively preserving the strands of a socially stable community but with a marked separation of public and private enclaves. The resulting Gini coefficient is lower than in major American cities, at 0.533.

The term "new town" covers a variety of situations, but these are essentially similar in their design solutions. Proactive investment in highways and rail transport have, in effect, led to an equitable balance between metro and non-metro areas, so that in recent years new town densities have been increased to meet housing program dictates, with a built form representation that is intensely urban but with reasonably high standards of open space, recreation, and amenity areas, befitting the strongly residential nature of these new communities. Their character has also been determined as much by single-use zoning as an overly standardized approach to building design. There is therefore an established community life but without the vitality or district-specific identity that is a traditional characteristic of the Hong Kong SAR's urban areas, in large part because of their contemporary role as bedroom communities.

Natural elements and physical constraints become informal determinants of identity, inherent in the urban setting.

Reshaping the Urban Identity

Only 24 percent of the Hong Kong SAR's total land area is used for all urban and new town purposes. The remainder comprises mountainous country parks, while its remaining areas of older village and agricultural land has tended to be used for questionable village expansion, purposes together with brownfield development. The value of land therefore drives the urban renewal process, less toward urban regeneration or rehabilitation and more toward comprehensive overhauling of older building fabric.

Various factors have conspired to bring about a physically fatigued environment in older areas, but unlike many other cities this has not led to severe levels of blight. In fact in many ways it is the older parts of the city that tend to underscore its essentially active character. The chief problem is the dilapidated older housing stock where rehabilitation and improvement has become secondary to the maximization of allowable gross floor area rat io potential.

In the older urban districts large parts of the housing stock still remain technically inadequate in terms of viable living standards, with an estimated 200,000 people living in what are termed "sub-divided" units. Urban renewal processes from the 1990s have effectively circumvented the need to realistically address the needs of established communities living in these areas in terms of social, economic, and physical processes. Supposed obsolescence has been addressed primarily through resumption, clearance and renewal, rather than the usability of older built fabric in sustaining its character. Older buildings, whatever their quality, are rarely derelict, they are simply run down. They do not represent wider levels of deprivation but rather interface directly with pockets of new development and economic activity, one type of use often benefiting from the other.

Thus, there exist different but overlapping urban vocabularies that have as much to do with perceptual aspects as with visual and physical ones. The Hong Kong SAR's fundamental urban component is its street configuration and lot pattern. An almost constant process of redevelopment over the years, some of it reflecting changes to the Buildings Ordinances, has tended to rationalize this pattern through remodeling the physical fabric, reflecting to some extent the unstable nature of contemporary urbanism, with its changing spatial imagery and condensed activity cores. The renewal process itself is more akin to redevelopment where owners are compensated and sites are assembled, and then tendered out to private developers.

The vertical stratification of uses, each with their associated activity and movement channels, underlines the essential difference between the formal framework of western public spaces and the more diffused and informal realm of the Hong Kong SAR's high density, compact city. Here the relationship between public and private is less tangible and the relationship between them works just as effectively in three dimensions as in two. The result is an urbanism

Narrow terraces become place for passive uses and informal gathering areas.

of edges and interfaces where urban space results from constant reinvention and complexity. Change and impermanence underlie the essential design language, while new and different values are superimposed on long-established spatial patterns, constantly extending the city's cultural reach.

The Culture of Compactness

We often refer to the culture of congestion with regard to New York, but Rem Koolhaas has also described Asian cities as embodying an equally pertinent signature—a tenuous quality of unrest that makes previous configurations expendable, but also each future state provisional. This sums up the Hong Kong SAR very well. Wherever we look, this Special Administrative Region of the People's Republic of China, which occupies only a little over 1,000 square kilometers, is marked by continuing growth, transformation, and change. Impermanence underlies its essential urban design language. This is manifested by substantial economic as well as cultural shifts, often representing new and different values superimposed on long established patterns. The representation of urban place is also open to radical change through the make-up and disposition of new spatial types, while evolving communications technology continually extends the reach and efficiency of economic activity.

The conservation of mountainous country parks that provide an imposing backcloth to all parts of the territory with their diverse array of flora and fauna necessitates the optimization of development opportunities in the urban area and existing new towns. Historically, this level of compactness goes some way to explaining its characteristic agglomeration economy, tall building and population density that makes public transport cost effective. In terms of achieving acceptable measures of sustainable urbanization, however, environmental comfort and urban design initiatives represent a challenge in the face of almost constant development intensification, where a high percentage of employment opportunities are focused on the urban core.

Western cities have long nurtured a realm of formal building elements and spatial configurations, including relatively high-density urban enclaves, that until comparatively recent times distinguished Western concepts of urban design from the less permanent and more spontaneous Asian city values. But the term "Westernization," now frequently used to describe the internationalization of business, finance, and technology development in Asian cities, has undergone a 21st-century transition. While much of the Asian urbanism we experience today stems from older and often imposed urban design frameworks, interwoven with indigenous

The textural ambiguity of older urban architecture built to accommodate the massive growth of population in the 1960s provides a complex array of features that extend well beyond an established design style.

building types, the modern Asian city is also a global one with decidedly international characteristics. The Hong Kong SAR is in many ways a special case, from its questionable beginnings as a treaty port through its fragmented growth via a succession of pragmatic responses to catalytic events.

The city's building objectives are elusive, and it is difficult to stand back at any one time and recognize a situation of completeness, or even a design or spatial distinction between the city's core urban districts. The city has, at least in physical terms, an intersection between high-rise enclaves and a residue of older but dense tenement blocks interspersed with the last remaining shophouses, that reflects an almost unique juncture of influences. Due to the new town building program that commenced in the early 1970s, urban area densities have, for the most part, almost halved. What remains in the older urban districts extends well beyond the normal conventions of urban grammar. Notions of urban form and visual address are blended with an integral matrix of compressed vitality, resonating surfaces and textures, coupled with dense older building fabric that offers flexible conditions of tenure and use.

High-rise urbanism brings with it an intensity of use that permits an accessible pedestrian realm that can only be realistically depicted in three dimensions—generally extending through interior and deck spaces, above and below grade, in ways that are not immediately apparent or legible in a strictly ordered sense. The result is contrast and complexity within a surprisingly intelligible pattern, which suggests alternative ways to engage with the city. Its value to the public realm lies in its intense levels of use.

The Energizing Ingredients

The Hong Kong SAR's older street design for the most part represents an architecture of expression over conceived form. In older urban quarters clip-on elements, signage, and video walls create a commodified sense of immediacy, both symbolic and sensory, thereby distorting established ideas of building aesthetics. There is, however, little firm conceptualization of urban space, which is a cornerstone of Western urban design. Building regulations permit 100 percent site coverage up to a certain level, so that urban renewal or redevelopment allows little leeway for regeneration of the public realm. Thus, new urban configurations contrast and yet co-exist with traditional place characteristics that relate more to patterns of activity than coherent physical form. This includes an emphasis on the street for social rituals, ceremonial uses, market trading, open eating areas, and the multi-use of small open spaces or pocket-parks.

Older street buildings are sporadically and deliberately transformed by their occupants in a fluid way through personalized building extensions and functional appendages to facades and roofs, generally on the basis of practicality and immediacy rather than design. This is not quite on the same level as Tokyo's *da-me*, literally "no-good" architecture, described by Kaijima, Kuroda, and Tsukamoto, which describes an urban reality of miscellaneous and overlapping functions having few orthodox design credentials. However, the Hong Kong SAR has, in its own way, evolved ambiguous functional combinations through the pressures of density, where supposedly incompatible elements are situated in curious yet dynamic juxtaposition—that is unless they are spotted by enthusiastic building control officers.

With good urban management, the constant presence of people becomes an essential ingredient for the compact city, energizing activities, minimizing threat, maximising use of public transport, and establishing a ready stream of users for amenities. Inevitably this creates a degree of tension between the complex and interactive workings of the city, particularly the need to synchronise certain levels of planning control, with the more indeterminate legacy of informality and spontaneity. Too little control, and informal uses easily proliferate into confusion and poor legibility, while with too restraining a hand, diverse and intricate street incident becomes steadily eroded.

The condensed metro area with its colossal land values and eminently flexible land-use zoning facilitates, and perhaps inadvertently encourages, a disjointed spatial juxtaposition of independent blocks with little contiguity. Yet these are unified by a kind of parallel universe of informal networks, both physical and electronic. In this situation the uniqueness of place is a biproduct of the city's essential dynamism where commonalities and interdependencies fashion the very image of the city through an intense range of consumption-oriented services.

This should ideally manifest itself in various functions and characteristics that relate to district image, changing cultural attitudes, and gradual gentrification. However, this puts older mixed-use areas on a collision course with economic forces whereby the potential plot ratio gain inherent in zoning plans and building regulations, which cover the entire urban area, means that in many cases the value of land is greater than the buildings that sit on it. The city's older street texture is therefore vulnerable to large-scale change and clearance, while at the same time modern commercial and residential towers require large floor plates, and consequently both redeveloped and new-build expansion areas replace the fine-grained older quarters with a more course-grained street matrix.

A Reconstituted Sense of Place

There are now virtually two forms of city character—the first emblematic of compartmentalization and high-rise efficiency that is gradually producing an undifferentiated city form of relatively standard blocks; the second offering an informal and adaptive response to changing

The graphic vocabulary of Chinese text takes on a strong urban design role in establishing complex urban imagery and fragmentary collage.

needs and temporary requirements that best meet the immediacy of the here and now. The first generally embodies a single-use complex at a monumental scale, under single ownership or management; the second involves areas made up of older street blocks and tenements and reflects an intangible realm of use and display that defies aesthetic categorization. Under the second category, complex layering and interpenetration of different elements is accommodated through constant adaptation. Regeneration objectives need to reflect many different kinds of emphasis in relation to older areas. These are not easy to pin down precisely and relate not just to the economic health of the city regarding the asset values of housing, commerce, and tourism, but to attributes of heritage, memory, and culture, all of which need to be reinforced rather than eroded, and which induce a range of secondary benefits associated with the preservation of vibrant communities. It is not a matter of bringing run-down areas back to life, but of respecting and reconstituting good city attributes.

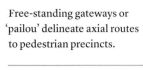
Free-standing gateways or
'pailou' delineate axial routes
to pedestrian precincts.

Thus, the spirit of place is elusive—it is rarely manifested in the empirical physicality of the city, but instead reflects the constant insertions and adjustments that invoke different qualities of use. These produce areas of special identity or urban signifiers that interact and change over time in response to prevailing constraints where there is little direct connection between sense of place and a localized aesthetic framework. In these situations the urban roots are more informal, stemming from qualities inherent in the historical fabric, social use, and the discernible visual appeal of color, street incident, and character that transcend time and place. These values open up possibilities to establish individuality within urban districts in a manner that sustains their capacity for change, and thus contribute to the personalized qualities of an urban locality.

The contemporary city has many layers of meaning and temporality accumulated at different stages of growth, stemming from historical imprints, colonial land policies, industrialization, waves of migration, property speculation, and former patterns of development. In addition, vulnerable urbanizing regimes made up of temporary components have become periodically insinuated within both the fabric and recent memory of the city—rooftop dwellers, the sub-division of space within tenements, and informal settlements, the latter often being subject to the hazards of fire, floods, and typhoons. In the urban area there is no *tabula rasa* where unconstrained new development can take place; urban design in a typical "quarter" must take as its basis the active history of the area in order to establish a relationship between urban uses, embedded cultural values, and new building elements. In a city where the average age of an urban building is less than 50 years, the city form itself needs to be considered in terms of both space and time components.

The cultural dimensions of the Hong Kong SAR are therefore intrinsically interwoven with a sense of immediacy, physical change, and fragmented incident. The emerging intersection of forces and economic priorities in the Pearl River Delta, and in the adjoining Greater Bay Area that provides the Hong Kong SAR with a future metropolitan framework, continues to superimpose a new collective identity on the region. This is helping to refashion both the physical and economic dimensions of the city itself, where post-industrial urbanism now enables a reinterpretation of city texture in ways that combine different design dimensions.

Urban Design Dimensions for the Compact City

The process of urban design is not really about pursuing prescriptive physical solutions but more toward integrative place-making that needs to reflect specific dimensions and contextual values. However, we have to recognize the inevitable forces that increasingly regulate this process. As a corollary to Ruskin's "Seven Lamps of Architecture," Jon Rouse incisively set out the "Seven Clamps of Urban Design" and these are particularly apparent in the Hong Kong SAR where the drivers of city growth tend to overwhelm and overcome both the behavioral setting and any kind of articulate community voice. The "clamps" include over-regulation, an over-emphasis on urban efficiency, and expedient means of funding large-scale redevelopment so that it is all too easy to end up with formulaic and undifferentiated solutions, reinforced by zoning plans that cover the entire city. When we superimpose on this the financial and bureaucratic expedients there is plenty of scope for city design to become abstracted from integrative urbanism and a changing notion of place.

In the Hong Kong SAR, as is many other cities, primary control over city development has become progressively diffused so that urban design is now less part of a coherent city building and regeneration process and more the outcome of various affiliated financial, land, and regulatory strategies, and therefore difficult to reconcile with other planning and community pre-determinants. The "silos" policy adds to the problem, so that the planning process itself has splintered into a maze of decision-making channels that are more responsive to functional engineering ends and property interests, than meeting the needs of an integrative urbanism. In addressing this the important role of urban design must be to safeguard a range of qualities that matter to the community. This is essential if the city is to maintain and reinforce the best of its urban characteristics—its traditional sense of diversity, drama, vitality, and an eclectic mix of uses—many of which cannot be planned for in the strict sense of the word. These are all factors that make the Hong Kong SAR unique from other world cities.

There also exist different but overlapping dimensions of urban design that underpin its workability and value, and that relate both conceptually and simultaneously to the development process. These have been categorized in general terms by Carmona et al. If we take this categorization with reference to the Hong Kong SAR, a number of factors emerge that reinforce the high-density city's giddy reputation for almost constant change. These are discussed in the following sections.

Morphological Dimensions
The configuration of urban form in the compact city is based on several key factors, the most prominent being the street pattern, adapted and consolidated over 150 years; the lot pattern that continues to change through subdivision or amalgamation; the built structures situated on these lots, and the prevailing land uses. In essence the older fine-grained street grids, influenced by topography and harbor profiles, have successively given way to a courser and less permeable organization of street blocks through both redevelopment and the requirements of new superblocks and rail-related sites on the new reclamations. This provokes a tension

...e ongoing process of urban
...ewal must take on a
...enerative role, seeking
...sponsive dialogue with
...city's urban traditions and
...ablished patterns of use.

Street interventions rarely for part of a composed totality bu mix historical associations wi contemporary social space an its symbolic expressions, alor with the designed identity of corporate capital.

Advertising structures perme the urban design language of the street in dense shopping and residential areas, inextricably bound to the culture of consumption.

between the older spatial and movement patterns that have endured up to the present time around the inner fringe of the urban area because of their essential robustness, for example the steep "ladder streets" to the south of the central business district, and the encroaching pattern of intensification through the development of large-scale, freestanding forms. These integrate new realms of movement and social space that can easily occupy an entire street block.

Successive stages of redevelopment, some of them helped on their way by changes to the Buildings Ordinance, have rationalized the street and block pattern through extensive remodeling of the physical fabric. We might say that this reflects the preternaturally unstable nature of contemporary Asian urbanism—somewhere between a traditional street-based morphology, and privatized enclaves. As streets lose their traditional character and social dimensions, the city is transformed by a new spatial imagery that in places extends to monolithic regimentation. At best this represents condensed activity cores related to stations and interchanges with a layered fusion of shopping, commercial, and residential uses. At a more questionable level it produces privatized enclaves of exclusion, several steps removed from the empirical reality of the urban realm.

In turn this raises questions that go beyond typological form, to the essential difference between the single-managed and developer-owned mega-complex, and the older tenements. While the latter offers the inherent potential to house a changing multitude of activities in response to demand, the former offers occasionally iconic but often only inwardly oriented landmarks with ambiguous public identity.

The city has an ambiguous relationship to ground level that recalibrates the normally comprehensive master planning approach, where choreographed pedestrian circulation can come to rely on a combination of the pragmatic and the piecemeal. While several hundred pedestrians might wait at any one time at a ground-level curbside for a favorable change in traffic light sequence, elevated networks of pedestrian movement stream above on overhead routes following less intimidating but often less than discernible alignment patterns through sinuous sequences of internal malls, atria, galleria, and commercial lobbies.

The "ubiquitous mall" is partly the result of building regulations that allow 100 percent site coverage up to a maximum of 50 feet on urban area sites, so that up to four stories of commercial retail and supporting uses within podia incorporate interconnected patterns of malls, voids, and bridge links. In central locations these collectively form intense matrices of circulation that can extend to sky gardens at roof level. Towers themselves establish a vertical and "joined together" urban design creating a stacked assembly of high-rise spatial entities with various forms of internal volumetric organization. As some of the highest development densities are associated with buildings that sit above mass transit stations, vertical correspondence with the ground plane itself can become somewhat elusive. While horizontal subway transit creates rapid routes between not-dissimilar commercial, hotel, and residential hubs, necessary vertical access requires banks of lifts and escalators that interconnect with a multi-modal selection of bus, taxi, and ferry routes, all forming part of a layered and networked pattern of rationalized movement.

Perceptual Dimensions

Perceptual factors should best relate to the link between community and locality with its store of meaning, relationship, and involvement. This combines cognitive values of association and experience, with the formal merits associated with expressive and symbolic aspects of cityscape. These help with an understanding of city environment in terms of knowledge and recognition that provide a mental image and perceptual frames of reference. In Asian cities this also includes aspects of unpredictability and spontaneity that permeate large parts of the urban environment.

Perceptual identity is heightened by constant changes in level associated with 'ladder' streets.

The high-rise identity of the Hong Kong SAR as a compact city might suggest at first glance that the conception of locality is subservient to that of tall buildings. However, in essence, the combination of sensory, formal, and symbolic values are intimately connected with the perceptual responsiveness of a place and the working patterns of the community itself, providing that these are physiologically comfortable. There is also a further factor—that of unpredictability and spontaneity. Patterns of use tend to be unified, not by building composition and formal identity, but though a more enigmatic vocabulary of interwoven detail and localized signifiers. Rowe and Koetter in *Collage City* have termed this "both the legacy and continuum of historical process that accommodates hybrid display."

Street environments are able to reconcile intuitive values with patterns of ad hoc activity evoking the local urban tradition of inventive bricolage that enriches and dramatizes the street frontage and establishes a dialectic between internal and external space. Within this process the tall buildings that make up the street wall tend to lose any individually expressive identity and become part of a collective and impersonal backdrop set against the elaborate foreground of the street, which is embedded in the complex framework of everyday life. Subliminal associations are to a large extent dematerialized from their physical boundaries, but grounded in local meaning and informal event.

eciality food markets become
sociated with certain districts,
formally inserted within
der and generally orthogonal
eet patterns, such as the
wrington Road Market
Causeway Bay.

Social Dimensions

Social factors are closely related to behavioral functioning that influences patterns of activity and association, giving rise to spontaneous interaction within a community realm that is accessible to all and where activities feed off each other. This underpins public life in the Asian city, even as localized forms of consumption now tend to re-emerge in a more socially reductive form of interaction through fast food outlets and chain stores.

The physical organization of urban space and its social functioning are closely intertwined. However, it is not so much environmental design that influences patterns of social or behavioral activity, but the public realm that develops spontaneously around flexible street fabric. Within this the local community has traditionally established its own sets of uses, events, and realms of transaction, shaped and animated by a wide range of users, and where activities feed off each other.

The very diversity of the public realm reinforces aspects of socio-cultural continuity that underpin public life. Left to its own devices, a continuing process of adaptation and interaction responds not merely to what is there, but also to what is lacking. While the urban street is by no means impoverished in terms of commercial use, its traditional connotation with localized forms of consumption re-emerges from the city's ongoing urban redevelopment processes in a more streamlined but socially reductive form.

Street-level spaces are increasingly layered into vertically stratified commercial channels that demarcate a sometimes-elusive divide between public and managed private space. This underlines an essential difference between the formal framework of Western public spaces and the more diffused and informal realm in Asia where the relationship between public and private is less tangible, and the routes between them work just as effectively in three dimensions

ne market street responds not
ly to the spatial ramifications
supply and demand but to
e community's preoccupation
th the availability of fresh
od. Shops selling flowers,
it, vegetables and fish extend
ross pavements with displays
at ensure all goods are visible
a glance.

as in two. The result is an urban design of edges, interfaces, and vertical channels of connection, rather than strict spatial demarcations and divisions.

Social patterns change in response to inventive superimposition and constant modification of the urban matrix. Although high-rise residential development forms the core use in these areas, it is less bound up with an identifiable local neighborhood and more with three aspects of urban scale: the city itself for employment, where public transport is both efficient and cost-effective; the compact high-density district with its choice of locales; and the localized street context for casual social interweaving and identity.

Visual Dimensions

We have to a certain extent been schooled to think that visual appreciation of urban environment is strongly geared to aesthetic considerations closely associated with cognitive understanding, consistent architectural typologies, and inherent cultural values. This generally relates to a well-articulated or formal organization of built elements, but generally leaves out the significance of the idiosyncratic that often permeates the less formal parts of the Asian compact city. In the context of the Hong Kong SAR's abstract urban forms and tight urban massing, built fabric cannot necessarily be read in an orthodox sense but through patterns of correspondence that presuppose the simultaneous existence of visual complexity and unifying elements. Sameness is alleviated by a multitude of irregularities, textures, signage, and giant crystal screens that sustain an engagement with the stacked and rhythmic patterns of the city that enriches sensibility. In this way streets establish a sense of expressive incident and kinetic unity rather than architecturally contrived space. This extends to the experiential dimensions of urbanism where there is a constant interaction between complexity and order, novelty and

Speciality retail and market outlets form identifiable distri[c] features.

familiarity—an ambiguous but flamboyant combination that Gordon Cullen has described as "the language of gestures."

In effect this creates a perceptual frame of reference for new development, but in the compact city there is always room for increasingly dominant features. However, in the Hong Kong SAR the scale of landmark buildings tends to be inverted, so that essential legibility comes from a low-rise presence that establishes a discernible quality of place. Voids in the high-density matrix become positively charged by temporary uses at ground level that somehow establish both a visual and functional sense of fit, where constant change compensates for largely anonymous architecture.

Functional Dimensions

Functional considerations are primarily concerned with the way in which places work, interrelate, and connect. Amos Rappaport whose research on the city focused on cultural variables and human behavior, stated that this comprises natural, constructed, and informal elements that allow for various levels of engagement between people and place. This can be broken down into social, in terms of communication and exchange; educational in terms of discovery; and cultural in terms of interface with the built fabric, activities, and events. In effect activities

and primary uses have a greater impact on the urban setting than the architectural fabric itself, which helps to forge a functional interpretation of social space.

In the compact city, spaces and circulation corridors reflect a complex assembly of natural, informal, and constructed components that facilitate various levels of social, cultural, and operational engagement. As much of the Hong Kong SAR's city building has been based on contingency and constantly changing physical delineation, the very neutrality of street walls and the lack of finite built configurations serves to fashion a situation where the definition of circulation and activity areas have a greater impact on the setting than the architectural fabric. In the metro area the total amount of public space is around 940 ha or 2.8 sq m per capita—however, virtually all major spaces, unlike Central Park in New York, have less to do with planning foresight than the obsolescence of large-scale uses under public ownership. For example, Kowloon Park and Hong Kong Park have emerged through the removal of older military facilities in the central areas.

But we must also remember that large public open spaces have never been a traditional feature of Chinese cities, and that at any time of the day or week one is likely to find more people in a street market, with its casual and informal affiliations, than an urban park. Of course, in the compact city, open space also acts as a visual, not merely a recreational relief. The city has

24 country parks, 22 ecologically protected areas, and five marine parks to choose from that occupy almost 50 percent of the entire territory and are easily accessible by public transport.

In the Hong Kong SAR, the busiest pedestrian connections are not derived from historic streets and axial movement flows, but from a sequence of interventions in the urban framework involving a complicated hierarchy of movement channels, the purposeful commercial incorporation of pedestrian linkage between intense activity nodes, and the reconciliation between public and private interests in bringing this about. These dedicated connectors extend their paths through lobbies, malls, and atria of commercial complexes, forming part of intricate and multi-level retail patterns. Public space therefore interfaces with a more ambiguous space that is to a large extent aimed at stimulating consumption through a strategically articulated system of navigation.

…e market in Stanley establishes
…formal connections with the
…aterfront café areas.

Commodity-oriented concourses have become the new cultural constructs in the city, providing condensed foci of urban ritual and encounter through themed and standardized patterns of consumerism. People interface both directly and indirectly with product, and the corporate typology of space often provides a more permeable alternative to the regularity and climatically challenged discomfort of the street. At the same time, the internal mall, atria, or galleria inevitably recast the way in which the city is experienced, purposely integrating episodic sequences of shopping channels and bridge links to connect with transit nodes, residential, hotel, or commercial towers that effectively exclude visual or spatial interface with the wider city realm.

Temporal Dimensions

The small seasonal variation in daylight and generally mild climate produce a sense of regularity to diurnal change and the expressive quality of this. The onset of darkness brings about an effective transformation where the user is not merely a recipient but a participant in a series of unfolding events. Streets that might have a mundane daytime character take on a new sub-realism through an assemblage of pictographic imagery and evocative associations that animate space with information overload. This convolutes the normal experience of urban space, although the greatest sense of change comes through the constant movement of people—the central ingredient of vitality.

Temporal considerations reflect the relationship between the passage of time and the urban environment. In the Hong Kong SAR the transition of uses throughout the day and evening means not merely changes in use, but different sets of users who inhabit urban space at different times for different purposes, where contrasting levels of responsiveness tend to imply a high degree of overlap. One result of compact city and neighborhood forms, together with high population density, is that this increases the attraction of available space in relation to the mix of users that have access to it. This includes designated recreation spaces that informally relate to morning exercise and passive activities, but are equally used for evening or weekend festivals, concerts, or temporary structures such as those used for Chinese opera. Similarly, the transition of daytime vehicular streets to night markets and street cafés produces dramatic diurnal change in the identity of place, texture, and public expression. In the compact city this cultural animation of space increases the attraction of people to places as locations are shared intermittently on a time basis rather than being used intensively by one particular interest group. Temporal change is therefore a function of the availability of space in relation to specific interest groups that have easy access to it.

This also introduces interesting aspects of urban time management—for example the connective escalator sections that snake through the local ladder streets, and across intervening road corridors on Hong Kong Island, carry workers downwards to the central business areas in the morning and are directed upward in the evening, dispersing users through adjoining streets at various levels, stimulating the growth and change of uses in neighboring areas, and promoting constantly evolving patterns of activity along their path.

Temporal issues raise an important question concerning the continuity of place and the prevailing approach to conservation. Preservation of its built heritage is not one of the city's greatest claims to fame, but the need to adopt a careful approach is not merely one that is directed toward aesthetic or heritage value, but the maintenance of functional and cultural diversity in the face of an unnecessarily narrow definition of obsolescence that is based almost solely on-site value.

The socio-cultural value of historic quarters is inadequately recognized, even as a potent economic resource related to cultural consumption and tourism, and where cities are in a constant state of competition. Every city needs its cultural permanencies that have strong local associations and that embody a tangible sense of city memory, together with flexible fabric

parts of the city, streets are
contextualised from their
roundings through layers
incidental use and display.

ildings in prominent
sitions can be granted a
nus' plot ratio for integrating
blic space at ground level.

Temporary 'stage sets' constructed for special festivities.

that can accommodate acceptable degrees of change. The Hong Kong SAR has traditionally thrived on its wide mix of ownerships and conditions of tenure. If this is accepted as a basis for continual regeneration, on the basis of preserving the underlying dynamics of the city and keeping its local communities together, then the Hong Kong SAR could well be a model for the Asian city of the future. Compact cities should, by their nature, be relatively sustainable, and the Hong Kong SAR is eminently so on a number of counts, but its historical trace elements must be respected in a similar way to a place that is said to embody good *feng shui*. In this environment of urban re-invention, complexity, and pluralism we need to recognize the need for a balanced co-existence between flexible and more static components so that the disparate parts can be mutually reinforcing during the challenges of the 21st century. A necessary role of urban design is to reinforce identity and to build continuity into the regeneration process. This must accommodate degrees of change while retaining permanencies that embody a tangible sense of community associations and traditional trace elements.

CHAPTER 8

Achieving sustainable urban design in the face of climatic challenges

Global initiatives reflecting sustainable concerns for the planet have, in recent years, helped to develop a clear ecological dimension for strategic planning, but the formulation of responsive urban design parameters to deal with this has been less reassuring. This requires a strong direction for change involving the integration of economic, environmental, and community interests in order to achieve the objectives of Agenda 21, which followed the UN Earth Summit in 1992. The environmental commitments made at COP26 in 2021 demonstrated the immediacy of global warming. The Glasgow Financial Alliance for Net Zero brought together 450 global financial institutions to work together to reach "net zero," including carbon trading and a global carbon fund.

COP27 held in Sharm-el-Sheikh registered progress on the use of renewable energy and electric vehicles, but minimal progress on legally binding naturally determined contributions (NDCs) aimed at cutting carbon emissions, coal phase-out, and deforestation. It focused largely on global commitments to make carbon credit schemes more credible and compensation for developing countries that face serious repercussions and damage from climate change. The UN Expert Group estimates that there is a need to mobilize at lease USD 1 trillion a year in external finance for emerging and developing countries, which suggests an enhanced role for multilateral development banks together with acceleration of external private finance.

Efforts to improve the environmental performance of Asian cities is possibly the most pressing issue to be addressed in the 21st century in terms of efficient and clean energy systems, recycling, eco-friendly architectural design, and new transport technologies. As Asian cities face the continuing challenge of accommodating increasing numbers of people and households, with the number of urban inhabitants rising to well above 50 percent of national populations, it is important that the achievement of sustainable human settlements must be matched by the environmental performance of cities themselves. A first glance this might not seem such a severe task by global standards where 100 cities now accommodate more than 5 million people each, and with the 20 largest conurbations having in excess of 20 million each. However, urban populations in general are now increasing three times faster than overall population growth. The UN projects that China will add 416 million and India 255 million urban dwellers by 2050.

The urban design approach must therefore be oriented around several key dimensions concerned with the husbanding of key resources.

Setting Priorities

There is both an urgent need and an opportunity to develop environmentally sound technologies including energy-efficient and pollution-free forms of transport, efficient energy supply systems, and the means to improve the clean energy performance of urban buildings. However, in any discussion on combatting global warming in Asia we must first take a deep breath and prescribe pragmatic measures that can also be effective to overall long-term health care and quality of life, rather than simply subscribing to overly ambitious short-term solutions to reduce carbon emissions and overly rapid transitions to renewable energy. While climatic change is an immediate challenge to combat the greenhouse effect, there is a need for smart rather than symbolic solutions with a continuous emphasis on energy efficiency. This is arguably necessary as implementation of the Kyoto Protocol, which became international law in 2005 and called for industrial nations to significantly reduce their greenhouse gas emissions, has been estimated by McKinsey to cost up to US$9 trillion annually. Actual economic costs must therefore be carefully equated with specific benefits that relate back to the cost of cutting CO_2 in proportion to the projected good achieved and the actual resources available to confront the problem.

Despite an acknowledgment that the use of fossil fuels must be dramatically reduced and largely consigned to their proper place under the planet's crust in the short-to-medium term, world coal and natural gas prices are presently at record levels, with 60 percent of the world's electricity generation being derived from fossil fuels. However, of all global investments in the energy transition, around one-third has come from China, which now manufactures a large part of the necessary hardware, including around two-thirds of all solar panels and half of all wind turbines. Meanwhile, India is using unprecedented levels of coal for its thermal power plants. While renewable energy is by far the favored alternative, present renewables fall well short of

meeting energy demands. The Global Energy Monitor reported in March 2022 that there are over 70,000 kilometers of natural gas pipelines in construction globally, with 122,500 km in the process of commissioning and a further 100,000 km scheduled between 2023 and 2030.

The Intergovernmental Panel on Climate Change Report issued by the United Nations in March 2022 stated that Asia is the biggest global polluter. It is also the most exposed to climatic risk, experiencing considerable hydrological changes in certain coastal areas and major river basins along the Yangtze, Ganges, Mekong, Brahmaputra, and others that house up to one and a half billion people. In these regions biodiversity and coastal ecosystems have a significant role to play in both socio-economic development and food supply. The Panel reiterated that emissions have to peak by 2025, and must be reduced 43 percent by 2030, and stressed that vulnerability to climate change varies in terms of geographical locations but in all situations the impacts have profound health, social, and economic implications, particularly in South and Southeast Asia. This might well affect up to 140 million people by the mid-21st century with different impacts according to age, gender, and ethnicity.

The ten years up to 2022 have been hotter than any sustained period in the last 125,000 years, and even with a reduction in greenhouse gasses, global temperatures are likely to take many years to stabilize. It is fair to state that costs of reducing carbon dioxide increase dramatically above a certain stabilizing temperature rise, while achieving commensurately less. An optimal model is therefore called for that encompasses a certain level of control over carbon emissions but in combination with other smart and more immediate initiatives. This is particularly important in the developing economies where the advancement of well-being is most important, and involves resolving many pressing issues that embody a moral purpose, such as communicable diseases, malnutrition, pollution, and access to proper sanitation and drinking water. The essential trade-off is to balance the costs of avoiding future catastrophe by means of low-carbon strategies, with the consistent costs of incurring harm in the present age. In less developed areas in Asia a primary objective in the medium term should be to improve the quality of life through investing in immediate cost-effective measures that combat existing

problems. The high populations as a result of continuing growth of many Asian cities have experienced the urban heat island effect in different ways, but are technically in a position to alleviate this through relatively simple but effective measures. This includes more urban greenery, installation of permeable and heat absorbing surfaces, and water features that act to reduce city temperatures.

While many might be forced to move because of lack of water and crop failures, some areas are already experiencing serious annual flooding. Intense monsoon rains in Pakistan in 2022 caused devastating floods that affected more than 30 million people and raises a salutary lesson that while the country contributes only 0.3 percent of global carbon emissions, this has little bearing on geographic impact. In Jakarta, rising sea levels in the Java Sea is having serious consequences as the city has an already high water table. In January 2022, the Indonesia parliament approved a bill to relocate the capital to East Kalimantan in Borneo, some 2,000 kilometers to the northeast.

While annual flooding does occur in certain Asian coastal zones, this is exacerbated because of the disappearance or degradation of natural coastal defense systems such as flood plains, mangrove areas, wetlands, and levees where reclamation for new development has acted to raise pre-existing water tables. This indicates a need for strong coastal protection measures as part of protective programs made cost effective through stringent planning, land management, and efficient water engineering that improves both quality and distribution. The global cost of climate-related disasters has increased but this must be equated not merely with climate change but with population growth in vulnerable and flood-prone coastal areas, inadequate zoning, and lack of development control, but also in many situations through inadequate building and construction codes that put property at risk.

The conclusion from this is that social policies are at least as important as climatic policies over the 21st century. At the same time, carbon emissions will continue in developing economies. It is also likely to become harder to convince national governments and their populations to spend enormous sums for environmental gains that are decades or even centuries away, and cooperation will be difficult to monitor. Short-term political gains are in many cases likely to come before meeting ambiguous long-term environmental goals, and most politicians are unlikely to be in office long enough to bear the consequences of over-commitment and sacrifice, or even the embarrassment of failure to meet stated targets. In addition there is a big question mark as to whether the planet is approaching anything like an irreversible climatic tipping point, however much we accept the physical symptoms of climate change.

A gradual transition to a non-fossil fuel economy must therefore be realistic and must emphasize investment in technology. This clearly requires collaborative research and development in the area of renewable and non-carbon-emitting energy production according to evolving visions, opportunities, and procurement programs. It would also require a sliding scale of investment with wealthier nations contributing the most, with collaboration on the potential across-board technological innovations and spin-offs that might be expected. At the same time, carbon taxes must be set at levels that are economically acceptable and achievable.

Developing a Sustainable Future for Asian Cities

The difficulties and costs of achieving a sustainable future for Asian cities indicate both the impending scale of the problem, and the hard choices involved. At a global level, two degrees of global warming represent an existential threat to massive numbers of people. In Asia, quite apart from the threat of rising sea levels, the heat island effect caused by large building densities also creates a significant impact on urban infrastructure. In achieving the goal of zero emissions by 2050, countries must adopt several core principles. The first is to establish binding targets with transparent monitoring, evaluation, and verification systems at all levels of the economy, focusing on electricity generation, traffic, and waste as being the source of most carbon emissions. This might comprise incentivization strategies, solar power installations, offshore wind farm construction, comprehensive waste-to-energy recycling agendas, and an energetic emphasis on carbon capture and storage strategies. A fundamental aspect of this is individual contributions from all parties, including sustainability curricula for schools.

The International Energy Agency in its "Net Zero by 2050" report, released in 2021, provides a road map to achieve established targets, but states that oil and coal powered plants must be eliminated by 2040. Investment in clean energy must therefore triple to US$4 trillion a year by 2030. This is to ensure that 90 percent of electricity in 2050 is generated from renewable sources that utilize solar and wind power. By the same date 86 percent of vehicles must run on electric battery-charging infrastructure, which requires considerable innovation in batteries and hydrogen power. International cooperation will be vital in reaching an agreement on both carbon pricing and investment in renewables.

Most concerns regarding sustainability are related to global ecological factors and the somewhat simplistic objective of limiting the consumption of renewable natural resources to within the capacity of their replenishment. The key consideration at an urban design level is to interpret these broad principles into practical design policies. The challenge in Asia is not necessarily in making sense of various disparate elements, but in evolving a culture of sustainability that must involve a greater degree of collaboration between various interests, in particular government departments and agencies, to ensure that sustainable measures work at a practical level.

Genuine urban sustainability is most likely to be achieved when environmental interests and good planning come together to ensure the integration of a whole range of design aspects meaningful to the wider environment. Established planning processes should provide the proper means by which public interests are defended and orchestrated through goal-oriented public participation. There is also a need to encourage new and innovative financial and institutional mechanisms in certain situations that might deal specifically with sustainable urban design and civic considerations.

The new direction represents a subtle shift in emphasis from pollution control to recognition that environmental and social guiding values have to be attached to development and economic policies. This indicates a need to focus on the planning and decision-making process, reflecting sustainable development concerns, and suggesting a need to impose values on which individual governments can make decisions and evaluate what is and what is not acceptable according to their situation and projections. Either way, the issue is essentially about needs and resources, and what is necessary to move individual countries onto a more sustainable footing in terms of development policy over long-term planning horizons in tune with economic growth. This is in line with the most simple and thoughtful definition of sustainability—that "development must meet the needs of the present without compromising the ability of future generations to meet their own needs."

Spatial and environmental planning is at the center of much of this debate both for its role in orchestrating how things happen and for its supposed responsibilities in safeguarding a range of environmental qualities. Concern over the environment is given added resonance by the recognition that an improved quality of places, localities, and regions is increasingly necessary not just for the health of the community but in promoting economic competitiveness in a global context. This suggests a need for collaborative, consensus-building practices. In particular, there is a need for a greater differentiation between the hard planning framework relating to the rules and regulatory policies affecting environmental quality, and the soft framework that needs to relate to a collaboration between all stakeholders. Genuine and long-lasting sustainability is only likely to happen where these levels are mutually reinforcing, and goals must be quality as well as target oriented. There is no point in generating massive planning and environmental machinery if the results that come out of this fail to fulfil their objectives.

Arcaded cafes line the street margin and animate the building frontage along Sisowath Quay in Phnom Penh reducing temperature and providing shade.

All aspects of sustainable strategies have some degree of spatial consideration in terms of their necessary practical application. It is therefore necessary to avoid blueprint solutions, but rather connective programs for integrated planning and management. In the industrialized city this cannot be disassociated from massive consumption of resources and generation of waste that needs to form a cyclic metabolism for cities in accordance with their ecological footprint.

"Change Management" is needed to incorporate environmental and social factors into the decision-making process in terms of policies, plans, and programs within an identified and agreed vision aimed at facilitation. This implies a strengthening of the institutional frameworks with respect to administrative procedures, and complementary participation and communication programs.

A number of policy considerations for decarbonizing buildings include the evolution of a regional green finance hub; stronger building codes; more frequent energy audits; publishing of building performance data; retrofitting existing public buildings and improving design standards in public housing; increasing renewable energy generation; implementing a carbon tax; and participating in a regional emissions trading system.

Responsive Design

In terms of city form, the high concentrations of people and development densities experienced throughout Asia have two advantages for achieving sustainability: first, the economics of scale this represents for the provision of infrastructure, public transport, housing, and jobs; and second, the general protection of non-urban environments.

Increased urbanization amplifies heat waves in cities, where low-density urban forms and vegetated areas have in many situations been replaced by large-scale building surfaces and primary roads that have a high absorption of solar radiation and a high thermal capacity. This leads directly to urban heat islands that can increase urban temperatures more than 20°C above rural areas. Mitigation strategies should therefore take into account the percentage of paved surfaces, together with wall and green area ratios, including green roofs to reduce solar reflectance and thermal emittance.

Urban design measures should encompass various levels of improvement, rehabilitation, and regeneration at a scale sufficient to incorporate comprehensive new layouts but with conservation or re-creation of resilient urban elements. If this process is carried out successfully, older communities with their capacity for adaptability would be left substantially intact, within rejuvenated and climatically responsive urban structures that reinforce their sense of place.

New development initiatives within Metro areas provide opportunities to consolidate a beneficial compact environment, with a typology of building forms designed to encourage flexibility of use, that can successfully offset, define, and animate the public realm and stimulate investment in green buildings. This directs the emphasis on urban design from a pre-occupation with architectural standards, to ways in which we can satisfy community concerns for environmental quality and to replicate, as far as possible, the inherent complexity and range of uses that meet public aspirations.

Historic environments to a large extent keep in place our collective memory of cities, and conservation objectives normally act to underscore a sense of continuity with the past. It is important, however, to differentiate between functional conservation geared toward the achievement of social aims, and its physical counterpart, which involves the retention and upgrading of buildings with sufficient historical merit. It is also necessary to ensure that contemporary needs are satisfied, possibly through a relationship with tourism initiatives, reflecting both the benefits of preserving important heritage sites, and the opportunities for physical regeneration of areas that might consolidate their identity through the integration of new attractions and amenities.

Comfortable and easily accessible places are more important than buildings to the public at large and good design, linkage and continuity of these means added value, and a high level of pedestrian use—essential characteristics of urban sustainability. There is a need to recognize the economic potential of listed buildings through mechanisms that incentivize their retention through compensatory procedures, along with a commensurate need to establish a self-financing approach for the conservation of listed buildings wherever possible.

Building Design

Climatic Responsiveness in a Tall Building Environment

The tall building is both a mainstay of city growth and a major determinant of urban design form in most Asian cities. There are no immutable rules to its design apart from the prevailing regulatory framework, which raises the issue of how high-rise urban environments should reflect sustainable objectives. At a city-block level, form and massing relate to the dynamics of street environment and micro-climate, and affects the way in which pedestrian movement systems are integrated at ground and other levels.

New technologies are liberating established aesthetic traditions in terms of possibilities for new urban design expression. However, there is clearly a need to relate sustainable energy policy both to what is technologically possible and what is economically practicable. For example, it is possible to open up semi-public spaces through sky courts, terraced gardens, and planting so that attention must be paid to designing them in an ecologically responsive way.

Population—dense cities contribute less greenhouse gas emissions per person than suburbs. The latter accounts for around 50 percent of all household emissions mainly in the form of carbon dioxide—best known as the "household carbon footprint." In large part this reflects the impact of extensive private vehicle use for commuting and virtually all household needs. It is possible to compare carbon footprints to create customized climate action plans with reference to a number of mitigation options, for example, emissions associated with transportation and the use and source of electricity. In The Hong Kong SAR the personification of a high-rise city, an interim decarbonization target was announced in 2021 to reduce emissions by 50 percent before 2035, in part by decarbonizing the power sector by scaling up domestic renewables and enhancing regional collaborations.

Colonnaded Street
in Margao, Goa, with family use
on the upper floors and shops
on the ground floor.

Environmentally Sound Technologies

Climate protection mechanisms in many older Asian neighborhoods adopted low-tech and sustainable devices such as colonnaded "five-foot" ways, louvred openings, balconies and verandas for cross-ventilation. These together with locally acquired building materials built up sets of architectural components that in themselves created a distinctive but flexible urban design vocabulary in their assembly. A compatible set of elements using modern technology can be used to create a not-dissimilar set of sustainable building tools that generate much the same tactile solutions for green buildings. For example, elements that provide shade can also act as solar collectors to generate energy.

The air-conditioned glass tower has become a symbol of profligacy, increasing energy consumption through the cooling load demand. New industrial techniques and technological advances offer creative potential and have, inherent in them, ways to enrich the city, and to transmit a new aesthetic and environmental dimension that interacts with the public realm in an expressive way. This must, however, be defined by different forces than in the past, with a greater respect for environmental context, low energy consumption, minimal operating costs and a generally green carbon neutral vocabulary. An ongoing vertical urbanism must involve the creation of "green places in the sky" that involve contact with the wider environment, not

dissimilar to those at street level. With major building programs underway in almost all Asian cities, this calls for methods to assess new and old buildings for everything from energy efficiency to the potential for "sick building" syndrome. This encourages the use of tried-and-tested energy-saving methods, from technologically advanced building materials to multiple electricity meters that inform all users where they are expending most energy. Types of rating can be harnessed to specific lease conditions in order to incentivize the use of improved technology that achieves set standards. At the same time established floor area ratios can be relaxed in return for energy efficient features, such as terrace and balcony areas.

It is necessary to act strategically, through the use of natural gas as a stepping stone to the use of green hydrogen in repurposed power plants. In Central Asia, much of the natural gas extracted travels across plains full of solar and wind farms. Off-shore wind farms are an increasingly viable technology, while large-scale batteries can be installed at major energy consumption users such as airports.

While there is no single criterion to the design of low-energy and bioclimatic building solutions, provision should be made for maximum use of natural ventilation, solar energy, and daylighting. Innovative bioclimatic buildings must be based on ecological design principles based on a consideration of the use of energy and materials in terms of various interactions and interdependencies, both external and internal. For example, shade, shelter, and ventilation can be provided by permeable street edges, large roof overhangs, connecting arcades, and brise soleil. These act to reduce environmental load in terms of energy consumption but also create responsive green features that can fashion evolving stylistic design patterns. This implies, first, a response to the siting, orientation, and configuration of the building in relation to ambient and environmental characteristics; second, a minimal use of mechanical and electrical systems; and third, effective management of energy efficiency, taking whatever advantage possible of climatic benefits and recycling of construction materials.

Designers can utilize a range of both high- and low-technologies. Nerve centers can continually gather and transmit information and program their own energy-saving response, complemented by the use of low-tech elements such as roof canopies and sun-screens. These can reduce glare and stretch the facade while providing a new design aesthetic of climatic moderators, which control light and heat energy. Outer building skins can also be designed to respond to changing climatic conditions by means of photovoltaics, photochromic glass, and shading devices linked to special sensors so that wall filters and blinds could be automatically inclined to reduce excessive sun penetration or react to typhoon conditions. Devices such as wind deflection shields or sun-scoops, activated by hidden neural networks, can also be designed to generate their own design repertoire.

Climatically responsive and eco-friendly solutions can combine to provide an expressive design vocabulary, both energy efficient and aesthetically interesting. Incorporation of soft landscaping through planting and introduction of organic matter associated with facade elements, sky courts, and balconies provide both ecological and design value.

Green Networks and Interfaces

Green networks can be incorporated through direct integration or in juxtaposition with major building elements. Asia's microclimate in the main calls for energy savings in mechanical cooling, so this implies a preliminary design diagnosis of sites including orientation in relation to the sun, shadow effects, and prevailing breezes. Planting can minimize heat-reflection and glare, while evaporation can help the cooling process on the facade and can significantly reduce summer ambient temperatures. Studies have shown that plants help to process internally generated carbon dioxide, release oxygen into the air, and remove some air-borne pollutants and chemicals. Internal spaces overlooking sky gardens and atria, for example, would receive air oxygenated by plants. Landscape at podium level, in the form of roof gardens, is an accepted part of open space provision in dense urban areas. Most plants can grow in 0.6m of soil with 0.2m for drainage, and trees of up to 7m can be grown in tree pits of around 1.2m depth, centered on the prevailing support structure. This also helps to reduce heat absorption on floors below. In a similar way, planting can be used in sky courts, recessed into the facade, that provide transition areas between internal and external spaces for use by building occupants, but can also serve as visual amenity and passive recreation and leisure facilities.

In terms of open space provision in Metro areas a distinction must be made between quality and quantity. Much existing open space tends to be poorly distributed and rarely forms part of a coherent pattern of distinctly urban elements such as squares and pedestrian precincts that might fulfill a wider and more meaningful design role. Many passive urban spaces are, in practice, simply left-over areas on awkward sites that offer little relief from sources of air and noise pollution. It is the design of open space as an integral part of the urban fabric that is ultimately of most value to the user and fulfills a strong connective function that can offset buildings in a civic sense.

Green areas have an important visual function in softening the impact of roads, flyovers, and other engineering infrastructure. This might include the integration of passive open space and other community uses beneath elevated roads, together with public promenades alongside major water bodies. Similarly, pedestrian environments can be multi-functional in nature and utilized for such functions as festivals, exhibitions, or weekend markets.

Distribution of open space, particularly in relation to large residential concentrations, is important. The quality of urban spaces is fundamental for their success, and proper linkage between activity areas is necessary to ensure both usability and workability in a wider urban and civic sense.

Efficient and cost-Effective Public Transport

Asia's compact conurbations technically place large concentrations of people within easy reach of rapid transit that can be optimized in a cost-effective way. The overall livability of the city habitat can be markedly increased by reinforcing the high use of public transport by pollution-free vehicles and the integration of pedestrian-friendly urban neighborhoods that accentuate the attractiveness of walking, together with cycle tracks that also have an intrinsic environmental value.

Forms of multi-mode public transport are available in the wealthiest Asian cities, where high densities make it cost-effective, and helps to keep car ownership to some of the lowest levels in the developed world. Nevertheless, a high proportion of public transport is by road vehicles, and the majority of licensed buses, taxis and ferries are driven by diesel fuel so that all transport modes contribute to overall pollution levels. Larger cities suffer the impact of imposing high traffic volume on inadequate highway infrastructure, leading to cities experiencing traffic congestion, badly maintained goods vehicles, and street corridors which inhibit dispersion of emissions. For example there are around 787,000 licensed vehicles in Hong Kong on approximately 2,130 kilometres of road space – an average of 370 per kilometre. The 160,000 licensed goods vehicles constitute only 20% of the total number, but they are responsible for approximately two thirds of all vehicle kilometres travelled. Feasible targets have been set by government to attain zero vehicular emissions before 2050, and fuel-propelled private cars will not be registered after 2035, along with the accompanying promotion of new energy vehicles and vessels.

All public transit systems are, by any standards, more energy efficient than personal transportation. Electric transport systems such as trams and trolley buses have cleaner emissions than diesel operated buses, and, because they are trackless, can use existing roads. A further

alternative is the use of compressed natural gas for buses with low emissions of suspended particulates. Greater use of electric transport might also result in balancing out the overall electricity demand throughout the day. However, the ultimate benefits in the 21st century must also resolve the means of power generation. China accounts for half of global electric vehicle sales and is the largest adaptor of EV vehicles globally, but EVs are dependent on precious metals required for rechargeable batteries, including lithium, nickel, and cobalt. China refines roughly 35 percent of all nickel and utilizes almost 70 percent of lithium and cobalt available globally to keep up with this demand and supply to other countries. This calls for an effective solution to metal resource policies, with a high rate of battery recycling and research for cobalt-free batteries.

For a genuinely sustainable strategy there is a need for a greater co-ordination of transport infrastructure and financing policies, together with more vigorous enforcement policies and investment in rail-based transport systems and other innovative forms of people movers.

Making the Best Use of Resources: Respect for the Natural Ecosystem

Recycling Techniques

Solid waste comprises municipal and construction material that can only be disposed of in landfill sites within territorial limits, or through incineration—although some wealthier countries are known to ship solid waste to poorer states for disposal. With an increasing rate of urbanization in Asia, the disposal capacity is unsustainable at present levels, even with a planned increase in incinerators. An overall reduction in waste generation and an increase in recycling processes are the only long-term solutions.

Landfill sites should be equipped to collect leachate and burn off landfill gas that contains CO_2 and other trace elements, or wherever possible recover the gas and use this for energy generation. As there can be major variations in development activity it is difficult to project waste arising from construction and demolition, but a significant reduction in this needs to be also matched by an increase in waste-to-energy incineration facilities and new disposal sites. Waste reduction scenarios include domestic recycling and public awareness matched by inducements for companies to produce goods that generate less waste in the first place. Economic incentives might also be necessary to reduce or avoid waste and encourage environmentally responsive behavior.

Incineration is generally the most efficient form of waste management but should be restricted to wastes that cannot be recycled and that can provide for energy recovery. Wherever possible, governments should adopt waste-to-energy polices. Many cities now favor a combination of recycling and composting facilities, aided in some cases by landfill taxes. Suitable sites can be identified for leasing to the recycling trade under short-term tenancies at concessionary rates, for example waste paper and metal recycling. To formulate separation and collection of recyclable materials, building regulations should specify that new urban buildings must provide sufficient space for waste recovery activities.

Ecological Protection

Asian cities are vulnerable to increasing population demands, environmental compromises to production, and to potential resource depletion or changes in pricing policy. This points to the need to bring about greater efficiency in the use of resources.

The so-called "ecological footprint," that is to say the carrying capacity of land area in order to sustain itself with food, energy, and other resources, varies between cities. In the Hong Kong SAR for example, this represents 4.6 hectares per capita or around 263 times Hong Kong's total land area, and is virtually equivalent to Hong Kong's ecological deficit of 4.5 hectares per capita. This clearly acknowledges the dependence of the Hong Kong SAR on neighboring Guangdong Province, which supplies around 80 percent of its water and much of its food. By comparison, London's ecological footprint extends to around 125 times its surface area, nearly 20 million hectares.

It must be obligatory for all developments to connect to some form of sewerage system and to ensure that all water treatment facilities are operated properly. Licensing must also cover all major waste treatment and disposal facilities. While governments must bear the capital costs for these, the introduction of proper user charges for waste collection and disposal is ultimately necessary to help fund environmental infrastructure, to encourage waste reduction, and to effectively instill the message that environmental quality comes at a price.

Design with Nature

Landscape planning can be considered as an essential precursor to urban design, where the best aspects of the setting can be harnessed to development opportunities. This should establish priority areas where growth can be absorbed while preserving the intrinsic qualities of the landscape for public benefit. The starting point must be an appraisal of the basic influences that make up the environment and, stemming from this, an identification of the value and quality of available resources. Studies therefore need to be carried out into terrain, agriculture, drainage, hydrology, existing areas of settlement, wildlife habitats, and areas of particular visual or scenic quality. This exercise helps to define properties that can perform a valuable planning or environmental service in their natural form and suggests areas where development should be regulated.

Street trees, at an appropriate scale, form an essential component of urban space, and can enhance its organization and use by providing enclosure and amenity, breaking down the horizontal scale and providing climatic protection. Planting alongside streets helps to oxygenate the air and contributes to a reduction in airborne dust levels and noise pollution, while acting to modulate light and shade. Together with lighting, seating, and kiosk elements, tree lines act to visually unify these spaces for passive uses, while double rows of trees provide shaded avenues, and help to demarcate spaces.

By regarding urban and rural areas as a continuum rather than two separate and irreconcilable entities the design of urban form and, in particular, its open space structure, should be based upon the natural elements that are dominant at the interface between the two; for example, hill forms, river channels, or areas of coastline. Every attempt should therefore be made to extend the influence of these elements within and through urban development areas where buildings, open space and landscape are equally important components of the environment.

Conversely building form and density should reflect the increasing dominance of natural elements, as distance from the urban core increases. The concept of an integral and continuous landscape and open space system is based on the premise that its visual and functional value in high density development situations is markedly greater than if an equal amount of open space were to be distributed in discreet units.

In planning for sustainable development, effective environmental management should extend the values that are currently placed on rural habitats. At the same time natural landscape and open space must be seen as vital elements of urban infrastructure, in effect an urban ecology that should ensure quality for the built environment and add value to it. Tree planting can, for instance, remove up to 75 percent of particulate pollution in the atmosphere.

The (RAMSAR) Convention on Wetlands of International Importance, especially as waterfowl habitats, provides a framework for the conservation of wetland as valuable breeding grounds for rare bird species. This is based on their important functions in maintaining water quality, reducing flood risk and damage by providing water storage and through shoreline stabilization. China has 64 designated sites, including one in the Hong Kong SAR, in all covering an area of 7.5 million hectares, while India has 46 sites—the largest network in South Asia. These act as nurseries and spawning grounds for many important species, as well as acting to conserve biological diversity. The overall objective is to establish an incentive structure for "wise use" as defined by the Ramsar Convention as "sustainable utilization for the benefit of humankind in a way compatible with the maintenance of the natural properties of the ecosystem."

A "design with nature" approach represents an ecologically inspired way forward and demands a respect for the role played by various factors on the natural ecosystem so that development itself achieves a sustainable fit and equilibrium with natural forces. The landscape planning approach must have built into it a set of urban quality considerations related to policies that underpin the fundamental values of the city and impel us to embrace resilient environments. Protection of the environment and biodiversity requires the development and utilization of formal classification systems and indicators for all natural habitats, including their state of health and interdependence with other aspects of sustainability, which will help to identify trends over time and assist in the identification of protection and remedial actions.

Environmental Management

The starting point for sustainable policies is in establishing the state of the current environment in all its forms. That is to say how much one aspect of environment is valued against others, and to what extent the creation and sustenance of environment is valued against economic and social criteria. Monitoring mechanisms therefore need to be extended to all aspects of habitat through environmental audits. This should involve information from a wide range of sources, so that these critical "thresholds" can then be a resource not only for environmentalists and government agencies but also for development bodies, in order to promote resource efficiency by working toward the production of integrated plans.

Measures must be aimed at reducing or eliminating the impact of development actions, and should form part of all urban planning and development studies. This should include a description of the existing environmental characteristics, impact prediction, evaluation of anticipated impact, and proposed mitigation measures. In many cases this requires not merely environmental controls but stricter planning enforcement. A major aspect of this is the need for a holistic approach, whereby environment is not merely a residual issue, but achieves a sustainable balance with development.

A range of possible indicators should therefore be assessed against specific criteria, including the ability to facilitate policy decisions. Under the categories of air quality, marine water quality, and solid waste, indicators can be translated into an understanding about the overall state of the environment at any point in time.

It is necessary to ensure that proper mechanisms are put in place, through a combination of environmental initiatives, to ensure the best creative care for the physical quality of the urban environment. This implies a high level of synergy between those responsible for lands and financial matters, transport, cultural provision, planning of the public realm, and environmental control.

Air Quality

Air quality indicators are based on various pollutants, of which the main one is Respirable Suspended Particulates (RSP), which mainly arise from traffic, industrial or power generating activities that involve a serious risk to public health. Carbon dioxide is emitted by power stations through the use of fossil fuels and contributes to the greenhouse gas effect. This is likely to rise due to increasing energy use, although it could be markedly reduced by the use of advanced combined cycle power plants using natural gas. Nitrogen dioxide and Ozone are the result of chemical reactions, the former arising through burning of fossil fuels and the latter being a secondary pollutant. These play a part in the formation of photochemical smog that can appear in response to certain atmospheric conditions and can cause serious respiratory ailments. Sprawling Asian megacities such as Beijing, Jakarta, and Delhi experience pollution at a dangerous level from toxic smog generated by power generation and traffic exhaust, particularly during the winter months. Delhi is ranked as the world's most polluted capital, with more than 13 million vehicles on the capital's roads despite an underground rail network, with road users spending up to four hours a day in traffic, and where buses share the roads with rickshaws as well as private vehicles.

Marine Water Quality

Pollution of marine waters is caused by discharges of inadequately treated waste and industrial effluent that have a direct impact on nutrient levels and therefore affect ecological conditions. As a result, the absorptive capacity of marine waters can be exceeded by polluted discharges. This can be assessed in terms of E. coli concentrations that determine health hazards, and total inorganic nitrogen concentrations that ultimately relates to ecological balance.

The latter emanates from human and animal waste and leads to eutrophication. This results in excessive plant productivity, oxygen depletion, and potential red tides as a result of nutrient accumulation, particularly in deep inlets around coastal areas.

The marine ecosystem is extremely significant in Asia. The East and South China Seas are some of the world's most productive fishing grounds, and parts of these waters are experiencing warming up to 10 times the global average. Fish is a mainstay of the regional food economy, and the depletion of key commercial species is made worse by unbridled exploitation of increasingly limited resources. Already some countries, including China, have instituted summer fishing bans in the South China Sea, and this situation is exacerbated by the prolific growth of the aquaculture industry that uses excessive amounts of fishmeal. Fisheries management strategies for marine resources need to be developed in tandem with climate-change mitigation policies.

The Need for Resilience

The ecology of urbanism is a continuing challenge during an era of concern for sustainable planning in response to climate change and rapid urbanization across Asian cities. With Asia accounting for approximately half of global carbon emissions, around USD 1.26 trillion is earmarked for projects in Asia's energy sector with the majority allocated to power projects that accelerate the global transition to renewable green energy. However, in the immediate future the use of coal and gas are likely to remain dominant, while carbon prices are well below the level needed to bring forward the low-carbon investment required for climate change mitigation through necessary technological change. This calls for an intersection between urban design, urban life, urban nature, and biodiversity, in situations where eco-collapse must be countered through various forms of resilience.

Greenhouse gas from burning of fossil fuels slows down planetary atmospheric waves and results in climatic extremes, from severe flooding to wildfires. COP1 was held in 1995 when atmospheric carbon dioxide concentration stood at 360 parts per million. By the time of COP26 this had climbed to 414 ppm with emissions rising a further 4.9 percent in 2022. The Intergovernmental Panel on Climate Change has stated that a reduction of 45 percent in global carbon emissions must be achieved by 2030 in order to achieve net zero by 2050, and limit global temperature rise to 1.5 degree Celsius. This means phasing out coal-powered generation by 2035. As it is estimated that at least 60 percent of Asian carbon emissions are derived from the low energy efficiency of existing buildings, improvements to this must be a priority, including protection from solar heat gain, and recovering waste heat for other uses.

The widespread melting of the Greenland Ice Sheet has led to a shift in hemispheric winds that carry warm air to the north, depleting sea ice. However, sea level rise is not due to melting of sea ice but from glaciers, and water expands as it gets warmer. The more precipitation in the atmosphere through warming the more ice is likely to be accumulated at the poles, but there is little notable sign of major ice-loss in Antarctica where the ice sheet is up to two miles in thickness. However, while many changes to ice sheets are irreversible, glaciers themselves have been receding for centuries. They act to accumulate water during the cold season, and feed major rivers through melting during the dry summer period, providing water for continued agricultural productivity. The world's largest ice sheet located in the East Antarctic is stable only so long as temperature rise is limited to two degrees Celsius. The ice shelves themselves, which extend into the water, act to hold back the glaciers that are thinning as a result of warming ocean water underneath. It has been estimated by scientists at NASA's Jet Propulsion Laboratory in 2022 that this process has reduced Antarctica's ice shelves by 12 trillion metric tons since 1997.

Chinese researchers have called for urgent action to protect the Tibetan Plateau and its surrounding mountain regions that represent the source of Asia's ten major rivers. It is known as the "Asian Water Tower," that delivers fresh water to almost two billion people, and accommodates most glaciers outside the Arctic and Antarctica. Climate change is accelerating glacier melt and thawing of permafrost in the region, and in the process is increasing both downstream flows of sediments and other contaminants.

Much of the Asian landscape was initially sustained by wetland and aquatic systems fed by stable groundwater discharge and periodic heavy rainfall. Coastal communities are particularly vulnerable, not necessarily from rising sea levels, but to storm surge and tropical cyclones. Flooding can also be triggered by catastrophic events such as earthquakes, volcanic action, tsunamis, and coastal erosion. This tends to effect areas that were settled precisely because of the advantages of alluvial soil conditions and sources of food so that coastal and river-side communities interfaced with the naturally protective preserve of marshlands and mangroves. As environmental concerns have increased, this has led to commensurate forms of socio-economic exclusion and contestation, with those most vulnerable inhabiting forms of temporary or stilted habitation along rivulets and coastal waterways. This requires risk mitigation strategies to counter what would, almost certainly, have a severe impact on those living in informal settlements. In a not dissimilar way, ecologically based wastewater treatment systems must prevent harm to receiving waters, as most areas are sensitive to certain chemical substances used for irrigation and farmland. It is therefore important that sustainable performance targets are established for individual development areas. The desirable end state is to create clean and reusable water from local wastewater that minimizes the use of mechanical energy and complicated infrastructure.

Contemporary urban and rural land use practices in and around Asian cities are responsible for surface water runoff that can cause both flash flooding, water quality degradation, erosion, and habitat loss. This can also act to lower the regional water table and reduce the capacity of utilizing water as a necessary resource. In many cases this needs to be corrected through restoring hydrological stability, with forms of stormwater engineering that act to absorb water and diffuse adverse impact, including the means to direct stormwater runoff, capturing of rain water, waste water recycling, canal and water filtration systems, and regeneration of vegetation areas that sustain important ecological landscapes. Integrated building and site design technologies such as recirculation and storage measures can be used in the application of resource management measures through utilizing the full extent of integrated water harvesting via porous ground treatment, infiltration and bio-retention systems related to the use of natural vegetation that reduce and cleanse water flow and enhance local aquatic systems.

As urban growth proliferates, low-lying delta areas and coastal wetlands together with high urban water tables are being threatened by uncontrolled reclamation, while previous wilderness areas or land devoted to agrarian pursuits are transformed through metropolitan growth. In Saigon, Manila, and Jakarta reclamation of low-lying and swampy land, together with impermeable surface treatment through overbuilding, challenges the prevailing ecosystem. This has tended to drain the water table creating subsidence, thereby preventing runoff and creating flood conditions.

Resilience to coastal erosion is a significant factor in future planning of the land-water interface. Mangrove forests together with tidal marshes represent a major defense against flooding, but these forests are declining through conversion to other purposes such as aquaculture, or destruction from natural hazards. A case in point is the Sundarbans, which straddle the boundaries of India and Bangladesh in West Bengal, and embraces the largest contiguous coastal mangrove forest in the world with unique ecological characteristics. It is controlled by the Ganga-Brahmaputra-Meghna river system and accommodates large rural farming populations living in coastal communities whose agrarian livelihood is threatened by regular inundation of agricultural and settlement areas. This situation is projected to worsen over coming decades. Around 58 percent of Bangladesh is less than six meters above sea level, and the country suffers from a tropical monsoon climate with three distinct seasons. Summer drought turns to a rainy season between June and September when up to two-thirds of the country is subject to flooding. The Bangladesh Delta Plan produced in 2018 proposes both flood protection and water conservation measures.

A report prepared by a UN Intergovernmental Panel on Climate Change issued in 2020 stated that as a result of human-made greenhouse gas emissions, an increasing area of coastline in Asia is now exposed to land loss, in particular the Mekong Delta, Bangladesh, Thailand, Vietnam, and large parts of Indonesia and the Philippines. In certain cities high water tables have caused particular problems. Bangkok, a city of 8.2 million built on land with a high-water table, is sinking at a rate of 30 millimeters per year due in part to the tapping of groundwater by industry. In Jakarta around 40 percent of the city has sunk below sea level, causing land subsidence. In the Philippines the same situation is affecting the coastline near the capital city, Manila. Floods in Malaysia are common during the monsoon season, and in late 2021 11,000 people were driven from their houses in Selangor, Malaysia's wealthiest and most populous region surrounding the capital Kuala Lumpur. More than 60 million people depend on Southeast Asia's largest river, the Mekong, which flows through China, Myanmar, Laos, Thailand, Cambodia, and Vietnam, but its banks are increasingly threatened by rising water levels and a loss of sediment due to upriver dams. With 20 precent of India's population living within 50 kilometers of the sea, the country's 7,500-kilometer coastline is considered to be the world's most vulnerable in terms of future impacts unless extensive mitigation measures are carried out. In Southern China's Pearl River Delta, one of the country's most important economic regions that accommodates 93 million people and includes the Special Administrative Regions of Hong Kong and Macau, much of the land is lower than the annual coastal floodline projected for 2050. A number of areas are now subject to 10-year disaster prevention schemes for key low-lying urban areas. China has brought together 17 ministries to cooperate on a national climate change adaptation strategy. Low-lying Singapore has budgeted some US$70 billion to construct barrages` and holding reservoirs in anticipation of future rises in sea levels by mid-century.

The devastating floods across some of China's longest rivers and their tributaries in 1998, caused largely by the clearing of forests to make way for available and industrial land,

necessitated a new "greening" program of sustainable forestry. Over the past 20 years several billion trees have been planted, which has helped to extend the global tree canopy by 25 percent, with forest stock projected to increase to 19 billion cubic meters by 2025. A target 88 million acres of forests are planned by mid-century, in part to stem the sandstorms that blow in from the Gobi Desert. Technically, this can significantly reduce the carbon footprint by up to one-third, and in theory should be viewed as wise investments.

An urgent re-appraisal of these aspects must address the intersection of city functions with necessary ecosystems that bind together urban parkland and cultivation requirements with flood protection, protection of biodiversity, the production of clean water, and the preservation of natural habitats.

Planning for a Sustainable Future

There is undoubtedly a high environment cost to population growth, and in the coming years the way in which this is contained is likely to be a critical indicator of environmental health. This suggests a need for all Asian countries to set out unambiguous and proactive environmental and planning objectives geared to the achievement of sustainability, and necessitates common goals with separate agendas to allow for individual programs of city building. This should act to inform the planning and development process itself, and in so doing generate actions that are most suitable for particular needs and requirements.

One solution is to capture and store the massive amount of carbon dioxide generated from major facilities such as oil refineries and chemical plants, financed by tax incentives. Other "capture and storage" initiatives applicable to heavy industry sectors such as cement, steel, and natural gas processing are arguably necessary to meet the International Energy Agency's net zero 2050 targets. However, this must be seen as complementing major green technologies such as wind and solar power, as success ultimately depends on whether carbon capture complements or undermines long-term environmental benefit.

Urban design processes must recognize and prioritize all these aspects, and ensure that efforts to reconcile the applicability of diverse sustainable policies with planning objectives do not subscribe to anti-urban policies that over-regulate and sanitize the city, reduce its sense of urbanity, and dilute the expressive potential of human activities that have always personified the Asian city. It is an inherent aspect of the sustainable agenda that it should assist inhabitants of cities to meet their needs while enhancing urban places that can stand the test of time. This is underscored by the International Union of Architects Charter that calls for an "integral architecture," sustainable and bringing together building, landscape, and city planning through the core of urban design.

One urban initiative to cushion the impact of variable temperatures, drought, and heavy rainfall is the "sponge city" concept that utilizes green water absorbing infrastructure to create water-resilient cities. These are effectively large spaces in low-lying areas that hold stormwater but also recharge groundwater for periods of drought. China has incorporated the sponge city as a national strategy aimed at recycling rainwater runoff in 80 percent of urban areas by 2030, including the cities of Beijing, Shanghai, and Shenzhen. Mini islands are created, held in place by plant roots that allow water to permeate, and during dry periods allows water to be used for plant irrigation.

To end on a positive note, new scientific discoveries perhaps point the way to future clean energy supply. Solar powered infrastructure is getting progressively cheaper in comparison with fossil fuels. While oil, natural gas, and coal are predicted to run out over the course of the next century and will command ever rising prices, by comparison, solar photovoltaic technology costs have dropped by 82 percent over the past 10 years. By 2020 more than 500,000 megawatts of solar capacity had been installed globally. In February 2022, it was announced that a green power milestone had been reached for the generation of fusion energy at the Joint European Torus facility in the UK, with the potential to deliver sustainable and low-carbon energy. In the same month a team at the Chinese Academy of Science announced that they had created a massively strong form of tungsten as part of their fusion reactor program that can be used to build the inner wall of reactors that can in turn produce an almost endless supply of clean energy through heating hydrogen gas to a temperature 10 times hotter than the core of the sun.

Achieving sustainable cities requires active citizen participation, geared toward long-term civic responsibility. Caring for places will ultimately impel us to embrace resilient environments. The word sustainable is derived from the Latin *subtenir*, meaning "to support from below." This is exactly what sustainable environments will mean in practice—something that is supported by all arms of the community in terms of care, concern, and inspiration.

ENERGY EFFICIENCY

- Utilise Renewable Energy Sources
- Energy Conservation Techniques
- Effective Site Planning
- Clean Energy
- Eco-friendly Buildings
- Plan for Pedestrians and Cycles

ECOLOGICAL PROTECTION

- Increase Green Environmental Networks
- Design with Nature
- Protect Natural Assets
- Maximise Bio-Diversity
- Preserve Habitats
- Reinforce Landscape Systems

ENVIRONMENTAL MANAGEMENT

- Reduce Pollution
- Urban Services
- Education Initiatives
- Building Maintenance
- Sensible Use of Controls
- Recycling of Materials

SUSTAINABLE URBAN DESIGN

RESPONSIVE DESIGN

- Adaptable and Resilient Building Forms
- Diversity of Uses
- Visual Quality and Legibility
- Design Places for People
- Maximise Defensible Space
- Robust and Permeable Layouts
- Preservation of Built Heritage

BUILT FORM

- Comfortable Interface with Public Realm
- Increase Densities around Activity Nodes
- Encourage Mixed-Use Developments
- Active Frontages
- Consolidate the Street Matrix
- Identifiable and Robust Features

MOVEMENT FACTORS

- Maximise Pedestrianisation
- Maximise use of Public Transport
- Encourage Route Connectivity
- Provide Modal Interchanges
- Recover Road Space for Public Use
- Maximise Linkage and Continuity

CHAPTER 9

The water margin

The majority of world cities evolved around navigable rivers, bays, and natural harbors as trading centers or deep-water ports. "New World" settlements such as the American 18th-century East Coast cities of New York, Boston, Philadelphia, Baltimore, and Charleston developed their early form and volatility as settlements built around ports and shipyards. During the 19th century the urban edge between city and water became essential production and transport staging posts, often with severe environmental consequences. As sail gave way to steam, railroads enlarged the flow of both cargo and passengers.

Urban waterfronts in older established cities played a major role in economic development, adapting to changing demands and circumstances through the 20th century as industrialization began to change their established characteristics. Shorelines and harbor fronts became increasingly complex as they had to accommodate the needs of industrial uses, along with ferry piers to accommodate the essential travel demand of workers and commuters. Seawalls and bulkheads were constructed to stabilize and regulate anchorages, docks, jetties, water basins, and rail-related land. In many cases these severed central commercial cities from their waterfronts and necessitated new surface infrastructure to service supply routes. Port operations have, in recent years, shifted to exploit necessary deep-water channels and ocean-side sites, which have affected the relationship between port and city, but have also influenced changes to the wider coastal environment, perpetually changing their functions.

As patterns of commerce began to change in the 1970s, mainly due to the inception of containerization, many older port uses and their associated facilities across the world became obsolete, leaving behind a residue of deteriorating buildings, wharves, and pier structures. In

Singapore River.

Sunda Kelapa in Jakarta dates back to its 14th-century role as a Hindu spice trading port and harbor situated on the Ciliwung River. The tradition[al] Bugis schooners continue to play a part in commercial links with cities through the archipelago.

many cases the relocation of port uses or industry from the mid-20th century led to stagnation of relatively large areas in prime locations. As waterfront industrial uses began to decline, the previously restricted "back door" of cities gradually came to be perceived as a potentially resourceful and welcoming "front door," redirecting the urban focus toward the water rather than away from it. As a result, regeneration has in many cases centered around the adaptive reuse of older structures and the integration of new ones, focused on consumption, cultural production, recreation, residential, and commercial uses. In most cases the built residue of heritage capital in the form of older industrial and warehouse buildings created opportunities to reposition and reconnect these areas. Many precincts were in close proximity to the wider activity setting, including growing business and residential cores, and were thereby able to meet demands for a range of new uses with a high degree of history and local identity.

Change in port activity, trade and shipping modes from the mid-20th century have reshaped the relationship between urban waterfronts and their home cities. This has also had

...e original shape
..the harbor at Sunda Kalapa
.now occupied by informal
..uctures, wooden piers,
..d fishing boats.

economic consequences for the city-region through a new infrastructure of goods, movement, and cargo terminals relatively impervious to other urban functions, but also the spatial reorganization associated with the reconnection between city, and newly available land and water in a more social sense. In the process the maritime connection has not been entirely lost. The urban design challenge is therefore about reconnection and the integration of new or regenerated physical forms that positively exploit opportunities available at multiple scales and involving many organizational networks and inter-dependencies associated with the reincorporation of the post-industrial landscape.

In general, the inspiration for new waterfront development, wherever it has occurred in recent years, has been closely linked with urban regeneration projects that had to overcome challenges of isolation that included preliminary interventions. These in turn established a new interrelationship between different uses. Contemporary forms of urban waterfront regeneration began in the USA where projects activated a sequence of new uses associated with the water edge, based on comfort, safety, and an optimization of sensory experiences for public consumption.

Across Asia, where the majority of large cities were settled and developed through their accessibility to navigable water bodies, harbors provided for new avenues of trade and immigration. Coastal seaports acted as terminals for a variety of purposes in a not dissimilar way to

their counterparts in the West, forming gateways that opened up countries and continents. In many cases these became outposts of Western entrepreneurialism that often disguised colonizing intentions that capitalized on existing port communities and their economic hinterlands.

The functions of urban waterfronts in Asia continue to reflect the characteristics, culture, and requirements of individual cities, which vary considerably. Large cities such as the Hong Kong SAR, Tokyo, Singapore, Seoul, and a number of cities elsewhere in China have long focused on international trade and were reliant on good accessibility through rail and road construction to support urban growth. Much unencumbered waterfront land turned to temporary uses such as storage of coal, oil, surface parking, and other municipal needs that required easy accessibility, while others were given over to single uses such as shipping, fishing, and commerce. From the mid-20th century, waterfront locations on the urban fringe of Asian cities also became reclaimed for essential large-scale uses such as new airports and ancillary facilities to avoid loud noise levels over settled areas.

The success of waterfront regeneration efforts ultimately depends on factors such as geographical location, environmental context, heritage qualities, the configuration and depth of water resources, and the opportunities determined by what is static and what aspects can be re-shaped. These dictate the types and potential range of water-related uses, and areas of possible conflict. The current emphasis on parkland and recreational uses associated with lagoons and marine uses such as boating stations have a more visual and functional relationship with water as its central element, and a number of cities have established authorities to manage

The Singapore River has been at the heart of the city's development since 1819 as the commercial lifeline of the emerging entrepôt. It has evolved from working quaysides to the site of major public buildings, leisure, and activity zones, such as Clarke Quay linked to Riverside Point and the Read Bridge.

and regulate these activities. In some cases there might exist problems over fragmented ownership and restricted property rights so that port authorities must exert management control over local operations, particularly over land use factors and means of cargo transfer.

Land resource is a further factor in terms of both area and extent, together with the ability in some cities to extend the waterfront edge through reclamation where land shortage is acute. This represents a reflection of both rapid economic change and opportunity in line with social forces and the need for places of urban vitality, but also social space and livability as city populations multiply. The city edge then becomes a city limit that demarcates a new and challenging boundary between entirely differentiated entities—outward rather than inward facing, and invested with potential for new and multiple meanings that act to counter the diffusion of the inner city, adding a new but occasionally contested dimension to the public realm. Many Asian cities have shorelines, rivers, and harbors that effectively act as linear channels for urban expansion, with opportunities for revitalized urban or recreational edges that wrap around the cities themselves. The inland boundaries can vary considerably and apart from abandoned port or industrial buildings, might also include underused or abandoned government, institutional, and community structures that embody older architectural configurations that can be repurposed.

The Hong Kong SAR has 80 kilometers of predominantly reclaimed waterfront around its central Victoria Harbour that are being slowly opened up to pedestrian access, while its reclamation of shallow bays in various parts of the New Territories accommodates new town development with waterfront parks and promenades. Over some 30 years, Singapore has added 40 percent of its land area through an extensive reclamation program. From 2010 the Singapore government has cultivated an upgrading program along the Singapore River as one of the region's most prominent waterfront regeneration initiatives, linking this with an outer harbor waterfront around Marina Bay. Its revitalization of Boat Quay adjacent to the Central Business District now forms part of a system of promenades around an aquatic park and was made possible by new port development that replaced the role of the old fleet of lighters that used to occupy the basin.

Characteristic Development Patterns

Two distinct development patterns characterize the Asian waterfront city, and some cities display elusive evidence of both:

— Cities located along one or more major waterways, or a central harbor:

· The Hong Kong SAR, where the urban area itself is bisected by a central harbor that acts as the physical setting for commercial, residential, recreational, port, and maritime activities;
· Guangzhou, the major city of Guangdong Province, is situated on the north bank of the Pearl River, which branches off the East and West Rivers. The Pearl River Delta consists of a number of Southern China cities including Shenzhen, Zhuhai, Foshan, Dongguan, Zhongshan, Jiangmen, and Nansha;
· Shanghai lies at the mouth of the Huangpu River with the bay of Hangzhou to the south. Hangzhou situated on the West Yue Lake is, by way of contrast, an example of China's traditional integration of water in its design;
· Bangkok on the Chao Phrya River, the established heart of the city once made up of waterways or "kongs," and which flows to the Gulf of Thailand;
· Phnom Penh bordering the Bassac River—a distributary of the Tonlé Sap and the Mekong River;
· Hanoi on the Red River that received its name of "Between the Rivers" in the Nguyen dynasty;
· Taiwan Region of China, which sits on an ancient basin, bounded by the Xindian and Tamsui rivers, south of the port city of Keelung;
· Delhi, whose main source of water is the Yamuna River that feeds into the Agra Canal to the south;
· Kolkata on the Hooghly River, which empties into the mouth of the Ganges at the Bay of Bengal;
· Kuala Lumpur, which lies at the confluence of the Gombak and Klang rivers, with its translated name meaning "muddy confluence"; and
· Singapore, on the Kallang River, which flows into the Kallang Basin.

— Cities that have grown along an expansive shoreline or bays:

· Manila, which occupies the plain of the Pasig River that flows into Manila Bay;
· Mumbai on Salsette Island, which lies at the mouth of the Ulhas River, and is bounded by the Arabian Sea;
· Macao SAR, which is situated on a peninsula on the western side of the Pearl River estuary with offshore islands of Taipa, Hengqin, and Coloane in the South China Sea;
· Georgetown in Penang, Malaysia, which is the seaport to St. George's Bay;

- Seoul, which sits on the Han River, the fourth longest river on the Korean Peninsula that runs to the Yellow Sea; and
- Jakarta, which developed around Teluk Jakarta and receives the flow of 13 rivers.

The relationship between a city and its waterfront is dependent on a combination of access conditions, shoreline patterns, environmental quality, and historical or cultural resources. A further factor in activating older waterfronts is the functional dependency of existing uses on the water frontage, and the extent to which these can contribute to regeneration in a compatible way. This can include essential amenities such as marine moorings, ferry piers, and terminals that might be combined with new public-oriented uses as recreational resources and can also serve to attract private investment and development allocated and integrated within a landscape open space framework, such as a fisherman's wharf or festival market. Such attractions can positively utilize the spatial resources of heritage structures that might include adaptive reuse and renovation of older industrial complexes, warehouses, wharves, and redundant municipal structures in terms of physical upgrading and support systems for new uses such as retail, commercial, entertainment, and residential units.

An important urban design aspect is visual interest and character, where waterfronts can be seen and appreciated from a variety of topographic features and urban spaces, and from the water itself. In particular, new waterfront buildings should complement the horizontal configuration of the land-water edge, in contrast to the vertical elements of the city behind. This contrast can be taken further in terms of building textures that best relate to the pedestrian realm, perceived in relation to distance, elevation, and movement. Features such as marina and ferry structures can stimulate interest together with the novelty of landmark focal points such as tall ship moorings.

As waterfront control mechanisms prevail in different contexts, development plans must respect geographic locations, and established boundaries. In this sense it is important that government jurisdictions dedicate and safeguard sites for public use, so that berths and other marine related facilities form part of promenades and associated open space. Equally, water quality must be the responsibility of Environmental Protection Agencies within coastal zone boundaries. In the Hong Kong SAR water pollution control ordinances are in place that govern aspects such as recreational use, navigation, shipping, and aesthetic enjoyment. Sensitive receivers include areas of ecological importance, marine life, beaches, and localized aspects such as the presence of natural habitats. In addition, waterfront uses must also accommodate sea water intakes and measures to deal with the dispersion of discharges, erosion, and tidal flows.

Waterfront character can
be emphasized by permanent
or temporary moorings for tall
ships, redolent of their older
maritime history.

In 2019, Singapore's Maritime and Port Authority developed a single information platform for consolidating marine, coastal, and land data and built a virtual twin of the city's marine and coastal space that allows data to be presented in both 2D and 3D formats. This assists in both monitoring of its coastal environment and facilitating planning of new waterfront areas and engineering works, together with conservation of marine biodiversity.

Remaking an existing older waterfront can consolidate the image of a city and act as an effective catalyst for city regeneration. For example, the Bund in Shanghai with its distinctive 1920s art deco and neoclassical buildings fronting wide promenades remains as the image of the city on the Huangpu River. Shanghai grew from a Tang dynasty fishing village to become the busiest Chinese port by the mid-19th century when it became a foreign concession area. After 1949 it became the industrial powerhouse of China but during the 1980s the city began to remove older industrial facilities along the riverfront through a transfer of land rights to raise capital for urban construction. It also commenced a program of improvement to the intersecting rivers and creeks that form a matrix of water features throughout the city. The Pudong area across the river from the old city was established under a new area administration in 1993 including a new port, a Finance and Trade Zone, and a new international airport. At the same time the waterfront along the Bund was reconstructed with the incorporation of an elevated riverbank that serves as both a promenade and a flood protection barrier. The accompanying regeneration of the river front and Suzhou Creek in the heart of the city forms part of an extensive parkland system, with scope for improvement of water quality, the preservation of historic buildings, and redevelopment of the old port properties. As a result the waterfront forms the image of the city, and a node of cultural and civic life.

Rising sea levels as a result of global warming also indicate a future where the land-water interface must be protected, which offers a further design challenge in reinforcing established partially enclosed water bodies, which themselves suggest opportunities to re-position forms of activity that are best able to recapture necessary investment through material incentives. A further factor is the relatively recent deployment of international waterfront networks such as the *Centro Internationale Città d Acqua* in Venice that act to reinforce necessary avenues of information exchange between cities.

Development Opportunities

A significant factor in the development or regeneration of urban waterfronts is that of improving environmental quality through clean-up operations as part of their new functional role. As urban area populations steadily increase, these factors become increasingly important.

The three phases of pre-development activity are overall project analysis, project planning, and project packaging, directed toward identifying opportunities and constraints, testing of alternatives, and establishing a strategy and program that satisfies both public and private interests. While a public-private partnership with a business-oriented outlook can involve different approaches for overall project development, the most conventional way forward is public-sector management, with a subsequent public-private joint venture agreement that must serve to make the proposal financially secure.

The Singapore River is spanned by a series of bridges. The Cavenagh Bridge is the oldest bridge across the river. It was named after the last governor of Singapore before it became a Crown Colony. The bronze sculptural figures evoke the memory of more recreational pastimes along the river.

While the economic conditions relating to existing waterfront uses are relatively straight-forward, the application of urban design initiatives are largely dependent on strategic development policies, and the condition or underutilization of an existing urban waterfront in response to its potential land value in meeting public sector objectives. This can dictate the complexity of development initiatives, and subsequently the priority given to amenity over economic priorities. In this regard, a number of requirements must be met including necessary public services, regulatory conditions including zoning and building approvals, design parameters regarding overall criteria in relation to different land-use parcels, attraction to investors, phasing, and the achievement of critical mass.

e resurrected waterways
the Qinhuai River that forms
rt of the Fuzi Miao heritage
ecinct in Nanjing.

Public sector development initiatives include the establishment of an overall management structure; specific zoning for preservation, redevelopment, regeneration, and mixed use; new or improved transit systems, including land exchanges; and favorable financing and taxation policies. The latter is of particular significance in stimulating the recovery of deteriorated or abandoned areas where federal programs might be necessary to fund new site formation, clearance, and service infrastructure. This is particularly so when special heritage districts are part of waterfront proposals. Specific goals for these areas are to widen the economic base, realize cultural potential through new uses, revitalize the wider city quarter, and preserve its historic character as a destination for visitors.

Space users such as hotel groups and cultural facility operators can also initiate development projects that might act as catalysts to stimulate further investment in amenities associated with the waterfront. This must combine both technical capabilities and financial resources with specialist experience necessary to handle design, marketing, engineering factors, and property management. A further organizational option is the establishment of a waterfront development corporation, either profit or non-profit oriented, in which property owners and member of the business and institutional community, together with relevant arms of government, can participate. This increases the ability to coordinate public and private actions and acknowledges that waterfront "destinations" require continuing investment from the private sector to meet the objectives of diversity and vitality that adequately reflect market forces. In so doing it is necessary to take into consideration the public contribution to the project, and cooperation through the design refinement and development period. It is particularly important to take into account interfaces with neighboring land and water uses.

Formulation of the development strategy itself must be receptive to the local social and economic context that might well involve certain trade-offs in order to finalize proposals and schedules for refinement prior to implementation. This should involve a detailed market analysis to include population trends, employment projections, origin/destination characteristics, and the likely demand for specific uses, in particular those that are water dependent. Planning and engineering analysis must in most cases extend to civil and structural investigations to assess immediate and long-range implications of land formation, reinforcement, and maintenance, particularly for water-related structures in the face of potentially corrosive environmental forces.

Necessary attributes are the characteristics and special amenities offered by the site that enhances its situation. An interconnected pedestrian environment, historic references, and an active land-water relationship can attract prime owners and tenants, where proximity offers

The drawbridge across the Ciliwung River in Jakarta was built in 1628 to connect the Dutch and English forts. It was known originally as Jembatan Pasar Ayam— The Chicken Market Bridge.

Urban recovery
The Cheonggyecheon
river in Seoul both restored
and transformed an ancient
watercourse along a central
line through the city
It involved the removal of
highway and re-programming
of traffic movement.

Waterfront destinations must accommodate a mix of uses and, where appropriate, heritage buildings that create a distinctive identity and over diversity.

all-round advantages, including a complementary mix of uses that optimize overall value. In particular, buildings should frame outward views to the water and can also act to define view corridors to existing urban features and the central urban area. Meandering or undulating walkways that offer a multitude of sequential visual experiences, together with a variety of public spaces, enhances pedestrian expectations. This can be increased through extensions over the water edge through quays or piers that house different attractions and distinguish the spatial setting and configuration of the waterfront alignment. Lighting is also important in emphasizing the nighttime atmosphere, in harmony with the setting and the promotion of its activities.

Existing urban waterfronts, including redundant or degraded areas, are nevertheless subject to regulatory and permit issues that meet the prevailing jurisdictional structure. Water itself is a resource that is likely to involve overlapping agencies and authorities. The more stringent the development controls over such fragile resources, the more that imaginative proposals can be stifled. It is in the public interest to control the process, and the production of urban design parameters can ensure that all participants and subscribers are responsive to available opportunities for cooperation. Water dependent uses must also achieve variety, contrast, and diversity while protecting public interests. Water-related uses include fishing industries, seafood markets, aquariums, marina-related activities, and single-user terminals that can be determined by site characteristics and prevailing economic conditions.

As waterfront development presents continuing challenges in Asian cities, new initiatives require forward vision that meets the demands for new uses, and the potential for further economic opportunities. As cities continue to grow in terms of population and with employment in new technologies, economic revitalization of undervalued waterfront sites is likely to offer continuing opportunities that contribute to the notion of livable cities.

Several constants can be listed as being necessary for waterfront revitalization while enhancing urban quality:

- Appropriation of the required area by the city as a prerequisite to opening up the waterfront as a public amenity;
- A common unitary sense to the different parts, both physical and functional;
- A multiple range of activities, including those that reference older and original uses;
- Pedestrian access channels linking the core city to the waterfront, together with modes of public land and water transport;
- An acceptable limit on vehicular traffic, helping to prioritize the waterfront as a predominantly pedestrian zone of activity;
- Maximization of water quality in order to encourage the development of multiple uses that touch the water;
- Encapsulation of outward views to the city and water; and
- Use of distinctive urban features relating to the existing waterfront whenever possible; including heritage buildings, piers, and wharves that can be converted to new uses.

The Need for Design Parameters

In major cities a Waterfront Authority can best be established through special legislation as an "enterprise zone" to drive the development agenda and might be exempt from normal planning controls. The bulk of the public realm might then be designed and constructed by the government with individual component uses by the private sector. This would reinforce opportunities for both public attraction but also necessary revenue, generating returns for investors

for large-scale uses such as hotels and commercial business functions that create opportunities for local employment and visitation. If it is considered cost-effective, cultural uses might include an aquarium or maritime museum with an orientation that embraces the waterfront, harbor, or bay, reflecting sea-going history and heritage.

To meet the criteria set out above, more is needed than a Development Plan in order to ensure as far as possible that overall urban design intentions, including multi-facetted and occasionally indeterminate aspects, can be achieved in practice. It is necessary to establish, in three dimensions, the underlying urban structure on which the land utilization and patterns of activities are based, but this must be geared to the achievement of a responsive overall solution. However, urban design must extend beyond this, and create opportunities for activities to happen naturally, or by chance. It is also important not to make the design process too prescriptive.

An informal level of complexity must at the same time ensure a fundamental order but can also be imbued with a variety of features that denote local character and encourage a degree of exploration. A vocabulary of design criteria can therefore be formulated that reflects local culture, economic conditions, and a necessary interplay between urban elements, in situations where implementation of neighboring sites might only take place over a number of years. Preliminary concept plans should therefore incorporate urban design requirements together with key connections and linkages that establish the interrelationship of use in three dimensions but allow for innovative interpretations in the mix and type of economic activities as a creative springboard for more detailed design.

ngqiao River
s constructed in Qingdao
ring the late 19th century.
e octagonal Huilange (wave-
pling) Pavilion was added
the 1930s.

Design parameters can be supplemented by guidelines, models, interpretive sketches, and CAD imagery, and shifts the emphasis on design control from a preoccupation with regulatory standards and prohibitions to community concerns for a dynamic public realm. A conceptual approach to spatial configuration that incorporates primary nodes, main retail avenues, and view corridors together with contextual information, is intended to convey an articulate urban design intention to which all participants can subscribe so that the whole is greater than the sum of the parts. Plans and design notes for individual tender sites establish development boundaries, access points, and necessary links to adjoining areas together with plot ratio, site coverage, height limitations, service requirements, and landscape responsibilities with regard to public areas at ground level. Design and disposition clauses can then be inserted in lease conditions as part of eventual tender procedures that should give special consideration to the criteria associated with both design and price. Urban design thereby becomes a means of reconciling private investment with public interests, as part of ongoing planning, implementation, and management. This should also be focused on the revitalization of neighboring older mixed-use areas with strong social and economic characteristics.

Essential Principles Derived from Non-Asian Cities

The first generation of urban waterfront transformation in the 1960s was on the American east coast cities that had retained a large part of their historic fabric. In this sense this reversed a long process of decline. The second phase in the late 1970 heralded a more global approach led by Sydney, Toronto, Cape Town, and Barcelona that were equally ambitious in their scope. This was followed by the establishment of the London Docklands Development Corporation in 1980, charged with the renewal of eight square miles of obsolete 19th-century warehouses, many of which were listed as heritage structures along with surrounding water basins in the East End of the capital. This entailed a series of local plans with the commercial business core of Canary Wharf at its center served by a new mass-transit rail line.

The third phase of large-scale historic waterfront preservation occurred in European cities including Amsterdam in Holland, Hamburg in Germany, together with Melbourne in Australia, Vancouver in Canada, Havana in Cuba, and Genoa in Italy that have capitalized on a new-found value of conservation-led regeneration as part of socially inclusive and sustainable strategies. In the United States, Europe, and elsewhere new waterfront destinations have formed part of downtown rejuvenation strategies—acting as an economic but also a cultural stimulus to growing communities—that go some way to answering the perennial question of who benefits. In fact, in some American cities one of the problems has been managing overcrowding on new waterfront amenities. All of these created precedents for an extension of waterfront regeneration initiatives to the context of Asian cities that speak to the future as well as the past.

As a starting point it is necessary to identify what the potential urban values are, and what can sustain them in terms of urban functions associated with the pedestrian level of activity—the transactional businesses on which Asian cities thrive, and that provide for interaction with people through genuinely mixed-use areas and which encourage the continuation of street life, diversity, and vitality.

If we use the example of American cities, where only five out the 75 largest cities are not associated with some kind of waterfront, the regeneration of derelict or abandoned buildings has been associated, in almost every case, with the revitalization of prominent downtown areas. However, it was not until the late 20th century that the effective re-use of what we might term industrial archelogy was adopted as a desirable means of reconciling heritage and memory of the city with practicable conservation as part of a collective approach to a new urban identity.

Urban waterfront regeneration in America began with the Fisherman's Wharf development in San Francisco, followed by a re-imaging of the Faneuil Hall/Quincy Market in Boston completed in 1978; the National Historical Park in Lowell; Baltimore Harborplace in 1980; New York's South Street Seaport in 1982; and Miami's Bayside Marketplace in 1987. Funding came from a combination of public and private finance. The introduction of Urban Development Action Grants provided for creative partnerships based on differing ratios of federal and private funding, with some injection of funds from the city. The essential key to success in these locations was to assemble land, including old buildings of some heritage value, to allow for a genuine mix of uses that helped the process of gentrification, bringing with them new residents, users and visitors. This in turn provided for an increased diversity of uses, easy accessibility and a distinctive type of new urban identity that has, in some cases, come to personify the image of the newly revitalized city. In general this has involved a determined political drive together with a positive urban development strategy which has brought new life and employment to downtown areas.

San Francisco began to undertake the regeneration of its waterfront wharves, warehouses, and railroad terminals around the bay area in the 1960s. This included the old chocolate factories of Ghiradelli Square that date back to the mid-19th century, and the Cannery, an old fruit packing plant. These form a collection of cafés, specialty retail shops, and related maritime attractions in a pedestrian environment that helps to attract a range of incidental uses and performers. A necessary evaluation of all these factors inspired the perception that the right balance of uses, set within an attractive spatial setting, could attract a high level of use from visitors and tourists that could set in train wider economic revitalization initiatives. Mission Bay represents the largest urban regeneration project in the city, adjacent to what used to be old rail marshalling yards and shipping terminals.

An important aspect of successful regeneration is the organizational body. The Boston Redevelopment Authority was established to manage the redevelopment of the waterfront and began with the redevelopment of Scullay Square, the older maritime quarter. Quincey Market was subject to a refurbishment program in the 1970s and linked to the waterfront by a new walkway and Columbus Park. The Fitzgerald Expressway, built between the downtown area and the waterfront, has been replaced by an underground roadway, with landscaped open parkland above to consolidate the relationship between the built-up area and the waterfront. The refurbishment of two older buildings, Faneuil Hall and the old State House was carried out in 1992. Together these provided a critical mass of attractions close to the waterfront, central business, and hotel district. The Authority successfully orchestrated a refurbishment program from some of the old waterfront warehouses, with a mix of condominium and low-income housing. A similar project was negotiated for the Charlestown Navy Yard, where the former barrack blocks have been converted into housing.

In New York the Fulton Street Market and South Street Seaport is situated in the old maritime area centered around the fish market and warehouse areas, covering a number of street blocks. The regeneration strategy was subject to an urban design master plan, with the objectives of reclaiming part of the river edge to create an activity center and public concourse related to a new setting for the Seaport Museum's collection of old ships. The Pier 17 structure and waterfront open space are built on reconstructed footings, with a structure that evokes the maritime history of the waterfront, with a series of terraces, open plazas, and a visual transparency between internal and external areas. The development has acted as a catalyst for private sector regeneration of adjoining street blocks.

Regeneration of Baltimore's inner harbor, once occupied by shipyards and steel mills, began in 1962 with the construction of new promenades and a dock for an old "tall ship" frigate. Harborplace, the two-story festival market, was completed in 1982. Its overall design and the World Trade Center and aquarium provides a focal point alongside the inner harbor with direct access from the downtown area. Part of the master plan involved the refurbishment of the adjoining older residential areas whereby derelict properties were sold at a nominal price on condition that they were rehabilitated within two years with low interest loans from the Housing and Urban Development Department. In this sense, projects that generate a new and highly visible image together with significant economic benefits to the city, tend to be

reliant on public-private partnerships with substantial public subsidies. These can succeed in acting as a catalyst to encourage a buoyant sense of purpose for both community organizations and city authorities.

The downtown area of Pittsburgh is divided into different sections at the confluence of the Allegheny, Monongahela, and Ohio rivers that provide around 50km of waterfront area. Part of the city's success has been the preservation and refurbishment of old buildings through the History and Landmarks Foundation set up in 1964, with a program of heritage building, conservation, and restoration for new uses. This was followed by the construction of waterfront landscape and parkland in the 1970s, largely through linking the greening policy to privately built commercial development.

Potential for Waterfront Regeneration in Asian Cities

In Asia, where more than 80 percent of major cities are located either along or around rivers, bays, harbors, and shorelines, most cites share many of the same values. As these have experienced significant population growth over several decades, social values have risen in concert with increased density and smart city initiatives. This has often been accompanied by sprawling development that continues to consume land and natural resources at a growing rate. At the same time older working waterfronts and derelict facilities along shorelines represent something of a final frontier for new and retrofitted destinations, with challenges for new urban placemaking offering opportunities for turning negative situations into rejuvenated and affordable locales, and as magnets for visitation.

A number of old Batavian houses are still located alongside the Kali Besar Canal in the Kula district of Jakarta. The brick townhouse on the corner site was built for the Governor General Van Imhoff in 1730 and acted as the Naval Academy from 17 to 1755.

The means to rejuvenate waterfront character might be elusive but is necessary in establishing urban variety and heterogeneity. It is dependent on generating atmosphere and contrast and even deliberate disorder, creating opportunities for spontaneity rather than prescriptive zoning, incongruity rather than sameness, and transparency rather than self-containment. Pedestrian precincts and promenades serve to unite portions of the site with individual features and gathering areas and should reflect local cultural traditions and associations with the past that allow passive interludes for reflection away from the busy city. Geography is an underlying determinant in terms of both the available site form, and its real or potential relationship with the core city itself. Urban waterfronts can come in separate forms, as coherent extensions to an existing urban area; as places to exhibit cultural uses; as part of wetland restoration programs; as a means of conserving historic but often redundant uses such as wharves; as an opportunity to protect and green the city edge with a fully accessible recreational focus; or as a mixed-use amalgam of some or all these that exhibit an appreciation of urban values. There also remains a potential need to protect against flood inundation from wave action and rising water levels.

Waterfronts in themselves are not enough to guarantee automatic success either commercially or from an urban design standpoint. The essential key to success in these locations has been to assemble land, including old buildings, with some heritage value; to accommodate a genuine mix of uses and a distinctive type of urban identity that attract existing residents, new users, and visitors; and which provide for diversity of uses within a predominantly pedestrian environment. Above all there must be a positive urban development strategy that tackles the underlying conditions and objectives realistically. Dynamic mixed development and regeneration do not happen by chance or by giving too much freedom to the whim of developers without some overall design guidance.

artially enclosed water bodies
ate opportunities to establish
w forms of waterfront
creational activity.

From the above we can extract certain initiatives relevant to all Asian cities:

- The preservation of older buildings of character and heritage, with new and public-oriented uses, that can help to provide strong neighborhood identity and induce a sense of belonging;
- Waterfront revitalization projects that improve the city image and act as a catalyst for renewed confidence in business and private oriented improvements;
- The need for urban design parameters for all new development sites that provide for a consistency of the overall architectural approach;
- Public funding to assist waterfront revitalization and upgrading that encompass improved landscape, new open spaces, and pedestrian circulation; and
- The incorporation of cultural uses that can, through their physical presence, social attributes, and community interface, engender a new and progressive image.

A key feature of large scale and recreationally oriented waterfronts is some kind of market focus that adds a symbolic identity to the location, visually linked with the central water body and functionally directed toward boat docking facilities as a central fulcrum that can play an essential role in the evolving waterfront community. Its design can be new build or retrofitted from an older heritage building. A striking feature, such as a festival market, works positively in matching downtown needs by complementing these rather than competing with them. The design should represent an interplay of internal circulation spaces and external terraces that accommodate a variety of establishments focused largely on cafés, restaurants, and specialty retail outlets. Its openness and permeability draw on the strength of traditional markets, harbor orientation, and accessibility to marine activities alongside, forming an essential catalyst for other related uses that form a critical mass of attractions centered around local retailers, arts, and crafts.

In certain high-profile locations there is likely to be various consent and decision-making authorities, including planning and maritime boards. In order to expedite development this might require the establishment of a Development or Foreshore Authority to reconcile the partial continuation of working waterfronts, such as quays and ferry wharves, with recreation uses and pedestrian promenades.

The ancient name of Benares in India's Utter Pradesh state was revived in 1947 to again became Varanasi. The city is said to be the home of the Hindu god Shiva, but has also played a significant part in the development of Buddhism. It lies on the left bank of the River Ganges and is one of the seven sacred cities of Hinduism, where pilgrims bathe in the river before worshiping Shiva.

An effective transformation of redundant uses revolves around the issue of place in the city and the continuing interface between urban design and regulatory frameworks, between land price and incentive subsidies, between commerce and culture, and between mega-projects and diversity. Indirectly it also touches on heritage, memory, historical processes, and a wide community of interests. Above all there is likely to be is a prolonged or constant tension between public and private interests, the first concerned with civic responsibility, and the second with necessary investment and returns. The urban design task is therefore to resolve a multiplicity of criteria within a forum of public debate.

Waterfront projects must be focused on a reconstructed place imagery and variety of uses that can attract ongoing investment while marketing the city's resources in a 21st-century competition with other cities. Architecture itself can therefore be a contested force in creating an authentic identity based on both urban design vision and the inclusive integration of older and re-branded entities. This invests new areas with public meaning for increasingly cosmopolitan societies, sustained by horizontal connections, through a mix of functions and dense pedestrian networks that capture the synergy of urban life through a mix of functions. In turn this encourages a symbolic conglomeration of uses and carries the potential of sustaining cultural and social capital.

The attraction of urban waterfronts as places of pleasure is rooted in a complex set of associations and symbolic identities. Not the least of these is their role as a means of liberation from the spatial containment of the city. It embodies a frontier that embraces the promiscuous Japanese ideal of the floating world to the water markets of Bangkok, the bay area of Singapore, and the dramatic Bund of Shanghai, all of which establish territorial boundaries and unleash creative energies associated with different site and water conditions. The surplus value of these must satisfy governments, investors, and citizens—the newly enabled consumers of urban space.

An important aspect is integration with its wider context, including a mix of housing types to achieve an intersection of social and functional public places, with a diversity of both formal and informal design solutions to achieve an identifiable urban character through patterns of experiences and events—something that Charles Jencks has referred to as "enigmatic signifiers." As new development itself impacts on urban character and historic references, this suggests an incremental approach to retrofit with height and massing controls that exclude a complete design transformation but emphasize an intersection between environmental performance and architectural expression. Urban design strategies must therefore be geared to maintaining or creating visionary urban character just as much as protecting and preserving it. This is the essential basis of place-making and the consolidation of better urban futures.

Good urban design of waterfronts must challenge community expectations, but also market precedents, in establishing new identities and values to meet changing suppositions that address issues stemming from climate change, and embrace opportunities associated with developing technologies. Kim Dovey in *Fluid City* stresses that the word "opportunity" is derived from *portus*, which both literally and appropriately translates as "the wind blowing into the harbor," indicating a gateway for new and possibly necessary ideas. Urban design is essentially a public activity, but it is also multi-disciplinary, and therefore implicated in prevailing political priorities, imposed control systems, the position of privileged or sequestered interests, and the ebbs and flows of market forces. Other more ambiguous factors to be resolved include existing communities whose self-interests are threatened, and prevailing reluctance on the part of older established communities to accept the inevitability of changing urban narratives.

CHAPTER 10

Spiritual heritage and sacred places

Sacred sites focus largely on spiritual associations, but have a large bearing on education and environmental factors. The sacred place associated with religious denomination does not necessarily indicate major societal forces, but a continuity of devotional practice that helps to shape cultural and social expression in different situations while respecting the plurality of traditions and their display. To a significant extent the sacred place represents a timeless construct in the face of change and accelerated economic growth in an increasingly competitive global context, where culture and tradition are largely marginalized from development activities.

Sacred places are the lens that we use to counter the secular forces of modernism, investing these special areas with a metaphysical intensity of spirituality that permeates through most Asian societies. An interpretive analysis must therefore seek to connect cosmological considerations about the origin of reality with presuppositions that act to shape fundamental values in regard to the natural environment. The designation of place as sacred or holy reflects both the spiritual characteristics of association with a deity or an event, along with the characteristics of the physical setting itself. This acts to link the natural world with the creationist process, with religion serving as a forceful bridge between time and space. In Buddhist practice this can also be linked to geomantic identification of auspicious environments. In Asia this provides for a cultural landscape that encompasses heritage and memory, even as cities continue to subsume rural migrants, transnational communities, and imperial points of reference.

Belief in the sacred goes beyond customs, legends, and traditions and as a heterogeneous entity it defies uniformity. Reality in terms of a single sacred place can be considered as an expressive consequence of a single established belief system. This arguably represents something

et Shrine, Bangkok.

Religious architecture in Myanmar stems from the continuous tradition of Buddhism, where acts of devotion are reflected in orna… design forms in the Shwedag… Stupas are located in central positions, while the *pyat-that* typifies the link between anci… royalty and Buddhism.

The stepped approach to the Shwedagon Pagoda in Yangon.

There are four approaches from the cardinal directions, with eight planetary posts around the base. Above this are the plinth and three terra… Pavilions and *zeidis* or golden pagodas amalgamate around the base of the central stupa.

beyond ordinary powers and therefore introduces an act of faith toward a "higher being" on the part of a devotional following, bound together by belief, ritual, and worship. This can nevertheless include both monotheistic and polytheistic faiths.

The temple is part of the Asian city heritage, but also encompasses its multiculturalism, interweaving the spiritual with secular, cultural and civic priorities, and where the essential importance of ritual forms a lingering empathy with the wider community. This must logically exclude belief systems such as atheism, which rejects a higher being's existence; agnosticism, which embraces uncertainty over this; and existentialism, which emphasizes subjective experience. However, temple compounds are used not merely for religious gatherings but for festivals and meeting places that extend to the management and maintenance of buildings and spaces.

According to a 2015 report on religious affiliation by the Pew Research Center, around 31 percent of the global population claim to be Christian, around 24 percent Muslim, 15 percent Hindu, and 7 percent Buddhist, with the remainder either belonging to other religions or unaffiliated. This does not necessarily translate into firm adherents, as geographic differences also play a major role in patterns of religious beliefs. For example, the majority of Hindus and Buddhists are in the Asia-Pacific region, while globally Islam is the fastest growing religious group.

The main religions that gave rise to sacred places in Asia were Buddhism, Confucianism, Taoism, Islam, Hinduism, Judaism, Shinto, Sikhism, and Christianity where space, design, and disposition are important factors. Architectural treatment itself reflects the different emphasis of worship, from the ornateness of Gothic cathedrals with their decorative and perpendicular emphasis, to the elaborate carving of Hindu religious structures, and the Buddhist temples,

pagodas, and monasteries devoted to different deities. Religious belief systems are to be found in all countries across Asia and reflect a persistent aspect of social society that permeates the cultural realm of cities through temple compounds, mosques, churches, monasteries, pagodas, gurdwaras, and shrines, where symbolism is a derivation of faith. In most parts of Asia religion is a determined and binding part of mainstream culture, exerting a unifying force on society and one where beliefs can be said to condition behavioral norms. Buddhism is most common in Central Asia, Islam in South Asia and the Middle East, Hinduism is predominant in India, and Christianity dominant in certain areas of previous European settlement such as the Philippines. Historical buildings fuse together culture and religion, demonstrably marked by the interaction of art, architecture, and the fervor of local communities.

Certain religions, including Christianity, have complex and hierarchical organizational systems, while others such as Buddhism, Taoism, and Confucianism are more philosophical, so that their imprint on society is markedly different. It must also be recognized that contemporary religious practice embraces considerable diversity, including pervasive "fundamental" and feudal forms that have a substantial overlap with social, gender, and revolutionary conditions. Increasing secularization in the cities continues to re-align past allegiances and in the process re-shapes urban values in the face of materialism and consumerism. This increasingly defines Asian society, sometimes creating a precarious balance between state and religion, but at the same time underscoring the significance of religious dynamics. The Silk Road, established during the Han Dynasty, introduced Islamic traditions into China as well as establishing trading links with its commodities of silk and spices. Buddhist beliefs and practices were introduced into China and the Far East from Nepal by Buddhist monks from India in the second century CE, extending through the Tang period, when Indian Buddhism began to decline with the rise of Hinduism.

The shrine of Data Darbar—the mausoleum of the 11th-century Persian saint Abul Hasan Ali Hajarari.

Across many cultures, certain sites have acquired special meaning because they are spatially identifiable and have become associated with ideas about sacred power that make them sources of spirituality, identity, and pilgrimage. Under Islam the hajj becomes an act of ritual obedience and religious unity. For Christians, travel to Jerusalem or Rome was associated with sites sanctified in the Old Testament, with pilgrims undertaking often arduous journeys and given aid and protection en route. Places associated with holy shrines, whether related to Buddhism, Christianity, Judaism, Hinduism, or Islam, have long been regarded as being sanctified through a combination of history and association.

Buddhist sacred places, particularly in India and China, were associated with scriptures that recorded worship of relics and housed in stupas that became the venues for pilgrims to attain enlightenment. In Japan the religious tradition of Shinto temples and shrines extended to sacred mountains, forests, springs, and bamboo groves.

Within the broad divisions that apply to religious tradition and practice in Asia there is considerable contrast and a wide spectrum of worship based on social and cultural contexts. This can be coupled with differences in the way that even the same religion can be practiced in different ways, for example the form of Hinduism in India is different from the Hindu Animist practice in Bali, where the majority of India's population worship a supreme being in three forms—Brahma the creator, Vishnu the preserver, and Shiva the most powerful.

Spirituality exerts a power on the imagination as it reaches beyond nature to the technical achievement of human influence over natural form and space, even as it inevitably creates a cultural tension with the setting. Characteristic imagery ranges from the Tawang Monastery founded in 1681 in India, to the Potala Palace in Tibet, the Taktsang Goemba "Tiger's Nest" monastery built in 1692—3,000 feet above a Bhutan valley—the Xuankong or "Hanging" Monastery in China's Shanxi province built on a wooden frame structure during the Northern Wei dynasty, and the Sikh Golden Temple in Amritsar in India's Punjab.

Sofia Church in Harbin
~~s~~ constructed in 1907. It is
~~e~~ best example of Byzantine-
~~v~~le architecture in China.

The Boan Gong Temple, Chinese Taipei.

The longstanding religions of Christianity, Buddhism, and Islam had their historical foundations in the city realm, while others were planned around cosmological principles. The Indian basis of Buddhism was closely associated with the notion of *Pravrajya*, the art of spiritual transcendency, resulting in a renunciation of society in return for an ascetic existence within a monastic community, and the supremacy of the *Dharma* based on universal virtue, morality, and duty. This took priority over the persona and established the duality of Kaya and Buddhism—the first consisting of the scriptural tradition of study and recital, and the body as a vehicle of insight and spirituality through meditation. Thus, all places can be considered sacred, becoming the abodes of deities responsible for certain domains that could be associated with the guardianship of mountains, trees, rocks, or water bodies—each the subject of different but equally elaborate rites as part of consecration rituals. Peking itself appropriated the notion of a cosmic center, the Forbidden City, as a sacred place, and Tiananmen Square later came to represent the secular center of political ideology.

The sacred place can be as lowly as a shrine on a street corner, or one distinguished by its remoteness and gravity-defying construction that constitutes a meeting point between heaven and earth. Additional significance stems from an attachment with a noteworthy deity or enlightened founder, reflected by history, and depicted through myth and association where devotees engage with the past through ceremonial activities. The symbolic representation of this gives rise to ritual participation in established procedures, although this might involve a merging of both religious ideas and practices.

e main stupa
the Shwedagon
Singuttara Hill in Yangon.

Diversity, even in minority religions, accounts for the wide range of sacred sites in cities and regions, along with an assortment of dedicated building structures, where diverse spiritual ideologies are celebrated even in the face of a growing cosmopolitan identity. The predominant religions in Asia also form part of constant spiritual rituals through accustomed practices and devotions. Sacred imagery of religious buildings, shrines, and symbolic ornamentation therefore become intermingled with community references. Spiritual beliefs extend and inform both urban settings and organizational aspects within the community, forming both a physical and social framework for everyday life linked to divinely ordained practices and associated deities. Religious traditions also stress a responsibility toward community enhancement, but also environmental stewardship, which advances social equity and wellbeing. For example, shrines that proliferate in public spaces and on-sidewalks in the vicinity of temples in Bangkok reflect

St. John's church in Kolkata, the original Parish Church of Bengal.

tree spirits, or *nang mai*, which are thought to inhabit natural or wilderness areas, and are dedicated to particular species such as the banana palm, tamarind, and banyan trees that are considered sacred. As sites gain fame from engagement with followers through forms of assumed messaging or revelation, they become the focus of ritual assembly, and take on a transformational and curative power.

The coincidence of 16th-century map making based on prevailing western religious principles and the global advance of Christianity, known as "ecclesiastical geography," tended to equate sacred sites with those referred to in the Bible, reflecting a bias toward the status of the church in the city. It took until the 20th century for the geography of religion to focus on its relationship with environment and society. In fact, sacred places have a reciprocal relationship with nature, geographical features and aspect, where religious activities are dictated by the setting just as monuments transform and configure the landscape, imbuing it with symbolic meaning. This extends to the shaping of fortune through the placement of key structures, entrances, and view corridors. For example, the Chinese system of geomancy stemming from the laws of "Heaven and Earth" are associated with *feng shui*, which embraces the healthy aspects of wind and water—a harmonization of energy flow.

The intersection of religion, placemaking, and building inspires a sense of reverence, but at the same time it pinpoints a long-held need to engage the public at large with iconic religious landmarks in terms of space, place, and divine purpose, and inevitably invokes the nature of the human condition. Lily Kong in *Mapping New Geographies of Religion* argues that sacred sites should be extended to memorials, shrines, pilgrimage sites, processions, and festivals on the basis that ritualization associated with sacred places hold different meanings in regard to different sections of the population, depending on such things as age and gender. In this sense

The Thian Hock Keng Temple, Singapore.

makeshift temple in Panaji, Goa.

Entrance Gate to the Quan So Pagoda, built in the 15th centu[ry] and the headquarters of Buddhism in Vietnam.

sacred places exhibit an intersection of spiritual and secular forces, reflecting the persistence of religious belief in the face of modernization, but also the association of sacred buildings, religious organizations, memorials, and domestic shrines as cultural attractions and sanctuaries in relation to a larger network of power relations. It could also be argued that the significance of a sacred place, as a manifestation of reality, is in how and in what situation it is realized or appropriated by social, economic, and political forces. In fact, discrimination over use and even restrictions on the entrance to certain religious buildings on the basis of gender continues to represent a point of contestation.

Many sacred places have been associated with worship through the centuries, where communities continue to congregate for a variety of purposes including sanctuary from disasters, poverty relief initiatives, education services, and assistance to the vulnerable in society. Others address sustainable development goals that become a potent force that binds together various programs. While places of spirituality—in particular monasteries, which are deliberately built in remote locations—the majority of sacred places have been built in cities for daily worship and adherence to regular activities that motivate a strength of purpose. They are easily accessible by the community and form familiar landmarks. Sacred physical structures are the result of belief systems and therefore convey an effectiveness and appropriateness even in remote situations, creating a sense of association through the process of pilgrimage itself.

The Gereja Cathedral was one time the tallest building Jakarta and now sits juxtaposition with the Masjid iqlal, built on the ruins the old Dutch fort.

The Interface with Society

"Life spaces" associated with sacred places provide a focus for culturally related activities by different groups. For example, courtyards within temple compounds provide a setting for both offerings, festivals, and tranquil reflection. They are therefore central to community interaction through a shared spirituality.

Religious processions are generally festive occasions in Asia and represent regular celebratory events, often linked to places of worship involving gods and goddesses. This includes Christian veneration of saints, Hindu bathing festivals, temple processions, Muslim Muharram or "mourning," Tamil funeral rituals, and those associated with marriage or cremation ceremonies. In all cases they involve movement to or from sacred spaces, streets, or grounds as the focus for transporting god-like statues. These communal events act to define or modify the status of religious sites such as important shrines, but also act to affirm boundaries, shaped by tradition, ritual, and public display. This provides opportunities for contact between followers of certain faiths and secular groups, but also establishes a compelling display of hierarchy in terms of the relationship between sacred sites and the wider landscape.

In celebrating joyful events, tragic ones, or even fertility rituals, music and dancing play a part, whether sad, loud, rhythmic, or dirge-like, according to the occasion. The Black Nazarene procession around the old Spanish city of Manila for example encourages participation by the urban poor. Religious variables dictate the interaction between ideologies and the often-complex understanding of protocol, community behavior, and expression of devotion. Space takes on a virtual but symbolic meaning often accommodating points of transition associated with specific forms of activity and association.

In the Hong Kong SAR, sacred places are associated with temples that have remained a physical constant through the flows of immigrants to the territory and emigrants to other parts of the globe who return to honor their ancestors. Of some 600 Chinese temples in the Hong Kong SAR, around half are Buddhist and 40 percent Taoist. The remainder are the *miu*—predominantly Taoist but with Buddhist practices. This underscores their broad relationship but also the generally relaxed attitude to worship, outside festival times. The main function of deities is to afford protection and proffer guidance, although it is shrewdly suggested that the most popular is the God of Wealth. The Taoist deity is Wong Tai Sin at the center of the territory's largest temple. The best-known group of divinities in the Taoist faith are the Eight Immortals who represent the different conditions of life.

Temples in the Hong Kong SAR all form the spiritual abode of a recognized deity, worshipped for conveying a protective role over the territory's inhabitants. Among the 235 outlying islands in the Hong Kong SAR are Buddhist monasteries and nunneries of which the largest is

The Kalighat Temple completed in 1809 on the site of a medieval temple and the site of the annual Kali Puja Festival in Kolkata.

the Po Lin Monastery on Lantau Island adjacent to the bronze Tian Tan Buddha statue erected in 1993, symbolizing the harmonious relationship between humans and nature. Processions are controlled by a Chinese Temples Committee under a special ordinance and focus either on a particular temple, where worshippers follow a route around its particular urban catchment area bearing a statue, or for a pilgrimage to a specific sacred place. New processional routes ostensibly promote Chinese heritage and strengthen community solidarity. The largest group of temples are dedicated to Tin Hau, the goddess dedicated to the protection of seafarers, and are traditionally located adjacent to the waterfronts around the territory including its off-shore islands, although most have become inland sites due to successive tranches of urban reclamation. The major annual festivity takes place on the harbor itself where a procession of fishing junks visit the main Tin Hau temple in Joss House Bay with its unbroken aspect over the South China Sea. The junks are dressed with flags, pennants, and silk banners together with a large bamboo shrine to be carried into the temple at the head of each group of worshippers.

The most famous religious procession on Hong Kong Island is associated with the Lin Fa Kung Temple dedicated to Kwan Ying, the Goddess of Mercy. It is culturally linked to the wider locality through the annual Fire Dragon Dance associated with the Mid-Autumn Festival, and commemorates the end of the plague that struck the Hong Kong SAR in the 18th century. To

Chinese Temples, whether Buddhist, Taoist, Confucianist are insinuated the urban and social fabric Chinese Taipei but with a strict adherence to a formalized layout around which new neighborhoods developed. Traditional customs, together with a profound belief in the power of iconic deities to improve earthly quality and ward against disaster, account for large-scale participation in spiritual activity within and around temples and shrines. Religion therefore interfaces with superstition, ancestor worship, and celebratory rituals where divine intervention must be met by an offering on the part of the petitioner. Both the Longshan Temple and nearby Qingsshan Temple contain shrines in honor of deities who were thought to intervene in staving off disasters and pestilence.

accentuate the cleansing ceremony the head of the dragon, adorned with incense sticks, is ultimately hurled into the harbor. The Fire Dragon ceremony receives a government grant as part of support for intangible cultural heritage.

The three Tam Kung Temples in the Hong Kong SAR are dedicated to a deity with a power to cure the sick, and each annual festival was at one time associated with a Chinese opera. Processions follow a route around the associated districts, the first in Happy Valley, the second in Shau Kei Wan—both on Hong Kong Island—together with the Hung Sheng Temple on Ap Lei Chau.

Kenneth Dean has examined Chinese temple networks in Singapore, a city of 5.5 million people and more than a thousand temples, churches, and mosques together with home-based shrines among a number of ethnic groups—Buddhist, Taoist, Christian, Muslim, and Hindu. His analysis has identified more than 800 Chinese temples, around 400 Christian churches, 70 Islamic mosques, 23 Hindu temples, and seven Sikh temples. The Singapore Tamil Hindu community, descended from Indian immigrants to Malaysia in the early 19th century, is centered on 24 temples. The main feature of these are towering "gopurams" or gateways and "vimanas" or domes which feature brightly colored figures and motifs from Hindu mythology

Temples dedicated to Confuci
are named according to their
location. One of the best
examples is the Temple
of Literature, Hanoi.

The Longshan Temple,
Chinese Taipei, renowned
for its wood carvings and ston
dragon columns.

e Imperial axis and
Temple of Heaven, Beijing
aid to symbolize the meeting
heaven (the circle) and earth
e square).

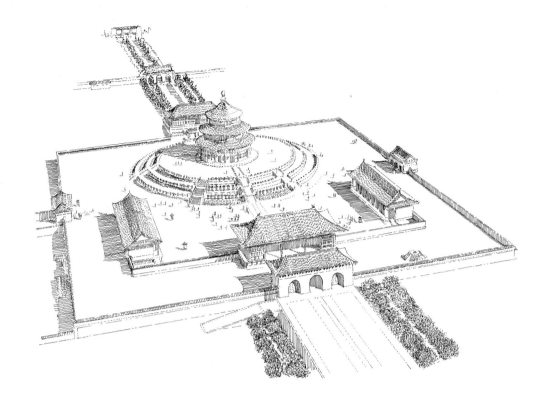

in the Southern-India style. They represent Singapore's pluralism, multicultural traditions, and a cityscape containing a multitude of churches, temples, and mosques. Hindu temples in the main are sustained by contributions from the community and payments made for various services. Associated with these are various public "chariot" processions, which embody both symbolic and spiritual values, originating from the transport of Hindu deities on wooden bullock carts. The three main chariot precessions, associated with the Festivals of *Jagannath, Koli Valarpu,* and *Maha Shivaratri Vizha,* are held in different parts of the island and are referred to as "walking temples." Spectators are thereby given the opportunity to benefit from the divine power of each deity, but temples also represent places where the Hindu community can reinforce its presence through conspicuous display along "sacred pathways," for which innumerable official permits and approvals are necessary.

The Muharram ritual in Mumbai forms a symbolic mourning procession that honors the memory of the martyred grandson of the Prophet Mohammad. This makes its way to the Rahmetabold Cemetery and is linked with the urbanization process of the city itself, led by ethnically diverse Muslim groups from around the Indian Ocean. Different Muslim groups participate, despite the ritual's accentuation on grief. The ancient procession provoked the

Temple compounds frequentl[y] embody public spaces that merge with circulation, and transactional areas, bridging the gap between secular and community activities, Wong Tai Sin Temp[le] Hong Kong SAR.

establishment of a separate Hindu Festival dedicated to Ganesh, the elephant-headed deity. This procession is now centered on the Bhendi Bazaar but follows a route through the oldest Shi'i buildings in the city, drawing on both the religious and social dynamics of the cosmopolitan city. The Parsi or Zoroastrian community in Mumbai, originally from Iran, are one of the city's largest landowners, operating as a charitable trust—the Bombay Parsi Punchayet that arose from their close ties to the British colonial government. The trust is used in part to administer annual religious rituals and a vast amount of housing that can only be sold to the Parsi community, with trust assets passed to new generations of beneficiaries but with a great deal of cross-subsidy.

The religious pluralism of Jakarta is reflected in a number of sacred places and religious buildings. These include the central Masjid Istiqlal adjacent to the century old Catholic cathedral, along with major Buddhist buildings associated with the Tzu Chi Foundation—the largest such organization in the Chinese speaking world, carrying out many philanthropic activities. At the immense Tai Chi Centre is a large porcelain Buddha situated above a map of the world. Religious space is highly contested in terms of its symbolic and ideological significance, particularly between followers of Islam and fundamentalist Christianity. In a country that has the largest Muslim population in the world, the Reformed Evangelical Church is paradoxically one of the largest of its kind with branches around the world—an intersection between local, global, and philanthropic interests where a national call for "unity in diversity" leads to an often-contested coexistence, underscored by socio-economic differences.

In certain cities such as Bangkok and Yangon, sacred space is culturally visible in its urban articulation, bound to a consciousness of the past where tradition cannot be disassociated from ever-present religious symbols, social geographies, and interrelationships that reverberate

through the practice of Buddhism and its embrace of both ideology and reality. Bangkok was, until the 20th century, a place of city walls with demarcated spaces irrigated by *khlongs*. In 1782 King Rama I formed Rattanakosin Island for the palace at the center of the city after the capital was moved from Ayutthaya. New water channels created opportunities for prominent temples such as Wat Arun, the Temple of Dawn named after the Hindu god Aruna and built under Rama II on the Chao Phraya River—the most sacred place in the city. The promotion of the Rattanakosin area as a heritage area from the 1980s gave rise to a number of conservation projects emphasizing its history but inevitably this gives rise to the interface between areas of cultural significance and socio-economic characteristics. The moral relationship between religious authority and society in Thailand is emphasized by the ritual support of monks through daily offerings, while the monarch officially establishes projects that deify Buddhist icons.

Religious ideology itself is administered by a monastic elite from older monasteries near the old city center together with more remote and isolated Buddhist communities, the source of many Thai saints. Religion is therefore a "lived experience" through an almost constant devotion to deities. An all-embracing social meaning is tied into places defined by their spirituality and visitation in relation to everyday life, despite increased secularization and new practices.

Jin-Heon Jung in his essay *The Politics of Desecularization* states that during the Japanese annexation of Korea its power structure was manifested in the Government General Building, built on the Gyeongbokgung royal palace complex of the Joseon dynasty where 85 percent of the original buildings were destroyed along with the Sungnyemun gate—an iconic national symbol. The Japanese constructed a large Shinto complex behind this on Namsan Mountain, completed in 1925, in order to purposely weaken existing religious influences. After their defeat in 1945 the Japanese tore down the Shinto shrine, and the Korean Government later converted the government building into the National Museum. Later reconstruction of the palace complex in 1990 was held to require demolition of the government complex in 1996 in order to restore the palace and to ensure the protection of its important *feng shui* gateway relationship with the city.

Inwang Mountain, close to the urban center of Seoul, is the site of important Buddhist temples, and South Korea's most illustrious shamanic shrine, Kuksadang. Won Buddhism, "Consummate Buddhism," represents a modern fusion of Buddhism, Confucianism, and Taoism and represents the focus of the South Korean government's program to promote

eet Shrine, Georgetown,
nang.

sacred places as visitor attractions. The emphasis is on its diverse religious culture and the variegated geography of Christianity and Buddhism in the capital area where a large amount of land is owned by Buddhist institutions. The diffusion of red neon crosses proliferates across Seoul through a variety of sacred institutions, with intimate religious spaces located in basements, markets, shops, and bars across a wide spectrum of denominations. This is something quite apart from the urban "megachurches" associated with a somewhat controversial version of Korean Christianity that leaves the state open to accusations of using religion as a state-aligned brand of theology. Satellite churches are also built on the periphery of cities as part of property interests, creating a further contested area of Christian corporate practices.

Buddhist Landscapes and Places of Pilgrimage

In Chinese culture, with its strong philosophical connotations of Confucianism, Taoism and Buddhism, the sacred place is less related with religious obligation and more with the diffused formation of ideas as to where the power of a deity is manifest. Association therefore takes the form of spiritual contact. Mountainous regions have long been associated with hallowed sites, both as natural homes of the gods as sanctified by human discrimination, and as suitable sites for spiritual dedication. In China sacred sites often involve a mountainous journey to destinations where the image of a deity is enshrined and where the *shan-men* entrance gate is an analogy of both the temple and the mountain peak. This reflects both its remoteness and the difficulty of the journey as a necessary challenge, so that sacred landscapes take on a therapeutic quality in terms of well-being. The presentation of incense then becomes a means of "introduction" to the deity, but where the belief system is not solely in terms of the devotional posture.

Confucianism, Taoism, and Buddhism have collectively been absorbed into philosophical systems of thought in China, developed and integrated from antiquity. In the process this created an ideology that spread across East Asia, in particular Japan, Korea, and Vietnam through religious traditions manifested in the natural life force of *qi*. The underlying principle of *yin* and *yang* is essentially complementary to this with many layers of meaning. Confucianism relates to an ordering system that reflects a cosmic interrelationship between the five metaphysical forces of fire, wood, metal, water, and earth. Its emphasis on social harmony and responsibility over individual "right" helps to underpin the modern workings of both society and China's prevailing political system as a source of order and stability but also acts as a measure of care and obligation between ruler and society set out in the Confucian classics.

Under Confucianism, filial piety requires a close link between the living, ancestors, and deities, so that veneration and offerings are reciprocated through good fortune and sustenance. Space that is designated as sacred therefore ranges from simple sites to complex rituals, while

Hanging Temple on Hengshan Mountain in Shangxi, China dating from CE 491.

Confucius is honored by twice-yearly offerings at temples built to reflect the order associated with Confucian teaching and at centers of Confucian studies. One of the holiest is the Temple of Heaven in Beijing where rituals are carried out at the winter solstice to align with the temporal forces associated with sacred times such as the Lunar New Year, Hungry Ghost, and Mid-Autumn festivals focused on family and community gatherings.

In China five sacred mountains were regarded as sites for annual rituals going back to the 7th century CE, and early rulers visited to pay homage to immortal beings that were thought to live there, so that this process legitimized their rule. Gradually the development of sites as the focus of pilgrimage evolved into a sacred geography, with relics to be worshipped by visitors, and stupas associated with temples that contained relics of holy figures. Pilgrimage occurs at a variety of scales and is a clear indication of both significance in terms of divine meaning, and deep-rooted devotion.

Monumental images and Buddhist sutras became the focus of devotions in the search for enlightenment. The most important mountain temples for the bodhisattvas of Chinese Buddhism were called *san-ta tao-ch'ang*, or the great seats of enlightenment. Mount Ermi in Szechuan, Mount Wu-t'an in northern Shansi, Mount Chiu-hua in Anhai, and Mount P'u-E'oin

lden Summit Temple,
acred site of Buddhism
Heavenly Pillar Peak—
e main pinnacle of Jizu
untain in Yunnan Province.

e Jiming Temple and Pagoda,
njing.

in Chekiang, in combination, formed a circuitous pilgrimage route that gained in popularity during the 16th century as it accumulated increasing importance, with temples that added Buddhist teaching centers. As Islam spread to China the tombs of Sufi saints within the Chinese empire also became important sites of pilgrimage.

While the advent of a sacred place implies the influence of a place on religious authenticity, it is also important to respect the ongoing influence of religion on the environment, in particular the implications for transformation of the landscape through new structures and access systems. The sacred motivation to transform often-remote landscapes can be said to reflect both a strong religious impulse but also a challenge to human capabilities in the promulgation

The Longmen Grottoes comprising many cave temple and Buddhas carved into the cliff face of Xiangshan and Longmenshan Mountains south of present-day Luoyang. These comprise more than 100,000 statues, 40 pagodas, and 3,600 tablets and steles from the 5th century.

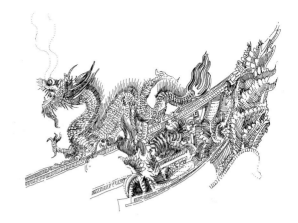

of belief into architectural form. This not only re-shapes the landscape but superimposes on it signifiers of historical actions and values, both purposeful and painstaking, while challenging the constraints of nature by imposing a new order. The temple in its various forms, complete with ornate decoration and artistic symbolism, has provided some of the finest monuments imprinted on both rural and city areas throughout history, underscoring both sacred identity and social significance.

The heterogeneity of sacred mountain sites as well as the built elements—the stelae, artworks, and inscriptions made over time—came from the diversity of the occupants and visitors: the monks, hermits, and pilgrims. These transmitted a range of descriptive accounts, drawings, prints, and tales of private miracles that immortalized the sites, heightened expectations, and reinforced the sacred attraction, but also contributed to an accretion of meanings accumulated over centuries, through forms of artistic expression. The Shanghai artist Zhang Huan has collected the light ash from smoldering incense sticks from the Jing 'an Temple in Shanghai where the residue of offerings from devotees formed the material for his paintings, reflecting a physical reincarnation or form of replacement that forms part of Buddhist philosophy.

The geography of Buddhist China is essentially marked by mountain sites where the most famous bodhisattva manifested themselves in human form such as Mount Wu-t'ai, the home of Wen-shu. P'u-t'o Shan on Mount Potalaka sits on an island and its significance as a place of pilgrimage goes back to the 10th century when the cult of Kuan-yin and the miracles attributed to her became popular, and later led to the creation of other Mainland pilgrimage sites.

Certain sacred mountain sites embrace innumerable destinations. Wu-t'ai Shan, for example, is a cluster of peaks and valleys some distance apart, the highest of which is 10,000 feet above sea level. The five sacred mountains that make up Sung Shan in Honan province contain the site of the Shao-lin Monastery where legend has it that the first bodhisattva meditated

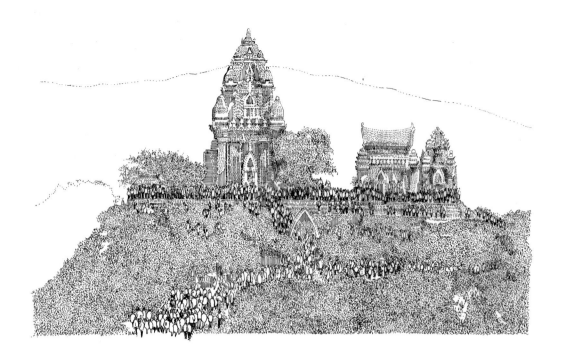

for five years. It earned its fame as a center for martial arts from the exploits of its monks who fought against Japanese pirates in the 16th century.

Landscapes of worship overlap with those of death, which adds a further dimension in relating the iconography of religion to graves, cemeteries, tombs, and catacombs that can in themselves create imposing spatial features from monuments to mausoleums. Buddhist beliefs that encompass reincarnation generate a means of continued veneration through various funerary practices. Followers of Buddhism assist the departed in their future existence as a benign continuation of ancestor worship. Chinese burial sites are chosen according to the energy forces dictated through geomantic principles, while Hindu practices on the other hand leave no trace of the deceased who is thought to enter a new body, so that there are no monuments to the dead.

The entire universe as well as the human body is considered as being composed of the four elements, the *mahābhūta* characteristics of earth (south), water (east), fire (west), and air (north). In this sense, sacred places cannot exist independently of the buddha-mind or "pristine cognition," which recognizes the quality of all phenomena united within the mandala. This functions as a chart that maps interrelationships, with consciousness at its center. Stupas functioned as funeral monuments and vehicles for internment of sacred relics that could be suitably venerated by followers, with their spiritual power occasionally subsumed by rulers to underscore their political authority. The erection of stupas accompanied the spread of

...grims along one of the ...ths leading to the Zhiyuan ...mple on Jiuhua Mountain in ...ngyang County, China.

Buddhism throughout east Asian countries. The extensive building of stupas, as at Borobudur in Java, represents a Buddhist tradition of marking a historical site. Pagan in Myanmar houses more than 2,000 such monuments and temples with an accelerated program of construction as their symbolic significance grew. Their component parts, superimposed on the structures with different dimensions and heights, came to represent the cosmos with 37 aspects of spiritual attainment.

The ideal sacred dimensions of Buddhist temple architecture are concerned with the tantric mandala as an expression of enlightenment, marked by a symmetrical square form and large triumphal archways, with the most sacred point at its center. This reflects the need to cater for necessary ritual requirements through a hierarchical and axial form suitable for assembly and worship. The stupa of Borobudur constructed in the 9th century is one of the earliest representations of the mandala form.

Sacred Buddhist sites include landscape features associated with both factual and mythical legends, and many that are well remote from recorded history. However, by attracting large numbers of pilgrims, sacred places have served as points of attraction where different perspectives could mingle and harmonize around sites that were set to contain important relics, such as the Shwedagon stupa in Rangoon, and temples in Luang Prabang in Laos, Doi Suthep in Thailand, Kandy in Sri Lanka, and the Jizu Wutai, Putuo, and Jiuhua mountain sites in China.

The significance of pilgrimage as an act of piety is much enhanced by the auspicious timing of regular festivals at points along the circuitous routes, where participation includes the opportunity for religious instruction. Different systems of pilgrimage have evolved around various sects and deities, with contrasting customs but with some features in common, such as purity of mind and intention. The unified tantric school of Buddhism—the Vajrayana—defines 24 sacred places of pilgrimage associated with the overthrow of a dangerous demon Mahesvara by the Bodhisattva, elected by an assembly of buddhas on Mount Meru. The sacred Himalayan mountain of Kailash forms the best known of the 24 places, and is said to be the sacred source of India's main rivers, the Indus, Ganges, and Brahmaputra.

Hinduism and its Sacred Temples

Hinduism evolved in the northern part of India around 2000 BCE on plains that are bisected by the Ganges and Indus rivers. The religion itself absorbed other belief systems as it came to dominate the sub-continent, later giving rise to Buddhism in the fifth century BCE and two thousand years later to Sikhism, reflecting the country's diffused multi-cultural identity. This reflects a long synthesis of different but complementary beliefs that represent the divine purpose of existence that runs through daily life. It includes a duality of specific places of worship

The Sri Srinivasa Temple—the oldest Hindu temple in Singapore dating back to the administration of the East India Company in 1827. Like other South Indian temples its major feature is a five-story gateway tower, or *gourami*.

such as temples and shrines, but also sacred natural environments that range from mountains, oceans, and woodlands noted for their serenity. Certain types of trees are considered sacred, in particular the Bodhi tree associated with spiritual enlightenment, while temple forests assist conservation of soil and water bodies to benefit adjoining areas of agriculture. The seven holy rivers have a special significance for their life—enhancing qualities, particularly the Ganges where Hindus gather to bathe in the sacred waters that are considered to bestow purification. In the oldest parts of Chennai, water tanks formed part of the city's water supply as part of temple complexes that were then associated with communal resources as well as sacred places. Their rejuvenation as temple-related ecological values have become central to the city's protection.

North Indian Temple architecture reflects the mountainous topography with its ascending assembly of peaks and crests that symbolizes spiritual attainment. Temples, grottoes, and caves cut out of the mountains are also associated with habitation of deities, expressing a progression of increasing sanctity toward a sacred image. The Himalayan temples are notable for being venerated as the abode of the Hindu pantheon of gods—in particular Durga, the Universal Mother, and her consort Siva set out in the epic tales of the *Ramayana* and the *Mahabharata*. Places of pilgrimage might commence through the sanctity and attraction of a particular location, and as visitation increases this prompts the building of a temple as a focus of devotion and as a meeting point or *tirtha*.

ndu temples in Goa gradually
quired characteristics
Portuguese ecclesiastical
chitecture, with Mughal
d Maratha references such
in the Temple de Mangrexa
mplex at Pondrá.

e Arunachaleshwara Temple—
mil Nadu, dedicated to Shiva.

e ghats along the Varanasi
ntage to the River Ganges
er a setting for Hindu
igious rituals which extend
m ancient times.

The Hindu-Javanese
cosmological model establishe
an urban form closely related
to established cultural
procedures that assimilated
the Hindu-Animist culture of
Bali, with Buddhism and Islam
reflecting ancient trading rout
This has evolved to reflect
both modern global forces
and a rejuvenated Javanese
spiritualism centered around
the royal palace of Surakarta.
The model of the cosmos itsel
centers on Mount Meru—
the abode of the highest gods-
where the stream of divine
power and good fortune is
encapsulated in both the spati
form of the *Kraton* or central
palace, and in the multiple
practices and habits of daily li

A section of Pura Besakih—
the mother temple for the isla
of Bali, Indonesia. It comprise
22 temples on parallel ridges o
the southern slopes of Gunun
Agung. Fifty-seven structures
in the temple sanctuary are
dedicated to various member
of the Balinese pantheon,
the principal deity being Siwa
It is the site of the Purificatio
of the Universe Ceremony hel
once every one hundred years

The city of Varanasi, previously Benares, is the sacred center of Hinduism, but is also associated with the Buddhist pilgrim Hsuan-tsang who visited the city in the 2nd century CE, when it had 20 important temples. However, it remains as a stronghold of Hindu philosophy set among ancient Muslim shrines that also serve as places of worship. The cultural traditions of the city are expressed through ancient forms of worship, rituals, and belief system associated with the sacred river Ganges, which flows from south to north, rendering the 84 ghats along the western riverfront as the center for all Hindu rituals and festivals. A number of Hindu sacred sites form part of a pilgrimage mandala that encompasses a cosmic equation of time, numerology, and space that establishes a relationship between the human and the divine.

Hindu temples are represented in a variety of ways in terms of their size, architectural design, and associated artworks. Temples themselves began to take on an elaborate form commensurate with the onset of image worship between in the second and seventh centuries CE, and few of the older ones remain. The Hindu term for a temple is *mandira*, which literally means a habitat housing an image of a deity. Worship replicates the daily life of the community equated with periods of rest and evening devotional music and dance.

Detail of an intricately carved gopuram or Gate Tower marking the entrance to a Hindu temple.

The Dakshineswar Kali Hindu Temple, on the eastern bank of the Hooghly River in Kolkata.

The Mahamariamman Hindu Temple on Lebuh Queen, Georgetown, Penang on land granted by the East India Company. The Hindu goddess is paraded around the local streets during the annual Navaratri Festival.

Architectural rules are based on a symmetrical interpretation of locational aspects, mathematically related to the cosmos and in harmony with the universe. The central square houses the prominent deity, and around this are additional squares dedicated to planetary divinities. The overall construction therefore becomes a miniature replication of the universe, where deities are symbolically reflected in the pinnacles of temple architecture. The tiered arrangement that encloses the inner sanctuary is usually, in contemporary temples, associated with images of prescribed Hindu deities and attendant figures that establishes a sculptural reference, but within a strict proportional geometry. Monumental entrances or *gopuram* also have extensive sculptural embellishments and often rise to a height of 150 feet.

Some of the art and carvings decorating the temple walls is overtly erotic and amorous, depicting acts of sexual congress, commonly supposed to reflect the everyday occurrences of human life while screening those who have the most liberal attitude for admittance. It also underscores the inseparable relationship in Hinduism between religious and secular activities, where the fundamental concept of a sacred place must be sanctified by individual encounters. The more austere the journey, the more the spiritual rewards.

Islamic Sacred Places

Islam, founded in Medina in 622 CE, represents a blend of Arab beliefs revealed in the Qur'an along with elements of Christianity and Judaism that were adopted as the basis of Islamic law. This spread across North Africa, Mesopotamia, Persia, and the Middle East into Southeast Asia, shaping the later identity of Pakistan, Bangladesh, Malaysia, and Indonesia, and through the Silk Road into China.

Islam balances the symbolism of its religious buildings with a practical designation of space that interrelates sacred traditions with a conviction that this must extend into the natural environment. The mosque therefore assumes a central position, assimilating different activities that connect and unify the process of worship and acts of prostration within the sacred confines, along with educational, recreational, and social space. In Islam, a sacred place is always linked to a prophet or holy man who has served humanity. One of the most respected shrines in Lahore is the Data Darbar mausoleum for the 11th century Persian saint Abul Hassan Ali Hajarari, where people donate food that is then distributed to the poor, so that the site becomes more than a center of reflection. The edifice itself acts to sanctify the integration of activities in a way that is made congenial while creating a prominent focus. The process of worship embraces five programmed times for daily prayer, interspersed with other daily commitments, establishing a natural rhythm that blends the distinctions between sacred and secular space. Such a regime also emphasizes a belief that mind, body, and soul are intertwined.

The mosque itself is a consecrated space that sanctifies its primary use for prayer, replicating the holy places associated with the Prophet Muhammad or his followers that fulfills something of a personal bond. The most prominent is the *hajj* pilgrimage to Mecca, a desert valley in Saudi Arabia and Islam's holiest city as the birthplace of Muhammad. The *hajj* commences on the eighth day of the twelfth month of the Muslim lunar year, and represents the fifth pillar of Islam where prescribed rites are performed in a defined order as a religious duty for all adult Muslims, at least once in a lifetime, accompanied by an inward commitment to the sacred revelations inspired by the *Qur'an*. At the center of this is the Ka'bah, the black stone shrine carved from a centuries-old meteorite, that indicates a symbolic connection between heaven and earth, and the direction to be faced in daily prayer. The sacred place associated with distant shrines can thereby be considered as a micro-manifestation of the spirit that radiates from Mecca itself, and what has been described as the "oneness of being" that represents a persuasive link between past, present, and future.

The main mosque at Medina continues to represent the design exemplar and embodiment of the ideal architectural expression, replicating its rudimentary form and courtyard with a diverse blend of individually distinctive and natural features. Muhammed and his followers

migrated to Medina, in 622 CE ostensibly to resolve differences between rival groups of followers, before returning to conquer Mecca seven years later. This marked the beginning of the Islamic calendar.

The Temple Mount in Jerusalem draws on its origins as an Islamic sacred place sanctified by the Dome of the Rock, constructed between 685 CE and 691 CE on the site of the Jewish Temple destroyed during the Roman siege of 70 CE. This symbolically embodies the evolving prominence of Islam, built as a shrine for pilgrims, and sacred to Muslims and Jews alike. The Dome was intended to represent the divine structure and unity of the universe, with its octagonal plan form influenced by early Byzantine architecture. The characteristic circular dome that embodies a bulbous momentum toward the heavens is supported by 40 columns that represent the saintly pillars of the Muslim world. The significance to Muslims is the Prophet Muhammad's supposed ascent to heaven, with Qur'anic inscriptions around the octagonal structure that contain some of the earliest proclamations of Muhammad. Muslim shrines and centers of learning elsewhere tend to replicate its symbolic features even extending to private domestic places as part of a cosmic absoluteness.

The forecourt of the Badshahi Mosque, with the Hathi Pol Gateway, Lahore.

The Eastern Gateway the Wazir Khan Mosque, Lahore.

The Badshahi Mosque was built by one of the last Mughal emperors, Aurganzeb, in the ancient walled city of Lahore. The Alamgiri Gate rises twenty-two steps above the Hazuri Bagh—the forecou for the Grand Mosque—lined with cloisters that acted as a ceremonial setting for the emperor and his entourage.

Sikhism

Sikhism is associated with the Punjab in Northwestern India, translated as the land of five waters in reference to its rivers. After "partition" in 1947, a large part of this area was transferred to Pakistan, which severed the Sikh community from many of their major shrines. This reflected a substantial shift in the Sikh population from Pakistan in the Western part of the Punjab to India, although Sikhs can travel to Nankana Sahib in Pakistan for festival celebrations.

Amritsar was founded by Sikh Gurüs in 1577, and the name translates as "pool of nectar" that imparted immortality—or at the very least liberation—to those who bathed in it. The temple, or *gurdwara*, known as *Harmandir Sahib* was constructed in 1776 and was covered in gold under the reign of Maharaja Ranjit Singh, becoming popularly known as the Golden Temple—the spiritual center of Sikhism. As a result of this Amritsar became a place of Sikh pilgrimage, and the temple compounds became surrounded by residential neighborhoods. The Harmandir was constructed at a somewhat lower level than the surrounding area so that pilgrims had to descend in order to gain entrance. A later building devoted to religious activity was the Akal Takht, the Sikh center of authority, and a focus for ceremonial and spiritual affairs. Like the Harmandir it has been destroyed and rebuilt over several centuries as a result of

destruction by invading Afghan and Mughal armies, and in 1984 by Indian troops, which led to the assassination of Indira Gandhi. The Temple's architecture, covered with gilded copper, reflects the periodic rebuilding and restoration process with a mix of Indo-Islamic, Mughal, and Hindu details. More than 100,000 followers visit the shrine every day, pilgrims following a path around the pool before entering the inner sanctum via a causeway.

Shinto

The Shinto religion is the native belief system of Japan encompassing not merely sacred space but the multi-layered harmony between humans, nature, and seasons that embrace a multiplicity of meanings and interpretations associated with the Japanese value system. It can be loosely translated as the "way of the gods" that has in part evolved from Buddhism, introduced from China in the sixth century CE. The written source for Shinto belief is the *Nihonshoki* written in classical Chinese and inspired by ancient imperial chronicles.

Under Shinto religious practices in Japan, natural places hold an essential nationalistic spirit and power. In practice, this blends with the Buddhist ideal of individual subordination to the wider community and is an embedded necessity for social cooperation within the fabric of society. The most basic factor is a sincerity of intention on the part of believers themselves through the transcendental interface between power and place. Overall, reverence is therefore free of both dogma and competition between sects. Religion acts as a set of rituals that mediate relationships between humans and spiritual presences, or *kami*, who created the sacred landscapes, of which the most widely worshipped is Amaterasu—the sun goddess. These were revived after the Meiji Restoration in 1868 until 1947 and includes a type of folk belief in earth spirits associated with a sacred landscape. Thus, natural features such as mountains, water bodies, trees, and rocks have a purity or *kiyome*, through a long association with divine power, and are often marked by symbols or are enveloped by a rope to establish the abode of kami as well as for aesthetic effect. Sites can also take on sacred implications through holy ascetic figures who imbue spiritual places with charismatic association. The pervasive nature of sacred space is therefore far-reaching in terms of its multitude of characterizations.

The term *Kami* represents a wide range of supernatural forces and natural phenomena that inhabit sacred places and shrines, and every distinctive feature has an association with a local temple where an annual festival, the Matsuri, centers on the Kami shrine. Certain temples

Formal ceremony at the Meiji Jingu Temple, Tokyo.

are dedicated to the malevolent fox spirit that can only be exercised by a priest, reflecting the need to reconcile the malicious with benign harmony. One of the most prominent kami is Inari, the rice god that ensures prosperity and is the subject of 40,000 shrines in Japan, guarded by Inari's guardian, the fox. The three most venerated sacred gods are Kannon, the protector of children; Jizo, who aids the suffering; and Amida, who represents purity.

Traditionally family clans, or *uni*, made up the basis of society, and the head of each was responsible for worship of its guardian deity or *urigami* as part of a unifying process. Its ethical teaching is to some extent influenced by Buddhism, Confucianism, and Taoism that reached Japan from China in the 6th century CE, and was systemized by the Taika-era reforms of 645 CE. Buddhist statues were then placed in older Shinto shrines, the most well-known being the Grand Shrine to Amaterasu at Ise in Mie Prefecture. However, the bond between Shinto and Buddhism became less influential after the Meiji Restoration, and this might be said to have later fueled the later pernicious military expansionism of the mid-20th century.

As a result of the ubiquitous endowment of sacred properties associated with natural phenomena, the physical environment became closely aligned with the spiritual one, and evolved into settings for pilgrimage and worship, marked by the familiar torri gateway that distinguishes the approach and boundary between secular and sacred space. Sacred places enshrine the Kami spirits and are approached through a succession of gateways that define each precinct and accentuate its sense of reverence. The two most sacred Shinto shrines are at Ise and Izumo. The former is dedicated to Ameratsu, while the latter is devoted to Toyouke the goddess of harvest. The Ise shrine is dismantled and rebuilt every twenty years as a sacred act of renewal on a site alongside the old one, with the old components distributed to other shrines throughout Japan.

Some of the most prominent mountains in Japan represent not merely a sacred geography but the residue of austerities first performed by legendary ascetics, and therefore evolved into holy places. These then became the focus of pilgrimages, the most visited being Mount Fuji, Mount Ontake, Mount Tateyama, and the Yoshino-Kumano range, where spiritual journeys are divided into 10 stages that represent the 10 realms of Buddhism, and subject to a sequence of rituals.

Buddhist temples have been constructed in both urban and rural settings that have been identified as relating to spiritual events or traditional sanctuaries, where the manifestation of a Buddhist deity or the enshrinement of a Kami has given rise to a permanent structure in which to house important relics, along with guardian statues to ward off evil.

In a similar way to Chinese festivals, the Japanese New Year is celebrated annually, but in accordance with the Gregorian rather than the Lunar calendar. However, the latter is used to determine the timing of the Obon festival to honor deceased family members.

The Christian Sacred Place

As Christianity emerged out of Judaism and absorbed many of its scriptures, Jerusalem itself is marked as a holy city, with a history as a "promised land" systematically described in the Old Testament. The destruction of a sequence of Jewish temples culminated in the Dome of the Rock, built on the Temple Mount, becoming a sacred place for Muslims. The commonly held Christian belief in heaven as the place of God and the Holy Spirit, is echoed by the Muslim faith through Mohammad's aspirational ascent from the rock, while the concept of heaven can be regarded as a promised land, common to Christians, Jews, and Muslims alike.

Christianity spread from the first century CE to Samaria, Syria, Turkey, and Imperial Rome, where its acceptance led to a rapid increase in its popularity through the Roman Empire via missionaries. By the 4th century CE under Emperor Constantine, the Roman Catholic Church spread the Christian message to northern Europe, which at the time was largely pagan. Christians are known to have visited China from the 5th century CE, mainly from Persia and Central Asia. By the 6th century Christian churches and bishoprics in the Western part of China coincided with trading routes that converged on the emerging Chinese Empire. Early Christian teaching scripts brought about a synthesis of cultures and faiths, evidenced by ancient scrolls discovered in Dunhuang and in caves along the Silk Road in 1907 that have been termed "Jesus Sutras" or "Taoist Christianity," setting out a sacred literature of the Church of China during the Tang and early Sung dynasties. This brought together the beliefs of Eastern Buddhism and Taoism with Western Judeo-Christianity as a model of spiritual thought.

The Christian sacred place in Asia from the 16th century is essentially associated with Western colonial activity, be this as intruders, infiltrators, or invaders, bringing with them realms of belief and imagination, as part of a proselytizing practice. Places of spirituality are therefore associated primarily with the city, although missionary activity followed a devotion to various branches of the Christian faith that extended from the Hispanic foundation of Intramuros in Manila to remote treaty port settlements in China. In this sense, sacred places can reflect a literal interpretation of the Bible as factual history, or a more allegorical elucidation of Christian theological opinion in terms of God's relation to the world.

In general, Christian sacred places bear comparison with other religions in terms of the spiritual relevance associated with holy relics, tombs of martyrs, and significant historical events such as the working of miracles. This is extended to the consecration of ground for burial purposes. Also in common with other beliefs is the rigorous pilgrimage routes that underscore the degree of ritual devotion or atonement, and from which indulgences can technically be procured. A particularly Christian aspect is the personal dimension of salvation.

athedral Square or Largo
a Sé in Macau SAR has been
bject to a rehabilitation
ogram to restore the status of
important buildings which
cludes the Bishop's Palace
d Catholic schools.

rines to various deities
present a body of beliefs
om gods, ranging from
ortal figures to earth spirits
sociated with both living and
atural phenomena, Wong Tai
n Temple, Hong Kong SAR.

As an "end note" it must be stated that there is a long association between geography and the divine purpose of creation, and sacred sites can only be deciphered in relation to people's perception, behavior, and belief system. This has brought significance changes over time as traditional customs and rituals give way to new modes of worship and propitiation. The ancient past continuous to establish persistent ideas that run ever deeper across time and give rise to wide variations in terms of what is included or excluded. The concept of sacredness also suggests different forms of human worship in relation to the meaning of place for different demographic constituents, for example, age and gender or attitudes in respect of shared views.

Acknowledgments

I would like to record my thanks and appreciation to Gordon Goff, publisher and managing director of ORO Editions, and to Jake Anderson, CEO of ORO, for his constant assistance with this publication and for his valuable editing skills from which the book has greatly benefitted. I would also like to thank Pablo Mandel for the graphic layout and design, and for his many positive suggestions.

In conclusion a big thank you to my long-time friends, directors, and colleagues at URBIS for their constant help and support. I am particularly grateful to my assistant Lily Tam for her massive help in typing and coordination of manuscript drafts and her constant assistance with the compilation and editing process. Lily has worked on all my eight books, beginning in 2006. Her commitment and dedication have been invaluable in achieving the end products.

Finally, my gratitude to the many people and organizations I met along the way in a variety of venues, events, and situations. As stated in the Introduction, the various subject areas have been distilled from a series of papers presented at various forums on aspect of city planning and urban design, and I remain grateful for both the opportunities these offered for discussion and feedback.

These are set out below:

- University of Sydney 2005: *Regeneration through Sustainable Urban Design*
- Metropolis World Conference 2005, Berlin: *Tradition and Transformation in City Futures*
- University of Calgary 2005: *Planning Cities in China*
- American Institute of Architects Conference, Hong Kong 2007: *Place Making as Value Added*

- FT Urban Regeneration Summit, Hong Kong 2007: *Sustainable Urban Regeneration: Economic and Social Impacts*
- Symposium on Vertical Density (HK-NY Urban Exchange), New York 2008: *The Culture of Compactness*
- Coalition of Professional Services Forum, Beijing, 2009: *Planning the Asian City*
- Urban Planning Institute, Macau 2011: *The Design of Urban Waterfronts*
- National Planning Conference, Nanjing, PRC 2011: *Vertical Density – Sustainable Solutions*
- Asia Society, Shanghai, PRC 2012: *Tradition and Transformation in the Chinese Treaty Ports*
- Barcelona Regional Conference on Sustainable Urbanism 2012: *Rethinking Cities – Framing the Future*
- HKIP Conference on Community Planning 2012: *Public Engagement in the Planning Process*
- Bi-City Biennale of Urbanism 2014: *A Dual Approach to Waterfront Regeneration*
- HKIUD Urban Design Symposium 2014: *Urban Design as Public Policy*
- Institute of Surveyors Annual Conference, Hong Kong 2014: *Smart Urban Design*
- EAROPH World Congress, Jakarta 2014: Towards Resilient and Smart Cities: *Smart Cities – Future Cities*
- American Institute of Architects Asian Cities Symposium, Hong Kong 2014: *Practical Urbanism – Utopian Horizons*
- Bi-City Urban Exchange Symposium, Barcelona 2015: *The Urban Waterfront as a Driver of Change*
- Nobel Laureates Symposium on Global Sustainability, Hong Kong 2015: *Urban Resilience: The Asian City Challenge*
- Global Seminar, Salzburg 2015: *The Sustainable Dimensions of Asian City Development*
- Savannah College of Art and Design (SCAD), Georgia, USA 2015: *Urban Design and the Asian City*
- Barry Society Symposium, London, 2016: *Building the Walkable and Healthy City*
- HKIUD Urban Design Symposium 2016: *Betterment of the City*
- Urban Design Conference, Guangzhou, PRC 2017: *Achieving the Livable City in Asia*
- Cape Town City Planning Conference 2017: *Progressive Strategies to Revitalize City Space*
- City Development Conference, Kuala Lumpur 2018: *Cities and Digital Transformation*
- Qingdao University, PRC 2018: *Urban Regeneration and Heritage Conservation*
- Strategic Approaches in Design and Environment Conference, Hong Kong: *Sustainable Placemaking – Achieving a Livability Paradigm*

References and suggestions on further reading are set out in the following section, by the name of authors in alphabetical order.

References
and further reading

Abbas, A. *Culture and the Politics of Disappearance.* Hong Kong University Press, 1998.

Abel, C. *Architecture and Identity.* Architectural Press, Oxford, 2000.

AI, S. (ed) *Mall City: Hong Kong's Dreamworlds of Consumption.* University of Hawaii Press, 2016.

AI, S. (ed) *Villages in the City.* HKU Press, 2014.

Aldrich, M. A. *The Search for a Vanishing Beijing.* Hong Kong University Press, 2006.

Alexander A., de Azevedo, P., Yutaka, H., and Dorje, L. *Beijing Hutong Conservation Study.* International Heritage Fund, 2004.

Allen, A. *Sustainable Cities or Sustainable Urbanization.* UCL's Journal of Sustainable Cities, 2009.

Arkavaprasettkul, N. *Gentrifying Heritage: How Historic Preservation Drives Gentrification in Unban Shanghai.* International Journal of Heritage Studies, 2018.

Ashcroft, B. *On Post-Colonial Futures: Transformation of Colonial Culture.* Continuum, 2001.

Ashihara, Y. *The Hidden Order: Tokyo through the Twentieth Century.* Kodansha International, 1989.

Askew, M. *Bangkok: Place, Practice and Representation,* Routledge 2013.

Aygen, Z., and Logan, W. *Heritage in the Asian Century* in *A Companion to Heritage Studies.* Wiley-Blackwell, 2016.

Badcock, B. *Making Sense of Cities: A Geographical Survey.* Oxford University Press, 2002.

Bae, C. H., and Richardson, H. W. *Regional Urban Policy and Planning on the Korean Peninsula.* Edward Elgar Publishing, 2011.

Beard, V. A. *Community-based planning, collective action and the challenges confronting Urban Power in Southeast Asia* in Environment and Urbanization, https://doi.org/10.1177/0956247818804453 2018.

Berger, P., and Huntington, S. P. (eds). *Many Globalizations: Cultural Diversity in the Contemporary World.* Oxford University Press, 2002.

Bishop, R., Phillips, J., and Yeo, W. Y. (eds.). *Post-Colonial Urbanism: Southeast Asian Cities and Global Processes.* Routledge, 2003.

Biswas, L. "Evolution of Hindu Temples," in *Calcutta Journal of Cultural Geography* 4, pp. 73–85, 1984.

Blussé, L. *On the Waterfront: Life and Labour around the Batavian Roadshed* in *Asian Port Cities 1600–1800: Local and Foreign Cultural Interactions.* Ed Haneda Masashi (ed.), NUS Press, 2009.

Boano, C., Hunter, W., and Newton, C. *Contest Urbanism in Dharavi.* The Bartlett Development Planning Unit, 2013.

Boxer, C. R. *The Portuguese Seaborne Empire 1415–1832.* The Calouste Gulbenkian Foundation, 1997.

Broeze, F. (ed.). *Gateways of Asia: Port Cities of Asia in the 13th-20th Centuries.* Kegan Paul International 1997.

Bryn, S. *A* "New Direction for Community Development in the United States," *in Real Life Economics.* Routledge, 1992.

Burdett, R., and Sudjic, D. (eds.). *The Endless City* Phaidon, 2010.

Business and Professionals Federation of Hong Kong. *Poor Housing Conditions in Hong Kong: Exte Distribution and People Affected,* April 2007.

Casault, A. "Endangered Street Life: Building Frontages and Street Activities in Hanoi," in *Public Places in Asia Pacific Cities,* Pu Miao (ed.). Kluwer Academic Publishers, 2001.

hakraborty, S. *From Colonial City to Global City: e Far-From-Complete Spatial Transformation of lcutta* in *The Urban Geographer Reader*. Routledge, 05.

hapman, W. "Too Little, Two Late: Urban anning and Conservation in Phnom Penh," in *The sappearing Asian City*, Logan, W. S (ed.). Oxford iversity Press, 2002.

arney, M. W. *A History of Modern Burma*. mbridge University Press, 2009.

atane, M., and Hou, J. (eds.). *Messy Urbanism: derstanding the "Other" Cities of Asia.*

iversity of Hong Kong Press, 2016.

hattopadhyay, S. *Representing Calcutta: dernism, Nationalism and the Colonial Uncanny.* utledge, 2005.

eng, C. M. B. *Macau A Cultural Janus*. Hong ng University Press, 1999.

arke, M., and Hatafoff, A. *Religion and velopment in the Asia Pacific*, Routledge, 2017.

lm, J., and Bowker, J. (eds.). *Sacred Place.* nter Publishers, 1994.

ates, A. *A Macau Narrative*. Heinemann ucational Books (Asia) Ltd, 1978.

mmunity Involvement in Urban Regeneration, ropean Union-Regional Policy and Cohesion, mmunity Development Foundation with support m the European Commission, 1997.

ok, A., and Ng, M. K. *Building Sustainable mmunities*. University of Hong Kong, 2001.

vis, M. *Planet of Slums*. Verso, 2006.

an, K. *Parallel Universes: Chinese Temple Networks Singapore* in *Handbook of Religion and the Asian y*. Van deer Veer (ed.), University of California ss, 2015.

nt, C. M., and Huang, D. W. F. *Northeast Asian ionalism*. Routledge, 2002.

uglas, M. *Globalization, Mega-projects and the ironment: Urban Form and Water in Jakarta Environment and Urbanization in Asia*. SAGE lications, 2010.

Duany, A, Plater-Zyberk, E., and Alminana, R. *The New Civic Art: Elements of Town Planning*. Rizzoli International Publications, 2003.

Dutta, K. *Calcutta-A Cultural and Literary History*. Interlink Books, 2003.

European Commission. *Community Involvement in Urban Regeneration: Added Value and Changing Values*. Regional Development Studies Report No. 27, 1997.

Evenson, N. *The Indian Metropolis: A View Toward the West*. Yale University Press, 1989.

Evers, H. D., and Korff. *Southeast Asian Urbanism: The Meaning and Power of Social Space*. St. Martin's Press, 2000.

Evers, H. D., and Korff. *Southeast Asian Urbanism: The Meaning and Power of Social Space*. Singapore Institute of Southeast Asian Studies.

Falconer, J., et al. *Myanmar Style: Art, Architecture and Design of Burma*. Thames and Hudson, 1998.

Falkus, M. *Bangkok in the Nineteenth and Twentieth Centuries: The Dynamics and Limits of Port Primary* in *Gateways of Asia: Port Cities of Asia in the 13th-20th Centuries*. Kegan Paul International, 1997.

Farmer, A. *Handbook of Environmental Protection and Enforcement*. Earthscan, 2007.

Fischer-Tiné, H., and Mann, M. *Colonialism as Civilizing Mission Cultural Ideology in British India*. Anthem Press, 2004.

Flores, J. M. *The Portuguese Chromosome* in *The Threshold of the Third Millennium*. Institute Ricci de Macau, 2003.

Florida, R. *The New Urban Crisis*. Oneworld Publications, 2018.

Fok, K. C. *The Existence of Macau*. Institute Ricci de Macau, 2001.

Frampton, A., Solomon J. D., and Wong, C. *Cities without Grand*. ORO Editions, 2012.

Freek, C. *Under Construction: The Politics of Urban Space and Housing during the Decolonization of Indonesia 1930-1960*. KITLV Press, 2010.

Friedman, J. *Place and Place-making in Cities: A Global Perspective*. Planning Theory and Practice, 11(2) 149-64, 2010.

Friedmann, J. *Life Space and Economic Space*, Transaction Books, New Jersey, 1988.

Fry, T. *Remaking Cities: An Introduction to Urban Metrofitting*. Bloomsbury Academic, 2017.

Fu, C. "Conserving Historic Urban Landscape for the Future Generation: Beyond Old Streets Preservation and Cultural Conservation in Taiwan." *International Journal of Social Science and Humanity* Vol 6 No 5 May 2016.

Ghosh, D. (project coordinator). *Urban Heritage in Indian Cities*. Indian National Trust for Art and Cultural Heritage: Compendium of Good Practices, 2001.

Glover, W. J. *Making Lahore Modern: Constructing and Imagining a Colonial City*. University of Minnesota Press, 2008.

Glover, W. *Making Lahore Modern*, University of Minnesota Press, 2008.

Goh, R. B. H. *Contours of Culture, Space and Social Difference in Singapore*. Hong Kong University Press, 2005.

Gouldson, A., and Roberts, P. (eds.). *Integrating Environment and Economy*. Routledge, 2000.

Ha, S. K. *Seoul as a World City: The Challenge of Balanced Development* in *Planning Asian Cities*. Hamnet S., and Forbes, D. (eds.). Routledge, 2011.

Hagiwara, S. *The Alley as a Spiritual Axis for the Community: The Hikitune Project, Tokyo* in *Public Places in Asia Pacific Cities*. Pu Miao (ed.). Kluwer Academic Publishers, 2001.

Hamnet, S., and Forbes, D. (eds.). *Planning Asian Cities: Risks and Resilience*. Routledge, 2011.

Han, Judy. *Urban Megachurches and Contentious Religious Politics in Seoul* in *Handbook of Religion and the Asian City*. Ed Van deer Veer (ed.). University of California Press, 2015.

Harvey, D. *Social Justice and the City*. Edward Arnold, 1973.

Hau, W. M., and Lau, J. *Heritage Places of Singapore.* Marshall Cavendish International, 2009.

Heitzman, J. *Network City: Planning the Information Society in Bangalore.* Oxford University Press, 2004.

Heitzman, J. *The City in South Asia.* Routledge, 2008.

Heng, B. L., and Hee, L. (eds.). *On Asian Streets and Public Space,* Singapore: Centre for Advanced Studies in Architecture. National University of Singapore, 2010.

Hidenobu, J. "Ethnic Tokyo," in *Process Architecture* 72, Tokyo, 1987.

Hidenobu, J. *Tokyo: A Spatial Anthropology.* University of California Press, 1995.

Hlaing, K. Y., Taylor, R. H., and Than, T. M. M. *Myanmar: Beyond Politics to Societal Imperatives.* Institute of Southeast Asian Studies, 2005.

Home, R. *Of Planting and Planning: The Making of British Colonial Cities.* E. and F. N. Spon, 1997.

Hosagrahar, J. Indigenous Modernities: Negotiating Architecture and Urbanism. Routledge, 2005.

Ian, Colquhoun. *Urban Regeneration: An International Perspective.* B. T. Batsford Ltd, 1995.

Imai, H. *Tokyo Roji: The Diversity of Alleys in a City in Transition.* Routledge, 2019.

Issar, T. P. *Goa Dowada: The Indo-Portuguese Bouquet.* 1997.

Jacobs, B., and Dutton, C. "Social and Community Issues," in P., Roberts, and H., Sykes (eds.) *Urban Regeneration.* Sage, 1999.

Jacobsen, K. A. (ed.). *South Asian Religions on Display.* Routledge, 2008.

Jayapal, M. *Old Jakarta.* Oxford University Press, 1993.

Jenkins, G. *Contested Space: Cultural Heritage and Identity Reconstructions.* Transaction Publishers, Rutgers University, 2008.

Jenks, M., Burton, E., and Williams, K. (eds.). *The Compact City: A Sustainable Urban Form.* E. and F. N. Spon, 1999.

Jones, G. W., and Douglas, M. *Mega-Urban Regions in Pacific Asia: Urban Dynamics in a Global Era.* NUS Press, 2008.

Jun, Jin-Heon. *The Politics of Desecularisation North Korean* in *Handbook of Religion and the Asian City.* Ed Van deer Veer (ed.), University of California Press, 2015.

Kakiuchi, E. *Cultural Heritage Protection System in Japan: Current Issues and Prospects for the Future.* National Graduate Institute for Policy Studies, 2014.

Kaplan, R. D. *The Revenge of Geography.* Random House. New York, 2012.

Kim, W. B. *Culture, History and the City in East Asia.* Clarendon Press, 1997.

King, A. D. *Colonial Urban Development: Culture, Social Power and Environment.* Routledge & Kegan Paul, 1976.

King, A. D. *Spaces of Global Cultures.* Routledge, 2004.

King, A. P. *Colonial Urban Development: Culture, Social Power and Environment.* Routledge and Kegan Paul, 1976.

Knapp, R. G. (ed.). *Asia's Old Dwellings: Tradition, Resilience and Change.* Oxford University Press, 2004.

Kong, L., and Yeoh, B. S. A. *Building a Nation: The Politics of Landscape in Singapore.* Syracuse University Press, 2003.

Kong, L. *Geography and Religion: Trends and Prospects* Vol 14, pp. 355–71, 1990.

Kong, L. *Mapping New Geographies of Religion Progress in Human Geographies of Religion: Trends and Prospects* Vol 25, pp. 211–33, 2001.

Kong, L. *Conserving the Past, Creating the Future: Urban Heritage in Singapore.* Singapore Urban Redevelopment Authority, 2011.

Kong, C. H. *From Port City to City State: Focus Shaping Singapore's Built Environment* in *Culture and the City in East Asia.* Clarendon Press, 1997.

Kostof, S. *The City Shaped: Urban Patterns and Meanings Through History.* Thames and Hudson, 1999.

Kurokawa, K. *Rediscovering Japanese Space.* John Weatherhill, 1988.

Kwok, R. (ed.) *Globalizing Taipei: The Political Economy of Spatial Development.* Routledge, 2005.

Lane, B. C. *Landscapes of the Sacred.* John Hopkins University Press, 2002.

Lee, H. Y. *The Singapore Shophouse: An Anglo-Chinese Urban Vernacular* in *Asia's Old Dwellings: Tradition Resilience and Change.* Ronald G. Knapp (ed.), Oxford University Press, 2003.

Liao, L., Chong Zhang, and Jianfengfeng. *The Involvement of Planners in Community Planning: A Promising Model for Chinese Local Governance,* https://doi.org/10.4000/chinaperspectives 9491.

Lim, J. C. S. *Post-Independence Kuala Lumpur: Heritage and the New City Image* in *Cultural Identity and Urban Change in Southeast Asia: Interpretive Essays.* Deakin University Press, 1994.

Littleton, C. S. *Shinto.* Oxford University Press, 2002.

Lo, M. Y. *1900 Chinese Names of Streets in Penang.* Journal of the Straits Branch of the Royal Asiatic Society. 33:197–246.

Logan, W. (ed.). *The Disappearing Asian City - Protecting Asia's Urban Heritage in a Globalizing World.* Oxford University Press, 2022.

Logan, W. S. (ed.). *The Disappearing Asian City.* Oxford University Press, 2020.

Logan, W. "Hanoi Townscape: Symbolic Imagery in Vietnam's Capital in Cultural Identity and Urban Change" in *Southeast Asia: Interpretive Essays.* Askew, M., and Logan, W. S. (eds.). Deakin University Press, 1994.

Luan, T. D. *Hanoi: Balancing Market and Ideology* in *Culture and the City in East Asia.* Clarendon Press, 1997.

Lynas, M. *Six Degrees: Our Future on a Hotter Planet.* Harper Collins, 2006.

Maki, F. *Investigations in Collective Form.* Washington University, 1964.

Manners, S. G. M., and Kumalasari, R. *Jakarta Dynamics of Change and Liveability* in *Mega Urban* gions in Pacific Asia. Jones, G. W., and Douglas, M. ls.). MUS Press, 2008.

arcuse, P., and van Kampen, R. *Globalizing ies: A New Spatial Order*. Blackwell, 2000.

arti, J. *The Meaning of the 21st Century: A Vital eprint for Ensuring Our Future*. Penguin, 2006.

arvin, S., Luque-Ayala, A., and McFarlane, C. ls.). *Smart Urbanism: Utopian Vision or False Dawn*. utledge, 2016.

ason, A. *Spiritual Places: The World's Most Sacred es*. Quercus, 2014.

cGee, T. G. *Cultural Identity and Urban Change in utheast Asia: Interpretative Essays*. Askew, M., and gan, W. S. (eds.). Deakin University Press, 1994.

cKinnon, M. *Asian Cities: Globalization, banization and Nation-Building*. Nordic Institute of an Studies, 2011.

cPherson, K. *Penang 1786–1832: A Province fulfilled*, in *Gateways of Asia: Port Cities in the –20th Centuries*. Kegan Paul International, ndon, 1997.

ehrotra, R. *Kinetic City-Issues for Urban Design outh Asia* in *Reclaiming the Urbanism of Mumbai*. annon, K., and Gosseye, J. (eds.). Sun Academic, 9.

etcalf, T. F. *An Imperial Vision-Indian Architecture Britain's Raj*. University of California Press, 1989.

sra, R. P., and Misra, K. *Million Cities of India*. tainable Development Foundation, Delhi, 1998.

ore, E., Mayer, H., and Pe, U. W. *Shwedagon: den Pagoda of Myanmar*. Thames and Hudson, 9.

mford, L. *The City in History: Its Origins, nsformations and Its Prospects*. Harcourt, 1961.

mtaz, K. K. *Architecture in Pakistan*. Concept dia Pte Ltd, 1985.

ito, A., and Hozumi, K. *Edo, the City that ame Tokyo*, Kodansha International, 1982.

uwirth, R. *Shadow Cities: A Billion Squatters, A Urban World*. Routledge, 2005.

Nitschke, G., and Thiel, P. *Anatomy of Lived Space in Japan*. Bauen & Wohnen, 1968.

Nguyen, K. C. *Preserving Hanoi's Architectural and Landscape Heritage*. Ministry of Construction, 1999.

OECD. *Environmental Outlook to 2030*. OECD, 2008.

Oldstone-Moor, J. *Understanding Confucianism*. Duncan Baird Publishers, 2003.

Ora-orn, Poocharoen, Poon, Thiengburanathum, and Kian, Lee. *The Smart City as a Complex Adaptive System* in *Smart Cities in Asia*. Yu-Min Joo and Teck-Boon Tan (eds.). Edward Elgar Publishing Ltd, 2020.

Ordner, J. *Sacred Places of Asia*. Abeville Press, 2001.

Oriol, Bohigas O. *Ten Points for an Urban Methodology* Architectural Review. September, 1999.

Osborne, M. *Phnom Penh: A Cultural and Literary History*. Signal Books, Oxford, 2009.

Osborne, M. *Southeast Asia: An Illustrated Introductory History*. Allen and Unwin, 1990.

Palmer, M: *The Jesus Sutras*. The Ballantine Publishing Group, 2001.

Paprocki, K: "The Village at the End of the World" in *Death and Life of Nature in Asian Cities*. Hong Kong University Press, 2021.

Park, C. C. *Sacred Worlds*. Routledge, 1994.

Pearn, B. R. *A History of Rangoon*. American Baptist Mission Press, 1939.

Perera, N. and Tang, W. S. (ed.). *Transforming Asian Cities*. Routledge, 2013.

Perera, N., and Tang, W. S. (eds.). *Transforming Asian Cities: Intellectual Impasse, Asianizing Space and Emerging Translocalities*. Routledge, 2013.

Perera, N., and Wing-Shing, Tang. *The Transforming Asian City: Innovative Urban Planning Practices in Asia*. Hong Kong Baptist University, 2007.

Price, M., and Benton-Short, L. (eds.). *Migrants to the Metropolis: The Rise of Immigrant Gateways*. Syracuse University Press, 2008.

Rakudi, C., and Firman, T. *Planning for an Extended Metropolitan Region in Asia: Jakarta*.

Revisiting Urban Planning: Global Report on Human Settlements, 2009.

Rappaport, A. "Pedestrian Street Use: Culture and Perception," in Moudon, A. (ed.), *Public Streets for Public Use*. Columbia University Press, 1987.

Redfield, R., and Singer, M. *The Cultural Role of Cities* in Economic Development and Cultural Change, 3(1), pp. 53–73, 1954.

Reed, R. R. *Colonial Manila: The Context of Hispanic Urbanization and Process of Morphogenesis*. University of California Press, 1978.

Revi, A. *Climate Change Risk: An Adaptation and Mitigation Agenda for Indian Cities*, Environment and Urbanization 20(1), pp. 207–29, 2008.

Rimmer, P., and Dick, H. *The City in Southeast Asia; Patterns Processes and Policy*. NUS Press, 2001.

Roberts, B. *Manila: Metropolitan, Vulnerability, Local Resilience* in *Planning Asian Cities: Risks and Resilience*. Hamnet, S., and Forbes, D. (eds.). Routledge, 2011.

Roberts, P., and Sykes, H. (eds.). *Urban Regeneration: A Handbook*. Sage, 2000.

Rowe, P. G. *Emergent Architectural Territories East Asian Cities*, Birkhäuser, 2011.

Rukmana, D. *Street Vendors and Planning in Indonesian Cities*. Planning Theory and Practice, 12, pp. 138–44.

Santiagpo, A. M. *Case Study of Land Management in Metro Manila in Megacity Management in the Asian and Pacific Region*. Asian Development Bank, 1996.

Sassen, S. *The Global City*. Princeton University Press, 2001.

Sassen, S. *Cities in a World Economy*. Pine Forge Press, 2006.

Scriver, P., and Prakesh, V. (eds.). *Colonial Modernities*. Routledge, 2007.

Selya, R. M. *Taipei*. John Wiley and Sons, 1995.

Sham-DH-M. *Heritage Resistance: Preservation and Decolonization in Southeast Asian Cities*. Centre for Cultural Studies, Goldsmiths, University of London, 2015.

Silver, C. *Planning the Megacity: Jakarta in the Twentieth Century*. Routledge, 2008.

Singh, B., and Manoj, P. *Smart City in India: Urban Laboratory, Paradigm or Trajectory*. Routledge, 2020.

Singh, B., and Parmar, M. *Smart City in India*. Routledge, 2020.

Skelcher, C. *Community Networks in Urban Regeneration, University of Bristol*. The Policy Press, 1996.

Smart, N. *Religions of Asia* Prentice Hall, 1993.

Soh, E. Y., and Yuen, B. *Government-aided Participation in Planning Singapore*. DOI:10.1016/j. cities.2005.07.011.

Soja, E. *Postmetropolis: Critical Studies of Cities and Regions*. Blackwell, 2000.

Song, J. "The Origin of Urban Heritage Conservation in the Specified Block System in Tokyo," in *Journal of the City Planning Institute of Japan*, Vol 52. No. 2, 2017.

Sorenson, A. "Subcentres and Satellite Cities: Tokyo's 20th-Century Experience of Planned Polycentrism" in *International Planning Studies 6*, 2001.

Sorenson, A. *The Making of Urban Japan: Cities and Planning from Edo to the Twenty-First Century*. Routledge, 2002.

Stiglitz, J. *Making Globalization Work*. WW Norton and Co, 2006.

Susantowo, B and Guild, R. *Liveable Asian Cities*. ADB, 2021.

Thant, M. U. *The Making of Modern Burma*. Cambridge University Press, 2001.

Tillotson, G. H. R. *The Tradition of Indian Architecture*. Yale University Press, 1989.

Tsukamoto, Y., Kaijima, M., and Kuroda, J. *Made in Tokyo*. Kajima Publishing Company, 2001.

UK Urban Design Group. *Urban Design and Community Issues*. Conference Proceedings, 1996.

UNCHS. *The State of the World's Cities Report*, UN Human Settlements Program London: Earthscan 2006.

Urban Design and Community Issues, Conference Proceedings, Urban Design Group, 1996.

Van Grunsven, L. "Singapore: The Changing Residential Landscape in a Winner City," in *Globalizing Cities: A New Spatial Order*. Marcuse P. and van Kempen (eds.). Blackwell, 2000.

VN-Habitat. *The State of the World's Cities Report*. Earthscan, 2006/2007.

Weng, L. *Hutongs of Beijing*. Beijing Arts and Photography Publishing House, 1993.

Widodo, J. *Historical Morphology of Coastal Cities in southeast Asia* in Handbook of Urbanisation in Southeast Asia. Routledge, 2019.

Woodman, D. *The Making of Burma*. The Gesset Press, 1962.

World Bank. *The Sustainable Development of Walled City of Lahore Project*, 2009.

Wright, G. *The Politics of Design in French Colonial Urbanism*. University of Chicago Press, 1991.

Wu, L. Y. *Rehabilitating the Old City of Beijing*. University of British Columbia Press, 1999.

Yatmo, Y. A. "Street Vendors as 'Out of Place' Urban Elements," in Journal of Urban Design, 13, 3:387–402, 2008.

Yeang, K. *Tropical Urban Regionalism: Building in a Southeast Asian City*. Mimar, 1987.

Yeoh, B. S. A. *Contesting Urban Space: Power Relations and the Urban Built Environment in Colonial Singapore*. Oxford University Press, 1996.

Yeoh, B. Contesting Space: *Power Relations and the Urban Built Environment in Colonial Singapore*. Oxford University Press, 1996.

Zargoza, R. M. *Old Manila*. Oxford University Press, 1990.

Zhang, L. *Strangers in the City: Reconfigurations of Space, Power and Social Networks within China's Floating Population*. Stanford University Press, 2001.